BAD BOYS

BAD  BOYS

ISIAH
THOMAS

with MATT DOBEK

MASTERS PRESS

Published by Masters Press, 5025 28th Street, S.E., Grand
Rapids, Michigan 49512

Photo credits:

Einstein Photo—10, 18, 23, 54, 60, 64, 68, 72, 75, 78, 83, 87,
91, 92, 96, 98, 101, 102, 109, 111, 112, 119, 128, 130, 133,
134, 140, 145, 151, 152, 156, 158, 161, 163, 171, 173, 176,
184, 188, 191, 193, 199, 200, 205, 213, 220, 222, 225, 226,
230

Noel Webley, II—7, 20, 24, 25, 26, 30, 31, 34, 35, 38, 40, 42,
44, 46, 48, 121, 122, 164, 168, 175, 181, 194, 218

Printed in the United States of America

ISBN 0-940279-10-X

Library of Congress Cataloging-in-Publication Data

Thomas, Isiah, 1961-

    Bad boys : an inside look at the Detroit Pistons'
1988-89 championship season / Isiah Thomas with Matt
Dobek.
      p. cm.
    1. Detroit Pistons (Basketball team) 2. National
Basketball Association. I. Dobek, Matt. II. Title.
GV885.52.D47T48 1989
796.323'64'0977434—dc20
                                          89-36235
                                           CIP

TO *our families and friends. For eight years we've been chasing a dream. And while we almost drove you insane playing this kids' game, we accomplished the ultimate: the World Championship.*

Putting up with us, especially this season, has been difficult, but I think we can all agree that it was well worthwhile.

The past is for remembering. Thanks for sharing all the memories.

CONTENTS

PLAYER PROFILES:

FOREWORD

HINDSIGHT IS SO CONFUSING. Even in Utopia there is myopia. The season is but a pair of tail lights off in the distance now. And yet there's still the low roar. A motor.

Chuck Daly doesn't look like a mechanic: the hair, those suits. That's a chauffeur. His basketball team—if it were a motor vehicle—would be a bus. It'd be a Badmobile, not very streamlined, but what a motor! And lots of seats. That fancy gym in Auburn Hills is simply never going to be mistaken for a service station either. But here's the work order anyway; the service job is done.

The ring job for the Pistons is completed.

So is the race. The checkered flag was waved. Wonder why there's a skull and crossbones on it. Anyway, the NBA's Car of the Year is taking its victory lap. All the others are in the garage, towed away, or hauled off.

So honk if you love the Bad Boys.

By the way, that glitzy hood ornament is really a trophy.

It belongs to the World Champions. It comes with a one-year warranty, parts and labor not included. And although that warranty is extendable, that's another race altogether.

The baddest were also the best.

But that's the ending; the rainbow also must have a beginning. For that's how the phenomenon of the Bad Boys can best be understood.

To skim over all the blood, sweat, and ginseng it took to reach that majestic moment is like hopping in an Indy car and cutting across the infield to the finish line, 500 miles too soon. It's like kicking the tires and deciding a used car is a beauty almost sight unseen and asking where to sign. Four straight victories over the Los Angeles Lakers in the Championship Series was an accurate microcosm of the Pistons' season; if that wasn't the real Lakers, it certainly was the real Pistons. And at their Microwavian best.

But that series, dramatic as it was, is insufficient to examine the depth and breadth of this faceless team of so many faces. You need a different kind of dipstick to measure what fueled the Pistons. To understand their final destination, you must retrace and

9

maneuver through the long, strange journey that was the NBA regular season.

So let us pop the hood on the 1988-89 model out of Detroit via their showcase in the suburbs and find out: What's that big ol' motor all about anyway? What do 82 games in the regular season and 17 more in the playoffs reveal? That Bad Boys can become good? Great? Badder? Adjectives are too argumentative, too subjective, too dependent upon interpretation, too susceptible to preconceived notions. Were the Pistons appealing or appalling? Probably both, depending on your point of view. And there's the rub.

What the long and winding and often bumpy road that is the NBA season did allow is the noun of opportunity. A chance to display the best defense since the league started using the 24-second clock. It allowed a work ethic that would make factory workers and assembly-line laborers salute. It provided a classic working example of the universal coaching ambition—to convince a gang of well-paid strong personalities with sensitive egos that the shelter of Team is the best of all possible homes. It showed how the self-governing, self-disciplining, almost self-coaching nature of athletes all dedicated to the same proposition can prosper and thrive and excel.

And lest anyone forget, it also provided a nine-month incubation period in which a robust and swashbuckling image grew to monstrous proportions. Their jack-o'-lantern smiles, their arrogant nature, their apparent love of being everyone's designated villains, became a calling card. And a signature. Bad Boys in town; lock up the women and children, get ready for their welcome wagon of elbows and forearms and good-natured aggravation. It was all a cardboard shield, but you take your intimidation any way you can get it.

So attach any adjectives you wish. But recognize that noun of opportunity. And check out the sparkling ring that tells you how that opportunity got put to use on each stop along the championship road map.

Defense, work ethic, peer pressure, unity. These were the hammers and wrenches in the Pistons' toolbox. Has any team ever played with so much mental toughness and intensity? Can any other team that ever played in the NBA ever insist seriously that throughout the entire season they conceded nothing, contested everything—every shot, every loose ball, every rebound?

When there were less than 30 seconds left in the season, when the Pistons were safely ahead in the game and the crippled and proud but weary Lakers dutifully removed the incomparable Kareem Abdul-Jabbar so that his final standing ovation could commence, the Pistons looked up from their timeout huddle and applauded. They aimed their respect toward the retiring legend.

But only for a few moments. For Chuck Daly had final instructions. They were familiar ones. Play harder. Play all 48 minutes. Never let up. And while you might expect that from a coach who confesses to be an Irish realist, a veteran pessimist and someone with an overachieving imagination, one able to foresee this finest of all moments turning into the most horrible nightmare, what was special and almost conspicuous was the Pistons players themselves.

They listened. Their intensity had not subsided. They were accustomed to these moments where caution and precaution and plain old fear of the unknown is supposed to be clutched so tightly that everything gets forged into safeguards. It was how they had earned the best record in the league. It was how they would win in a few seconds the championship that had eluded them ever since the franchise was formed.

Yes, they would maintain their menacing countenance. And play hard till the end. All 48 minutes. The Pistons Way.

Chemistry is how you describe success that cannot be explained. And that image of Bad Boys was the chemical reaction that riveted this team. Forget that the surly image is nothing but a lovable disguise. Forget that their bully mask is really a brand of basketball every player should aspire to master. Focus on the result that comes when you are branded and put on one side of a line and everyone else is on the other side. The wagons circle closer.

There is the feeling of being put on the same boat and put to sea. So why not make it a pirate ship?

The image bonded them together. The Honor Among Knaves camaraderie never let up. It was like the Pistons' defense. Like the way they pounded the boards. It was like their penchant for finding the player with the hot hand on offense. They'd take on all comers, but you were dealing with all five of them. Their way was not caring who gets the credit. So long as they won.

Of course the ability to play basketball, to execute, to excel on every foot of the hardwood floor is the essence of the championship flag that flies high above The Palace. Mindset and attitude and iron-clad will are nothing but greeting-card verse unless there is talent stuck in the envelope as well. The Pistons are very good basketball players, first and foremost.

But look around the league. Everyone's a good player. Look at the quality of the athletes. Look at the talent level. Then look back at the Pistons. Something besides talent separates them. No Piston was named to the first, second, or third All-NBA teams. No Piston was among the league's top 20 in scoring. No Piston averaged 20 points a game or collected 10 rebounds a game. Isiah Thomas was ninth in the league in assists, Bill Laimbeer ninth in rebounding. Even on defense, where Joe Dumars and Dennis Rodman were named to the NBA's All-Defense team, no Piston was among the league leaders in steals or blocked shots.

Individual brilliance for the Pistons was a nightly thing; you wore the special hat only when it fit. Numbers go down, values go up. The car with low mileage is more valuable. Daly kept telling them they all were heroes, but it was his job to fine tune the engine every night. Sometimes there'd be combinations of heroes, enough to fill the starting grid of a Grand Prix road race. Everyone's got a role to fill, so be ready. And work harder. And when it's your turn, go to it. Pedal to the metal.

There were too many of them. So many Pistons, so little time. They were a swarm, an army of foot soldiers, a flock of birds, snipers and tanks and long-range bombers. Sneak attacks, frontal assaults. Worm warfare. Hoo's next. Wham bam, thank you Lam. Ohhh Isiah. . . . And hey, when did this guy Dumars start playing offense too?

It got kind of crowded on that Wheaties box. That's how it was during games too. Only five at a time. But somebody was always at the scorer's table, fresh legs and lungs, ready to step forth. The Pistons Way.

Coming at the enemy from all angles, everywhere, in gangs. Daly had his Rhinos, the limbering starters. And his Thoroughbreds, the sleek speedsters off the bench. That's working the double-team to perfection. It added up to team totals. To victories. Daly's favorite image of his team was how versatile they had become. Interchangeable parts, like a Swiss Army knife. The point guard's also a shooting guard, and vice-versa. The power forward will guard anyone down low. McHale, Sikma, Cartwright, Worthy. Bring 'em on. Dennis Rodman played four different positions: he'll guard anyone anywhere. Watch Vinnie rebound. Watch Laimbeer nail the three-pointer. Is that really Mark Aguirre throwing a blind pass to a teammate for an easy layup?

Ever seen anyone who could run the floor like Rodman? Work harder than Joe Dumars? Play more together than the Detroit Pistons?

And the beauty of it is, nobody cared who got the credit. Because now, all of them get it. They went through the White House greeting line together, as a team. Collectively Bad.

They've even ganged up to write a book. Public Relations Director Matt Dobek and team captain Isiah Thomas feel this most glorious of seasons actually began during the ignoble moments of last year's failure. In the locker room of defeat, with walls thin enough to hear the other team, the champions, celebrating, the lessons never to be unlearned were sensed. This book is a chronicle of the Pistons' unanimous obsession to find that championship locker room. And live in it.

It's a most accurate look behind those masks and facades. It's a voyeur's view of grown men thrown together in a job that is already performed in a giant spotlight. It's a vivid account thanks to the candid voice of the narrator, and it strips away the monotony of a long season. It comes at you in bursts, like a real

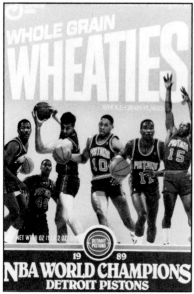

game, like a real season. It reveals how complex and diverse and harrowing and traumatic even a championship season can be.

As you will discover, it was a foot race that turned into a marathon. Time healed some wounds along the way but the Pistons poked and gouged themselves enough so that not all the pain ever subsided. They did not want to reach Heartbreak Hill again and be forced off the last exit ramp like before. They did not want to forget the gnawing pain of being only second best.

It was in training camp that Chuck Daly immediately noticed this incandescent determination boiling and churning just beneath the surface. He might not need a whip for the season, only a harness. His veteran players, Isiah, Laimbeer, Vinnie Johnson, Rick Mahorn, barked as many directions as he did in the workouts. A good sign. A coach who sets his philosophy, reinforced by his players, finds undivided attention easier to maintain. What other players were listening to but not hearing came at them again and again from within their own ranks. In stereo. To sell a team on such unglamorous facets of the game as team defense, rebounding, and unselfishness isn't easy. But the four veterans became a barbershop quartet and the harmony paid off. Then the chorus grew and grew, until it was 12-part harmony making the most beautiful music the basketball world has ever seen.

As a coach, you start the season knowing everyone would like to play 48 minutes and average 35 points a game. You soon realize there are not nearly enough basketballs or minutes on the clock to go around. Daly recognized quickly that quality depth is a double-edged sword. Keeping everyone happy could be a problem. Twelve simply does not go into five easily. And certainly not evenly.

While there were plenty of nights when someone's pouting jaw drooped to the floor over a lack of playing time, the prairie justice of this team quickly took over. Peer pressure had big muscles and a loud voice. Think beyond yourself. See the bigger picture. And

F O R E W O R D

the loftier goal. And if that carrot in front of you doesn't seem so appealing, remember that bench behind you.

Respect wasn't going to come easy. Too many bizarre things had happened to the Pistons. Too many times, they'd failed in big games. But failure is an event, not a person or a team. And the wisdom gained from those failures, some of them so ridiculous they defy explanation, became another layer of cement for their relentless approach to every second of every minute of every game.

They knew that nothing was guaranteed. They knew from experience. Then they grew from experience.

The Pistons won their first eight games. However, Daly was concerned as January approached. His team seemed sluggish on offense. The Pistons were having difficulty scoring points. When Joe Dumars broke his hand January 12, it seemed like they were in real trouble.

You don't have a good bench unless you use it. Vinnie Johnson, the hired gun whose instant-offense abilities were the stuff of folklore, became a starter. And the overlooked parts of his game, his ballhandling and passing and defense, were "discovered" by opponents. And the interchangeable parts clicked into place smoothly.

But something was still bothering his team, Daly felt. The team seemed to bog down even more. An 8-6 record for the month was proof. Other teams, like Cleveland, New York, and Milwaukee, were beating up on the Pistons. And there were whispers inside The Palace walls. Adrian Dantley, the 10th most prolific scorer in the history of the league, was the subject of most of the whispers.

Trade rumors flew everywhere. On February 15, the day after Valentine's Day, the other sneaker dropped. Dantley was gone, and Mark Aguirre was a Piston. It was a bombshell. The cynics and critics and agnostics screeched. The Pistons had just lit a match to see if there's any gas in the tank, they complained. Mark Aguirre? He's one of the known bad guys in the league. What made the Pistons think he'd be a good Bad Boy?

And when the Pistons lost the first two games Aguirre played, the protests became deafening. But Daly kept calm. McCloskey kept calm. The Pistons kept calm. You don't know a player until you coach him. Give him time to learn the system, get used to us, know what is expected. Then pass judgment if you must.

The Pistons suddenly started winning. And *Rolling Stone* magazine came out with a splashy story, salty and succinct and playing the outlaw image to the maximum. Nobody in the organization liked it. The team kept winning anyway. The league office kept handing out fines and suspensions for infractions like fighting and flagrant elbows and other misdeeds of a highly physical nature. But the Pistons kept winning. After losing the first two games following the trade while Aguirre was making the adjustment, the Pistons posted a 46-6 record the rest of the way.

Mark Aguirre? Well, he got taken under four overbearing wings his first night on the team. The Committee of Four, with Captain Zeke, Aguirre's best friend from their hometown of Chicago, leading the lecture, quickly let him know how things got done on the Pistons. Freedom of speech exists in this clubhouse, they said. Daly's a player's coach; you're allowed to be yourself. But there are some rules. Team rules.

Dumars' hand had healed; his initial disappointment at the trade (he was Dantley's closest friend) had never interfered with his approach to the game or his team. Joe Dumars' play blossomed. He was free to be . . . a budding MVP.

The absence of Dantley also allowed Dennis Rodman more playing time. Aguirre would play when offense was needed; Rodman would take his place when defense was in demand. Neither complained. John Salley figured into the equation. James Edwards as well. Depth to the Nth degree.

The Pistons kept winning. Trailing the Cleveland Cavaliers by five full games as late as February, they won their division by six games. Salley broke an ankle. Isiah broke his hand. Somebody always picked up the slack. The Pistons kept winning.

The league was looking over its shoulder now. How good were the Bad Boys? And how many of them were there?

Detroit swept the Boston Celtics. And the alibi was, Sure, but the Celtics were without Larry Bird. The Pistons then swept Milwaukee, and there was a swift finger pointed to the Bucks' injury list. They'd knocked off a team that belonged more in a hospital than a playoff series. Besides, the Lakers were also sweeping through the West with a dizzyingly familiar style, and were more impressive, more dominating. Like a Ferrari. And they were beating healthy teams. Beating them into the floor and stomping them flat.

Of course, a close victory and a lopsided one both count the same. And playing styles between East and West were vastly different and until the championship series, never the twain would meet. And nobody would know for sure.

Then the Pistons took on the Chicago Bulls for the Eastern Conference Championship. And that meant you-know-who, Michael Jordan, versus the static-cling Pistons. What a matchup. When Chicago won the first game of the series, the Team Everyone Loves To Hate suddenly found itself under familiar fire. The Detroit guards had shot horribly. Someone suggested they should be nicknamed Dr. Airball, Mr. Brick, and the King of Clank. Not only that, but Dennis Rodman's back was acting up, reviving memories of last year's Finals and Rick Mahorn's sad vigil, spent mostly belly-first on the sidelines. And Isiah Thomas could feel the piercing zing in his hamstring. And the refs were calling fouls in critical moments. Storm clouds were everywhere. And to top it all off, Jordan was lighting up the skies in a fashion spectacular even for him.

The Pistons' preoccupation with Jordan had messed up their offensive rhythm. Channeling their intensity exclusively to the defensive end of the court yielded ragged and erratic results at the other end. Isiah, however, bailed them out with three terrific offensive games. The defense, with Dumars and Rodman and Vinnie pulling the dirty duty, eventually neutralized Jordan to a bearable extent. And Detroit was back in the Finals.

The Bad Boys by then were everyone's Public Enemy Number 1. And little wonder why. Defrocking so-called saints was a Pistons' specialty. Ripping away a demigod mask and exposing an opponent's mortal side is not going to win any popularity contests anywhere outside of Michigan. The assorted death threats and tasteless incidents, like the time Mahorn received a dozen red roses and black balloons in the mail, were taken seriously. And FBI agents found themselves with courtside seats, but not to watch the game.

The veil of smugness did not help. Or hurt.

They were ready for the Lakers. They were confident. The home-court advantage had been earned by posting the league's

best record. That, they were convinced, was why they'd lost the championship the year before. And as the oddsmakers made the Lakers slight favorites to win the title anyway, the Pistons hunched their backs in their customary way. Still, it seemed, nobody would give them any respect. So, they glared in typical fashion, they'd have to seize it themselves.

Chuck Daly knows all about injuries. He'd seen Isiah struck down by an ankle sprain the year before. He'd seen Mahorn almost helpless. He'd groaned when Dumars, Thomas, and Salley were injured. But then he'd shrugged and looked at the healthy list and made hasty plans. It seems the league has this rather quaint rule—you play when you're scheduled. And the goal is still to win. Win with what's left. When the Lakers lost Byron Scott to a hamstring before the first game, the Pistons picked up a huge advantage.

And they ran with it.

And when fate's lightening crackled again and stabbed Magic Johnson's hamstring in Game Two, the Pistons ran even faster. Empathy, but no sympathy. Play with what's left. Tough luck, the Bad Boys chirped, but the game is out there on the court. It wasn't the Lakers they were playing, it was the game itself. The Pistons' guards ran wild. Rodman grabbed every rebound Laimbeer and Mahorn didn't. Salley blocked every shot. Edwards scored every point. Or so it seemed.

The Lakers were worn down by the rank and file of the Pistons. So many of them. In the clincher, as Edwards came forth in the fourth quarter, Daly said to him, "Jimmy, go and get us the ring."

The final hero. Just a face on a faceless team. Working-class heroes. Buddha, Horn, Zeke, Lam, Spider, Worm, Joe D., Hoo, Mark, John, Fennis, Michael. Big Daddy Daly. His willing and obedient henchmen, Suhr and Malone. Mike Abdenour, the hardest-working man in show business; Jerry, the equipment man; the clubhouse boys. The big man in the front office, Jack McCloskey, his scouts. The even bigger man, Bill Davidson. Even that damn flying hospitality suite the Pistons use to get around. Faceless domination.

The whole organization copped this attitude a long time ago. Shared it. Slapped each other in the face with it. Grab the wheel early. Work your dream to the bone. Pistons. Make it Bad to the bone. Show your motor.

A nice unselfish ride. Everyone else in the rear-view mirror. And a great parking place too. Especially for such Bad Company. The baddest ever, in fact.

Shelby Strother
The *Detroit News*

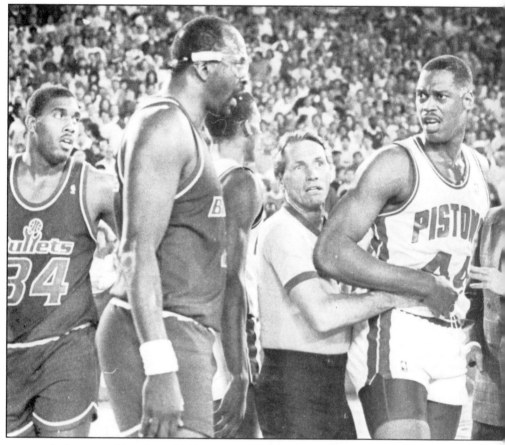

Is there a problem here, Rick?

BUILDING THE TRADITION

WHEN I FIRST CAME TO DETROIT EIGHT YEARS ago and straight out of college, I promised myself that I wasn't going to leave the league until we had won an NBA Championship. Not only did I promise myself, I made the same promise to the people of Detroit.

The first thing I noticed about Detroit when I started with the Pistons was that we had no tradition to build upon. In all the other major sports there were teams and cities with great traditions. In football, there were the Green Bay Packers, the Oakland Raiders, and the Dallas Cowboys. In basketball, everyone talked about the tradition of the Boston Celtics and the Los Angeles Lakers. In baseball, you had the New York Yankees, the Cincinnati Reds, and the Detroit Tigers. In hockey, the talk for years centered around the Montreal Canadiens and, more recently, the Edmonton Oilers. All these teams had tradition; they all had something they could sink their teeth into. When a new player would come to Boston, for example, he knew exactly what style of play was expected of him. The same thing would happen with the Lakers: a guy fresh out of college had a good idea from day one what his new role would be.

Back then, the Pistons had no particular

style of play. We were just another NBA team with a bunch of average guys playing the same 82-game schedule as everyone else. We really didn't have anything to set us apart from the rest of the teams in the league. Boston and Los Angeles had their winning traditions and were the class of the NBA. Their values in terms of winning and losing were at a much higher level than all the other teams because they won with consistency. Everyone else just came and went. Houston might rise up one year with Ralph Sampson and Akeem Olajuwon, put together a pretty good season, then fade the next year. Seattle might surprise everybody and be highly competitive for a year, then they too would fade away. Dallas would do the same thing. In the 1980s it was only the Magic Johnsons, the Larry Birds, and the Julius Irvings who won championships consistently. Julius won with the Sixers, another team with a tradition to build upon.

So, for the first six to eight years, we wanted to build a winning tradition. We wanted to make people in the community aware of our playing style, of our determination to play a specific brand of basketball, and of our commitment to being successful. We wanted to make the community understand what it is like to be a Detroit Piston, and to show them what sets a Detroit Piston apart from everyone else. Enter: "The Bad Boys."

How did the Bad Boys tradition begin? We went to Chicago during the 1987-88 season to play the Bulls. And we played hard. That's one thing about me: if you're a member of the Pistons, you'll never have a problem with Isiah Thomas as long as you make every effort to play hard the entire time you're on the court. But if you don't go all out and don't compete, you are going to have problems with me as an individual.

Now, our basketball team plays hard and we compete. We were playing the Bulls in Chicago on January 16, 1988. Michael Jordan went in for a layup and Rick Mahorn fouled him. It was a hard foul; it wasn't the nastiest foul I've ever seen, but a fight broke out right in front of the Chicago Bulls' bench. Actually, the whole scene was kind of funny, because Rick had his back to the Bulls' bench, and the next thing he knew there were five or six guys surrounding him. All you could see were Chicago players flying off the bench. Usually, when anyone grabbed or even touched Ricky, he'd throw the guy off, reacting first and asking questions later.

He even bounced Doug Collins around twice. Rick was tossed out of the game and fined—just what we'd expected.

Traveling to Denver the next day, we read in the papers that Michael Jordan had called us the dirtiest team in basketball and said that we intentionally tried to hurt people. We'd been labeled a dirty team before, so this was nothing really new. Red Auerbach had had the opportunity to express his opinions about our team and he'd said the same type of thing as Michael Jordan. Now, Red's a pretty smart individual, and he was planting the seed in people's minds that Laimbeer and Mahorn were two of the dirtiest players in the game. You have to give him credit because he was setting the stage

Rick Mahorn (right) defending Karl Malone of the Utah Jazz

for later in the playoffs, when we played his Celtics.

I was a criminal justice major in college, and I minored in sociology. I learned in my sociology classes about the labeling theory. When you apply labels to individuals, they tend to stick, and people begin to form opinions about these individuals based on those labels. Soon, these opinions become closer to fact than mere opinion. So, my first reaction was, "Here's our niche; here's our hook." I realized that this "Bad Boys" reputation could be our handle and separate us from the rest of the league. This would put us in the same category with Boston and Los Angeles. When you talk about L.A., you talk about Showtime and the fast break. When you talk about Boston, it's the mystique, the leprechauns, and the banners. Now, talking about Detroit, other players would have to answer questions about the Bad Boys, and that suited us just fine. When you're a player, this puts something else on your mind. For example, when we'd go to Boston, reporters would ask us about the Celtics' mystique. They wouldn't ask questions about Larry Bird or Kevin McHale—who would then promptly go out and kill you. Bird would score 40, McHale 26, and the reporters would be asking questions about the leprechauns.

Now it's the same for us. Those players—our opponents—have to answer questions about the so-called Bad Boys. That's our hook, our niche in this league. That separates us. So, when this all began, I said to myself, "We better let this work for us, because if we don't it's going to work against us." I knew that the way we handled the Bad Boys image could be the most telling part of our professional careers.

The way I saw it, we would be like the old Oakland Raiders. They had all the characters on their team, they were a bunch of

Bill Laimbeer tangles with Larry Bird of the Celtics . . .

misfit guys just grouped together. That's the same portrait that had been painted of our team: a bunch of crazies all assembled on one basketball team. The implication was that none of us really belonged, that our locker room was a padded cell, and that Chuck Daly was coaching in an insane asylum. But we as players knew that wasn't the case at all. The old Oakland Raiders were the same way. You want an image? We had an image. I was Kenny Stabler, the left-handed quarterback, "the Snake." Laimbeer was Lyle Alzado, Dumars was Lester Hayes, Mahorn was Otis Sistrunk, Dennis Rodman was Cliff Branch, and Salley was "the Stork" Ted Hendrick. We just let ourselves have fun with it.

We adopted a line from the movie *Scarface*, because I love Al Pacino. In that movie, Al Pacino was sitting in a restaurant eating dinner, just after he'd cursed out the waitress and everyone else in the place and made a fool of himself. He then said, "Say hello to the bad guy, because you'll never see another bad guy like me."

For the first few games, we'd walk onto the court and get into our huddle, and we'd all say, "Say hello to the Bad Boys, because you ain't never going to see Bad Boys like us again." It went on from there. We developed a closeness, a bond, a sense of trust and understanding—all the elements a team must develop to win. Basketball is not played simply with X's and O's, it's played with both trust and confidence. We all have talent, we all have skills,

. . . and one of his teammates.

B-a-a-a-d boys Dennis Rodman and Rick Mahorn

but we also must have trust and confidence in each other. As the Pistons, we developed a toughness for defense and a toughness for offensive execution. We became one. It was almost frightening, because we were so focused and into our jobs that nothing else seemed to exist. And that's how it should be, because basketball is a love, a passion; it's a game that consumes you. Not only did it consume us as a team, it consumed a whole city. In fact, the whole state of Michigan and thousands, maybe millions of other people across the country began to focus on the Bad Boys. It was a beautiful thing to see this develop, just as it is a beautiful experience to still be part of now.

The Bad Boys have established a style of play to which every individual wearing a Detroit Pistons uniform must conform. If that person doesn't live up to the type of performance expected of him, then he's out. That's what being a Laker is all about, that's what being a Celtic is all about. Now, that's what being a Piston is all about, too. It's a certain style of play, a tradition to follow and build upon. But it didn't come easily. We earned it. It took the Detroit Pistons eight long years of hard work to establish and develop it, and we started the 1988-89 season prepared to guard it jealously.

Michael Jordan drives on Vinnie
Johnson.

BAD BOYS

1988 EASTERN CONFERENCE
FINALS

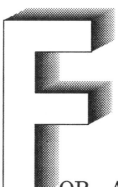

OR A GOOD UNDERSTANDING OF THE 1988-89 season, we really have to go back to the Eastern Conference playoffs in the spring of 1988. It was our post-season play after the '88 season which put us in a position to contend for the 1989 NBA Championship. Even though we had won the Central Division that year, I don't think we were given a legitimate chance of winning an NBA Championship by the so-called experts.

Over many of the previous seasons, the Celtics and Lakers had been playing in the Finals so often that most people took it for granted they'd be there again. We were the new kid on the block and few people gave us a realistic chance of emerging from the Eastern Conference to play in the Finals. After the first couple of games in our second post-season series, against Chicago, we almost believed it ourselves, but ultimately it was making it to the Finals and coming within a couple ticks of the clock of our first ever NBA Championship which laid the foundation for our success in 1989.

Those were an exciting couple of months, and the two series against the Celtics and Lakers are etched in my memory forever, not only because of the way we matured as a team and played great basketball, but also because of unforgettable events in my personal life.

Chicago Coach Doug Collins believes that our series with the Bulls is what really put our team in a position to contend for the NBA title, and I think he's right. After a tough and very physical series against the Washington Bullets in the first round, we entered the second round confident against Chicago. We started the best-of-seven series with an easy victory, but in Game Two we came out flat. Chicago led from start to finish and evened the series. We didn't know it at the time, but that game was a turning point, and our future was about to change dramatically.

Isiah down but not out during the Chicago series

Brad Sellers can't get a reach on the Spider, John Salley.

Doug Collins was right. The loss in the second game made us a better team and propelled us to within seconds of the NBA Championship. We came out for Game Three fighting mad, because it seemed like many had written us off for the remainder of the playoffs just because of one bad game. There already was talk of a Chicago-Boston series in the next round, but we were ready to show the entire league what kind of character our team had. The problem was, we had to do it in Chicago Stadium, one of the loudest and most difficult arenas to play in anywhere. I grew up only a couple of blocks from the Stadium, and used to sneak in when Jerry Sloan, Norm Van Lier, Bob Love, and Chet Walker were playing for the Bulls. The Bulls are always tough at home, and we all knew the next game would be critical, especially with Michael Jordan leading the way for the home team.

What happened in the next two games made people around the country stand up and take notice of the Detroit Pistons. In the first minute of Game Three, Bill Laimbeer and Jordan were involved in a minor pushing incident. One thing about our team: When there is a fight, in most cases it only gives us incentive to play that much harder and better. The incident did not affect our team's play, but it seemed to upset the Bulls. We led from the start, taking the crowd out of the game and controlling the tempo. We won by 22 points (101-79) and immediately began preparing for the next day's game. With a team like ours, which has eight or nine guys who can step in and not only play but really contribute, it's an advantage to play games on successive days. The next afternoon we were right back in Chicago Stadium playing the Bulls.

In Game Four of the Chicago series, we again led from start to finish on our way to a 96-77 victory. It was a great weekend, and when we returned to the Silverdome on Wednesday night, May 18, we were single-minded in our determination to close the door on the Bulls immediately. That's exactly what we did, winning 102-95, and winning the series 4-1. Unexpectedly, we had a few days off as we awaited the winner of the Atlanta-Boston series in the Eastern Conference semi-finals.

I remember sitting at home watching Game Six of the Boston-Atlanta series, not really sure whom I was rooting for. Each team created a different problem for us, but inwardly I guess I was hoping for a rematch with the Celtics. The year before, Boston had beaten us in an incredible seven-game series in the Eastern Conference Finals which we all thought we should have won. Against Atlanta, Boston needed to win the final two games to advance and make a repeat trip to the Conference Finals. True to form, the Celtics won by two points in Atlanta, and then won the seventh and deciding game in Boston, again by two points. Bring on Boston.

Because Boston had a better overall record during the regular season, we had to play the first two games in historic Boston Garden. Talk about the weight of the world on our shoulders! We had not won in Boston since 1982, and the streak had reached an incredible 21 straight losses. If we were to get the monkey off our back, we absolutely had to win one of those first two crucial games. Everyone talks about the ghosts in the Boston Garden and how the Celtics put some sort of hex on their opponents. As far as I'm concerned, it's a numerical hex, as in 33 (Larry Bird), 00 (Robert Parish), 32 (Kevin McHale), and the rest of their outstanding players. They're just a great team, and that's why they win. It has little to do with the arena; no matter where the Celtics play, a team with their talent is going to win.

For the second straight series, we were playing back-to-back games on consecutive nights. Again, because of the depth of our team, and because Boston was playing basically five players, this gave us a decided advantage when fatigue became a factor.

In Game One, the contest was close throughout. Laimbeer hurt his shoulder in the third quarter and had to stay in the locker room for the remainder of the half, so for the first time since he joined us in February, James Edwards had a very important role: he not only had to score points, he also had to defend against Robert Parish. He responded in a big way and helped us down the stretch. When we traded for James, we wanted him to be the additional player who could help us against teams like the Celtics. James can score in the low post (near the basket) and this is especially important against the Celtics because their front line of Bird, Parish and McHale is one of the best ever to play the game. When James was with Phoenix he was a starter, but in coming to Detroit he was asked to play a back-up role. He responded terrifically and gave our team another weapon, adding a new dimension with his inside scoring since Laimbeer is basically a jump shooter. With this game alone, I think the trade for James paid off.

The game was close until the final minutes when we were able to pull away and win, beating the Celtics 104-96. Not only was it important from a mental standpoint, knowing we could win in the Garden, but more importantly, we gained the home-court advantage. Because it was now a six-game series, we were one up, and three of the remaining games would be played in Detroit. Every other time we walked into the Garden, a loss seemed inevitable, but going into Game Two we were confident. We were winners.

Vinnie Johnson goes defensive against the Celtics' Dennis Johnson.

Laimbeer has always said that our team has a knack for doing things the hard way. Nothing comes easy for us, and I think he's right, especially when I look back on Game Two. For the second game in a row, the score was close the entire way. Boston had a chance to win in the final seconds, but we stopped their last play. What happened in the first overtime almost defies description. With 24 seconds left and the score tied, we called a timeout to set up what we hoped would be the winning play. The play broke down, but with Kevin McHale guarding me about 25 feet from the basket, I hit a three-pointer with 19 seconds left, silencing the crowd. We were in the driver's seat, up 109-106 with seven seconds left. Timeout Celtics. The ball is inbounded at half-court, intended for Bird. He misses the pass, and somehow the ball winds up in the surprised hands of Kevin McHale who barely has enough time to turn and shoot before the buzzer. Not only does he make it, but it's counted as a three-pointer, despite a considerable dispute about where his foot actually left the floor. We lose in double overtime. Maybe there are ghosts after all.

Game Three, back in the Silverdome. Memorial Day weekend. It was unseasonably hot in Detroit, and most people were thinking about vacations, long weekends, and outdoor barbecues. Playing in the Silverdome, with no air conditioning, it was almost unbearable, especially since the game was in the middle of the

A.D. and Bird go one-on-one.

afternoon. Over the past several seasons in playing Boston at home, a trend has emerged. Our starters keep the game close, and when both coaches start substituting, we go ahead and maintain the lead. That's what happened in Game Three. We kept it close for the first period, pulled away in the second and third quarters, and hung on for the victory and a one-game lead in the series.

Game Four was on Memorial Day, and the only memories I have of that day are terrible ones. In probably our worst performance of the playoffs, we lost a 79-78 decision and also the home-court advantage (three games to go, two in Boston). It was a weird and thoroughly forgettable game. We scored only 10 points in each of the first and last quarters. Sure, the Celtics were playing great defense, but we couldn't have thrown the ball into the ocean. Even so, we led by eight points after three quarters, but in one stretch of the game we missed 21 straight shots. No team can survive that much futility and expect to win a basketball game. Even at the end we had two chances to win despite all our mistakes. It was tied with 50 seconds left, but with only two seconds on the shot clock, we called timeout and set up an alley-oop play for John Salley. Adrian Dantley inbounded the ball, aiming for the rim, and as luck would have it, he made the basket from out of bounds! That, of course, was a violation. Even after Dennis Johnson made a free throw, we could have won it on the final play. But our shot was short. There was some question about whether or not Parish goaltended, but the officials said he did not. We lost another controversial game, the series was tied, and we headed back to the Garden for Game Five, facing our biggest challenge of the playoffs.

We all knew the whole series was riding on this game. If we didn't win it, the best we could hope for would be a seventh and deciding game back in Boston, and none of us relished that prospect. Early in the game, the Celtics played like the Celtics of old, and we dug a big hole for ourselves to climb out of. I felt like I was largely to blame. In the first half, I missed a lot of easy shots because I was forcing the ball. At halftime, I told myself to relax and let the game come to me. That mental discipline paid off, because even early in the fourth quarter when we were down by 16, I was sure we were going to win.

In most big playoff games, defense is the key to winning, and this game was no different. Ronnie Rothstein, our top assistant coach at the time, said this game was probably our best defensive effort ever. We held the Celtics to just 38 points in the second half. Near the end of the game, it was almost impossible to score—in fact, neither team scored a single point in the last minute and nine seconds. Overtime again, with the score tied at 92. Fortunately, this time it was different than Game Two. Although Boston scored the first basket, we reeled off eight straight points and won 102-96.

If the victory at the Garden in Game One was big, this one was enormous. We were maturing as a team, winning big games when we had to, which we had not done the year before. In the '87 playoffs, it seemed that no matter how well we played we always came up just short when we needed to win a big game.

Chuck Daly is fond of saying, "Never let another team off the hook when you got 'em there." With a 3-2 series lead over the Celtics, we needed to close the series out at home and not allow Boston another chance back in the Garden. They had just come back from exactly the same position against Atlanta, and they were capable of doing the same thing against us. The memory of Game Two haunted all of us. We knew we had to do it at home.

It wasn't the most exciting game we ever played, but we got the job done. We started sluggish and trailed throughout the first quarter, but we caught up in the second and began to pull away in the third and fourth. Vinnie Johnson really carried us, scoring 24 points in leading us to a 95-90 victory and our first ever Eastern Conference Championship.

The Silverdome erupted and it was absolute hysteria on the court. I still don't know how I ever made it to the locker room without being crushed by the wall of humanity. I do remember that just after the final buzzer Kevin McHale came up to me and said, "Zeke, don't be happy just getting to the Finals, go out there and win it." But like I said, at that point I was happy just getting to the locker room! There was no wild celebration for us that night because we knew the biggest challenge of all still lay ahead: The NBA Finals.

For the second time, we had to await the outcome of another series to see who our opponent would be. Los Angeles and Dallas were playing the next afternoon in the seventh and deciding

Isiah soars over Dennis Johnson and Larry Bird.

game of the Western Conference Championship, and I didn't sleep a wink all night in anticipation of the game. Magic Johnson and Mark Aguirre, two of my closest friends, were playing against each other to see whose team would win the right to oppose the Pistons for the coveted championship ring.

Isiah gets the jump on James Worthy.

BAD BOYS

THE 1988 NBA FINALS

ONE GAVE US MUCH OF A chance in the series against the Lakers. If you look back at the newspaper accounts before the first game, and at what commentators were saying on radio and television, you'd have thought the series was already over and the Lakers had swept us in four straight games. Deep down inside we knew that we were a better team than they were. But so what? I thought we were a better team than the Celtics in 1987, and they had beaten us. Judgments in the court of human opinion can always be suspect. We had to go out and prove it on the only court that really mattered.

James Edwards concentrates on moving around Michael Cooper.

Game One was scheduled for Tuesday, June 7, and after a Sunday practice we left for Los Angeles on Monday morning. The whole experience was going to be a first for all of us. On the way to the West Coast at 33,000 feet in our private plane, Roundball One, I remember Chuck telling us how much national media attention we were going to receive, and that we should try to handle the demands as professionally as possible. The only thing I could compare it to was when our Indiana University team played for the NCAA title in Philadelphia in 1981. It's fun to be in situations like that, but it makes it hard to concentrate on the game itself.

We played the role of underdog going into the first game, and even though we were mad as hell at what we thought was a lack of respect for us in the media, we knew the only way to win that respect was to beat the Lakers on their home court in the first game.

All the hype before the game should have benefited the Lakers and bothered us because they had been there before and we hadn't. We were expected to be uptight and tentative, but instead we were loose, and we opened the game by scoring eight straight points. We came out smoking—we were like a bunch of wild animals that had just been let out of their cage. We were going for the kill right from the beginning of the game. I remember when Thomas Hearns fought Marvin Hagler a couple of years ago, he tried to knock him out in the first round. We were trying to do the same thing to the Lakers, and I think they were hoping we would run out of gas and be too tired to stay with them at the end.

The Lakers were, after all, the defending champions, and they certainly weren't about to go down without a fight. They came within one point after the first quarter, but it was the closing seconds of the second period that virtually decided the game. We had moved out to an 11-point lead, and with three seconds left in the half, Laimbeer hit a three-pointer. Then, as Kareem Abdul-Jabbar inbounded the pass, I stole the ball about 25 feet from the basket and hit another three. Instead of being down 11, and within reasonable striking distance, the Lakers went into the locker room down 17 and they never recovered. Adrian Dantley had what was probably his best game as a pro. During the season we had given him the nickname "Teacher" because he so often takes his opponent to school. He was incredible in the game, making 14 out of 16 field goals and scoring 34 points, leading us to a 105-93 victory.

I remember walking into our locker room after the game and our attitude was, "OK, we won the first game, now let's get the second one."

For the fourth straight time, we had won the first game of a playoff series. This is always crucial, because if you're down by one game right from the start, you sometimes make moves you wouldn't normally make. We had accomplished our goal of getting at least a split in the Forum, and now we were in a position to really put the pressure on the Lakers by going up 2-0. Even though we had won, everyone acted like it was no big deal and the series would still belong to the Lakers. I did nothing between games but sit in my hotel room waiting for the next game.

Over the course of the season, I talk as often as possible to my high school coach Gene Pingatore of Weschester St. Joseph's. Coach Ping taught me all the fundamentals and skills, and

Kareem exhibits his famous sky hook.

when I called him, he reminded me how important it was to stay sharp by concentrating on basics. Good advice. On off days during the playoffs I practiced drills he taught me in high school.

In Game Two the Lakers took it to us early, but we hung close and in fact tied the game with eight minutes left. We were making another good run at them when Dennis Rodman stole the ball and we had a chance to cut the lead to two points, but on a fluke play they reset the shot clock and gave the Lakers the ball. As he so often does, Magic took over in the final seconds and the Lakers had tied the series 1-1. At least we had our split, and with the 2-3-2 format, the next three games were to be played in the Pontiac Silverdome.

With those two games, I learned a valuable lesson about the playoffs for the first time. When you're playing teams like the Lakers or the Celtics, the series isn't just about basketball. The opponents try to play with your mind as well, and whoever is the strongest mentally is going to win the series. If we were to beat the Lakers, we had to understand this psychological warfare and have the mental edge that would help us to victory. That's why guys like Magic and Bird are so tough. They're not only great basketball players, they're also strong enough mentally to excel for a full season plus two months of playoffs.

We all knew Game Three was going to be tough mentally. We thought we should have won both games on their court, and now we had three straight at home. We had to win two of them to have any kind of a chance. We did not get off to a very good start. Neither team played well in the first half, and the one-point difference at halftime made it anybody's game. It turned into a defensive war, which is our kind of game. If we're going to get beat, I'd always rather have a team beat us at our own game than in a full-court running game.

We only shot 41 percent from the field for the entire game, and you don't win much shooting that poorly. In the third quarter, the Lakers scored the first eight points and remained in control the rest of the way. James Worthy showed why he's an All-Star, scoring all eight of those points. We attempted several comebacks throughout the second half but were never able to mount a successful challenge. Referee Earl Strom ejected Chuck (Daly) in the fourth quarter and a couple minutes later I got injured. When you're trying to make a comeback, you really have to turn

Joe Dumars performs his defensive two-step against Magic Johnson.

up the defensive intensity a notch, which we definitely did. With about four minutes left in the game, I tried to block a Mychal Thompson jump shot. Not only did I foul him, I came down very awkwardly and landed flat on my back. I didn't come out of the game, but my back really began to bother me. The Lakers won 99-86, thereby regaining the home-court advantage.

Monday was an off day with a late morning practice scheduled. My back really started to bother me late Sunday night and I was unable to get out of bed on Monday morning. My wife Lynn, nine months pregnant with our first child, was helping me with massages, icing down my back and trying to alleviate the pain. I missed practice Monday, staying in bed all day. Tuesday was game day, and I missed the shoot-around scheduled for the morning, just hoping to make it to the game itself. From the end of the game Sunday until Tuesday night, all I did was get treatments for my back, look at game films, and worry about how effective I could be with a sore back. Oh yes, I did one more thing: I said a lot of prayers, hoping that God would get me through a very difficult situation.

When Game Four started, it must have been 95 degrees in the Silverdome, which really helped me because the heat loosened up my back. I was grateful, because I didn't want my teammates to know how much it really hurt. The game was close in the first half, but we opened up a seven-point lead at halftime. With seven minutes left in the third quarter, Magic committed his fourth personal foul, which turned out to be one of the biggest plays of the game. From that point on, we outscored the Lakers 15-4 to close out the period with an 18-point lead.

Before the series, Magic had told me that even though we were friends, if I came down the lane trying to score, he'd slam me if he had to to stop me. Well, in the fourth quarter with our big lead, I think frustration set in with the Lakers. I drove the lane and sure enough, Magic slammed me. I probably over-reacted when I shoved him, but those things happen when you're in an emotional game. After the game we talked and we both agreed that it was nothing personal, that we both had our jobs to do. Many followers of the series believed that the best part of the series was just beginning, and they were right. Tied at two games apiece, the final three games to determine the champion were going to be exciting.

My back was still causing me serious pain. I was on painkillers and had to miss practice the day before Game Five. Lynn was expecting any day now, and as luck would have it, she began having contractions that morning. The pain pills put me in a daze for most of the day. Just one or two really mess up my mind because I don't do drugs and try to stay as far away from them as possible. I finally fell into a deep sleep, but Lynn woke me up and said her water had broken and she was going to the hospital. I honestly remember thinking I was dreaming the whole thing, and I certainly wasn't in any shape to understand what was happening. Because I couldn't drive, Sondra Nevitt (Chuck's wife) drove Lynn to the hospital.

Isiah makes it tough for Byron Scott to pass the ball.

Lynn at the hospital about to give birth, me at home in a fog, the only thing keeping me awake the pain in my back. The phone rang, and it was Mike Abdenour, our trainer, checking to make sure I was OK. The phone again, this time Lynn, telling me I'd better get to the hospital right away. Now I was in shock. I sat on the couch thinking of all the things I had to prepare for her. From the prenatal classes we took together, I was trying to remember what my responsibilities were in this situation we had rehearsed so many times. I guess I was a typical nervous father like in a TV sitcom, because other than call my mother in Chicago to tell her she was about to become a grandmother again, the only thing I managed to do was get myself to the hospital.

Everything happened so fast, I barely remember the actual birth of our first child. I do remember giving Lynn my best coaching routine trying to get her through labor. I was in the delivery room while the doctors were working on Lynn but I couldn't really watch because I have a weak stomach to begin with, and the condition I was in, I was afraid I'd get even sicker. The next thing I remember hearing was the doctor's voice. "Congratulations. It's a boy!" I started to cry with joy, because I've never been happier in my whole life. We named him Joshua Isiah.

If the last 48 hours had been chaotic, the next two days were to be even worse. It seemed like everyone in the country wanted to congratulate Lynn and me. I decided right then and there to guard my son's privacy jealously. I know for a fact that not everyone likes Isiah Thomas, and that there are a lot of crazy people in the world. Terrible and bizarre things have happened to children of famous people, and I hope and pray that nothing like that ever happens to us. That's why I will never allow a television crew or newspaper photographer to get a picture of my son. In fact, I'm not even comfortable with the fact that Lynn has been photographed simply because she's my wife.

I stayed in the hospital with Lynn and Joshua for the next day and a half, and I was on a natural high. It's funny how you put things in their proper perspective when something like this happens. Here I was, living every schoolboy's dream, playing in the NBA Finals, facing the three biggest games of my life, and suddenly basketball didn't seem quite as important to me. My basketball career wasn't the focal point of my life anymore. My wife and my son meant more to me than anything in the world.

But the show must go on. Next up, Game Five of the series, and if we had any hope of winning it all, we had to have this one so we could go back to Los Angeles needing just one win. I was physically and emotionally drained going into the game. I hadn't slept much for four straight days and had too many things on my mind other than basketball. My poor play showed at the start of the game.

The Lakers scored the first 12 points of the game and led 15-2 with just four minutes gone. Chuck realized I wasn't at the top of my game (to say the least) and brought in Vinnie Johnson. Vinnie really sparked us, and we trailed by only three at the quarter and led 59-50 at halftime. The game tightened up in the third, and the Lakers made a couple of runs at us in the fourth, but each time we responded with key baskets of our own. We won 104-94, and were now just one win away from the NBA Championship. That game marked our final appearance in the Silverdome, and in all my seven seasons with the Pistons, I've never seen a more frenzied crowd. A playoff record crowd of 41,732 witnessed the victory and celebrated long into the night.

We were finally starting to get the respect we thought we had deserved all along. Most of the writers and broadcasters had thought the Lakers would win the series easily, but now the pressure was on them rather than us. We had the momentum and all the confidence in the world, believing our time had come to do the unthinkable. The hard work, dedication, and effort each one of my teammates had invested was about to pay off with just one more victory. I had mixed emotions about leaving my wife and baby because I thought it was a time when we should all be together. Lynn listened to my argument for all of about five seconds. She told me the team needed me and to hit the road for L.A.

As in the Boston series, we knew we didn't want to face the Lakers in a Game Seven, so we wanted the first one. I was feeling better than I had at any time since the first game of the series, and knew I could make the big plays I hadn't been able to make in the previous three or four games. I felt like a new man. We led by six after the first quarter and were confident.

Then Earvin started working some of his magic, and it turned into a chess game again. Part of the reason he's such a great player is that whenever you make a mistake, he makes you pay for it. They outscored us 33-20 in the second quarter and led at halftime 53-46. During the intermission, I decided that if we were to lose this game, I personally was going to go down shooting. I came out in the second half with a lot of confidence in my jump shot, and I was determined not to lose passively. They were giving me the long-range jumpers, and I started making them pay for it. We closed the gap after I had scored 14 points early in the third quarter.

Then it happened. On a fast break, after passing to Joe Dumars, I landed on Michael Cooper's foot. I was down with a severely sprained ankle. As I lay on the floor in excruciating pain, I thought, "I can't believe this is happening. Not to me. Not now. Not fifteen minutes away from an NBA Championship." I thought my ankle was broken. I hadn't been seriously injured all season, and now this was the second time in a little over a week. When I went down, I tried to grab the official's leg to tell him I was really hurt. As I lay there waiting for the game to stop, I got angry thinking how lucky the Lakers were. If I were healthy for the rest of the game, I knew the championship would be ours.

A few years ago, when Norm Nixon was playing for the Lakers, he missed a game because of a separated shoulder. Mark Aguirre and I were watching the game on television and we both agreed that if either one of us were in that situation, we'd play no matter how severe the pain was. I told him I'd have to be dead for them to keep me out of the lineup. Brave words at the time, but now I had a chance to put them into action. I said to Mike, our trainer, "Tell Chuck I'm ready to go back in."

During the last four minutes of the third quarter I scored another 11 points, and we led 81-79 after three. Twelve more minutes and the championship was ours. I later found out that my 25 points in the third quarter was an all-time NBA Finals record.

We couldn't put them away in the fourth quarter, but with exactly one minute to go, we were leading 102-99. Byron Scott hit a big jumper with 52 seconds left to cut our lead to one point, and we couldn't score on our next possession. The Lakers had the ball to take the lead, and as they had so often during his great career, they went to Kareem for the possible winning points. He was fouled and made both, but we still had 14 seconds left, and all we had to do was score to win. We called a play during our timeout in which I was the first option, but our luck had run out. I collided with Adrian Dantley and the Lakers won 103-102, forcing a seventh game.

After the game, I looked at my ankle and it was the size of a basketball. I knew I had messed up big time, and everyone told me it was doubtful I'd be able to play. Needless to say, the only thing bigger than my ankle was my depression. Two days away from the biggest game of my life, and I have to sit on the bench. I sat in the locker room trying to accept it before going to the hospital for X-rays. I remember a security guard at the hospital taunting me, saying, "Isiah, you're not hurt," and the doctors and nurses, all Lakers fans of course, telling me the Pistons were going to get their butts kicked in Game Seven. Everyone told me I was risking a possible serious long-term injury if I tried to play, but I was determined to play if it killed me.

If it had been a regular season game, there's no way I'd have been ready to play in two days, but fortunately, a few of our friends came to the rescue. Earlier in the season, when our team was getting a reputation as "the Los Angeles Raiders of the NBA," Raiders Owner Al Davis had sent us shirts and sweaters from his team. As it turned out, many of us from both organizations had become good friends, and now the Raiders put their entire training facility at our disposal for the next two days as we attempted to reduce the enormous amount of swelling. The only help the Lakers offered was a bucket of ice. To this day, I have nothing but the greatest respect for the entire Los Angeles Raiders organization, and I'll never forget the help they gave me. I lay in their training room almost the whole two days receiving treatment, and their trainers tried every conceivable method to alleviate the pain and swelling. The ankle responded somewhat, but I was still going to have a big problem playing. And to make matters worse, Rick Mahorn was also hurt.

There must have been a thousand media personnel covering the last game, and my injury seemed to be the biggest story. The night before, our Public Relations Director, Matt Dobek, decided we should have a press conference to end all the speculation, and even at that time I didn't think I'd be able to play. Someone asked me if I believed in miracles, and, thinking of the recent birth of my son, I didn't hesitate in saying yes.

I must have set the NBA Finals record for number of practices missed in a series. I missed six days of scheduled practices or shoot-arounds for one reason or another, and after a full day of treatment before Game Seven, I went to the Forum not really knowing whether or not I could play. After I suited up, the old determination took hold, and I was going to give it a try. The score stayed close in the first half, but we led 57-52 at intermission even though I was ineffective. During halftime the ankle swelled up again and began throbbing worse than ever, and in the third quarter we were outscored 36-21. We never quit, but even though we cut the lead to one point late in the game, the Lakers held on to win their back-to-back titles.

Looking back over everything that happened during those two weeks, I believe our team accomplished an awful lot. I don't believe there's another team in the league that could have survived the adversity we did and remained so competitive. If either Rick Mahorn or I had been healthy for the last game, I know it would have been the Detroit Pistons with the rings and the trip to Disney World.

But as I said at the beginning, that playoff experience is what laid the foundation for our success in 1988-89. Sure, we thought we were the best team in 1988, but the best team doesn't always win. "I'd rather be lucky than good," as the saying goes. Well, the Lakers were both, and now we had a whole off season to think about it, even though we wished the new season could start the next day. Come hell or high water, we were determined to win the championship we felt cheated out of, and we didn't want to face anyone in the '89 Finals except the Los Angeles Lakers. We had discovered how important home-court advantage is in the playoffs, and for the new season, our first priority was to guarantee that. We began looking ahead immediately, and preparing for another run at our first ever NBA Championship.

Two of the best: Isiah against Michael Jordan

THE 8-0 START

HE ATMOS-
PHERE IN TRAINING CAMP
was surrounded by optimism and an air
of high expectancy. We were focused, dis-
ciplined, and motivated, and we all had
only one goal in mind: a return trip to
the Finals, but this time walking away
with the prize that we had had in our
grasp the year before, but which had
eluded us at the last moment.

The first week was highly competitive.
Everyone had worked on their game over
the summer, was in good physical condition,
and played extremely hard. Our team was
basically intact from the year before, and
everyone was eager and hungry. We did

make a couple of moves to give us added depth. We added rookies Michael Williams and Fennis Dembo. Michael looked good in camp; he's quick and aggressive, and he's eventually going to be a good guard in the league. He helps me out a lot, because for the first time in my eight years with the Pistons, I have someone to compete against in practice.

Fennis, on the other hand, may have some problems, simply because in college he played forward and was used to playing with his back to the basket. Chuck moved him to guard in camp, and it takes some time to make that adjustment. He's a very talented player, he has a great attitude, and he works hard. These attributes will eventually make him a contributor. I just hope he has enough time to develop into a good basketball player. Sometimes in the pros you just don't have enough time to let players develop to their full potential.

In camp, despite the optimism, if there was a cloud hanging over everyone's head it was William Bedford. He's been a disappointment to all of us, not as a person or a basketball player, but as a result of his involvement with drugs. I know from my own experience in dealing with people who have this problem that no matter how much you want to help them, they can only help themselves, and then only if they are ready and want to recover. Unless and until William Bedford decides that he wants to be a changed person and lead a clean life, I think he's always going to have the same problems he had leading into training camp.

The only other new player in camp was Darryl Dawkins— the Chocolate Thunder from Lovetron! He had been with us for a while the previous year, but things just didn't work out for him and he left the team. Darryl is a veteran and a very smart basketball player. We looked for him to make key contributions down the stretch, because he's physically intimidating which fits well in our style of play. With his reputation preceding him, that could only add to the already good chemistry on the team. Sometimes when you're winning, you win not just with talent and smarts, but with reputation and experience. That's what Darryl added to our team. Most of us felt that if he had been with us in Los Angeles in June, we'd have won it all.

We came out of camp to play our first pre-season game at Portland, and we were hot. We picked up defensively right where we had left off in the playoffs, and our discipline and hard work in camp paid off. We started strong during the exhibition season and were further along at the beginning than most teams because we're a veteran team. But as the exhibition season wore on, we began to fade a little. The playoffs had lasted until well into June, and we were right back at it in August getting prepared for the new season, so we really only had about a month off. In addition, we were on the road for most of October. We finished with a 6-3 record, but the coaches and players all knew we had accomplished our goals for the pre-season. We were ready.

Our season opener was in Chicago, and we were nervous. Michael Jordan can make any team nervous. He's capable of scoring 60 or 70 points in a game, especially at home, thoroughly embarrassing the opposition. We didn't want that to happen in our first game of the new campaign because we're a veteran team and take a lot of pride in our performance.

Before the game, some of our players thought we might not be ready for Chicago. We play an aggressive, gambling defense which can be risky if we're not familiar with the other team's offensive tendencies. It's very important for us that all five players know what each of the others is doing defensively at all times. If there's a breakdown, it usually results in an easy score for the other team, and this is doubly true against Jordan, because he's not only a scoring threat but a great passer as well.

We got into Chicago on Thursday night, November 3rd, and I called a team meeting in the hotel. We looked at game films of the playoff series against Chicago and decided we would try to duplicate the way we had double-teamed and rotated on defense against Jordan. It worked, because the next day we moved out to an early lead and then kept the crowd out of the game the rest of the way to win it. It's always a big psychological lift to win the first game of the season, especially on the road in a tough place like Chicago Stadium.

After the game, we immediately started to think about our own home opener in The Palace the next night against the expansion Charlotte Hornets. It's amazing, and a bit unfortunate, but it seems in pro basketball you never really have time to savor a victory. We did our interviews, showered quickly, and jumped on the bus for the airport. We did make time for Home

Run Inn pizza, though. It's absolutely the best pizza in Chicago or anywhere else. After every game in Chicago, I make sure our flight crew picks up the pizza for the guys. When I was growing up on the west side of Chicago, we used to shine shoes in local clubs and bars every Friday night, save our money, then eat Home Run Inn pizza. It's truly my favorite.

While we ate and watched films of Charlotte, the mood of the team was upbeat. Everyone had worked hard, in addition to staying up late Thursday night watching game films.

Now it was time to focus on Charlotte. Chuck gave us the next day off by not scheduling a shoot-around, but we had a 6:00 p.m. team meeting before the game. As an expansion team, Charlotte has several young players mixed with a few veterans, and I'm sure that in time they'll be very competetive. They were all juiced up about playing the Detroit Pistons in the inaugural game at The Palace. We didn't know much about them except from the scouting reports, because of course we had never played them.

Everyone showed up about a half hour before the team meeting. This was a big occasion for the whole organization—opening night at The Palace, the first game in a brand new arena for a team with high expectations. There was a buzz in the air and a festive atmosphere. A lot of people worked very hard to make sure everything—the music, the ceremonies, the promotions—ran smoothly and were done in a first class manner. We hoisted the banners from the previous season's Central Division and Eastern Conference Championships and all the pre-game festivities went off without a hitch. Unfortunately, the game didn't live up to all the hype and hoopla that preceded it. There seemed to be a letdown once we tipped the ball up. Why that happened I'm not sure. Whether because of the opponent or because we had expended so much energy in Chicago, we were missing something and seemed flat. Certainly Charlotte was much better than any of us had expected. But even if it wasn't artistic, it turned out to be a win all the same. Charlotte stayed close until the middle of the third quarter, but then we opened up a big lead and hung on.

For the first time in six years, we were 2-0 after the opening weekend of play. In my first two seasons we had won our first two games only to struggle the following week. In the last five years we sometimes won opening night but fell apart the next game. We weren't about to let that happen this year. We were determined that there would be no letdown.

The next game was in the Spectrum in Philadelphia, Vinnie Johnson's home away from home. The way the Microwave heats up and beats up against the Sixers, I'm surprised they haven't traded for him yet. Every time we play in the Spectrum, Vinnie seems almost unstoppable, and it's been like that ever since he's been with the Pistons. We knew Vinnie would be a key factor, as would the Sixers' Charles Barkley. Charles is a player made from the same mold as Jordan, because once he gets rolling he's almost impossible to defend against.

Rick Mahorn drew the task of defending Barkley and did a good job. We gave him plenty of help and again were on top early in the game. Even though Charles finished with 31 points, he had to earn every one of them. Vinnie had been in a two-game shooting slump, but once he hit the hardwood in the Spectrum he was his old unstoppable self. Joe Dumars had a great game as well, with a career high 31 points and a number of clutch shots to key the victory.

During the course of an 82-game season, there are a lot of "big" games, and even though it was only our fourth of the season, our next game was big. This was our first real checkpoint to judge where we were as a basketball team, because we were to play Atlanta, one of the league's best teams. Atlanta had received more pre-season hype than even the Lakers or ourselves, because during the summer they had acquired two seasoned veterans of proven ability. Adding Moses Malone and Reggie Theus to a team that had won 50 games last year made them a favorite for the title. We both came into the first meeting undefeated, but at least we were playing in the friendly confines of The Palace.

For the second straight home game, we came out flat and played uninspired basketball. We went into the fourth quarter down by 12, but then the crowd came alive and the home-court advantage propelled a great comeback. We outscored Atlanta by 12 in the final period, forcing an overtime. We jumped out to an early lead in overtime and hung on to win by six points.

For the past three or four years, our season series with Atlanta has been extremely competetive, and there was no reason to

A young Piston fan

believe it would be any different this season. There would be five more games with the Hawks, so it was important to get the upper hand right out of the gate.

Next came our old nemesis, the Celtics in the Boston Garden. Not since my second year in the league had we won a regular season game there, although we beat them twice in Boston in the playoffs. We had to get this particular monkey off our backs, but Boston was bent on revenge for the Eastern Conference Finals. Boston was struggling, trying to adjust to new coach Jimmy

Rodgers, who had replaced K. C. Jones after last season. The Celtics wanted to prove that last season's playoff loss was a fluke, and we wanted to show them it wasn't and also win in the Garden for the first time since 1982 after 19 straight regular season losses.

Laimbeer and Robert Parish did most of the early scoring. Over the last couple of seasons, those guys always seem to get into a fight or two during a game, and this one was no different. Bill went up for a shot late in the first quarter and on his follow-through made incidental contact with Parish. The two squared off, and even though no punches were landed, both were ejected.

We stayed close and entered the fourth quarter tied at 81. Boston took an early lead in the final period, but then we started making some big shots. They were within six, but when I hit a triple with the 24-second clock running out, we had our biggest lead of the game and coasted to victory. We had finally done it, clearing the hurdle we had stumbled over so often in the past, and we had also won the important first game of a six-game road trip.

Our six-game road trip really kicked into high gear with our next stop in Dallas. The Mavericks are one of the best teams in the NBA, and this was the start of a stretch of four games in five nights in four different cities.

When we're on the road, most of the hotels we stay in have extensive health club facilities. When I walked into the health club in the Dallas hotel, I saw Darryl Dawkins working out. I was amazed to see a guy who's been in the league for 13 years working this hard to stay in shape, especially since he rarely plays. He worked out for several hours the night before the game against the Mavericks, and the next morning I called him to ask if he'd like to go to breakfast with me. When we met I told him how impressed I was with his work habits and desire. He said he really wanted to contribute to the team effort so he wanted to be ready at all times.

Surprisingly, that night Darryl was called on to play some important minutes during the third quarter. He responded in a big way, scoring eight points in just five minutes, denying the Mavericks an opportunity to make a comeback. Laimbeer carried us down the stretch, finishing with his best game of the season (23 points and 21 rebounds) as we went to 6-0 with a 108-99 victory.

After the game we got some discouraging news: Adrian Dantley was going to miss about a week of action and was being sent home. In the first quarter, Mark Aguirre had the ball on the wing for the Mavs and was making a move toward the basket. Mark's elbow caught Adrian in the mouth, fracturing his upper jaw, dislocating two teeth, and requiring 15 stitches to close the cut. This was the only downside to an otherwise good game, and now we had to make the necessary adjustments for playing without Adrian.

Back-to-back games can really wear you out. We flew a couple hours in the middle of the night and arrived in San Antonio at 2:30 a.m. It still amazes me that you can fly two hours in a jet and never leave the state of Texas. Bleary-eyed and exhausted, I got to the hotel, picked up my room key and headed for my room. I couldn't figure out why my key wouldn't open the door until I realized I had gone to the room number I had had in Dallas the night before. It's nights like this that you have to stop and think to even remember what city you're in.

Dennis Rodman replaced Adrian in the starting lineup and played well. The Spurs are a young team, and they played aggressively. They're going to be good, especially when David Robinson joins them. Although we never really took control of the game, we were ahead the entire second half. Again Joe Dumars was the key to the game, making several spectacular plays in the fourth quarter.

The next stop was Phoenix, one of my favorite cities. They always seem to have warm weather when we play there, and it gives us a chance to sit in the sun by the pool. This time it was 3:00 a.m. when we checked in from San Antonio, but Thursday was an off day, and I was even able to locate my hotel room on the first try. The Indiana Pacers had played the Suns the night before, and the hotel didn't have any more rooms with king-size beds. Because mine had twin beds, Mike (Abdenour) was gracious enough to give me his suite. While we were sorting all that out, Herb Williams of the Pacers came walking through the lobby and mentioned that something strange was going on with their team. They had just lost their seventh straight, and he had a feeling something drastic was about to happen. As it turned out, he was right, because Jack Ramsay, their coach, resigned later that day.

Talk about two teams going in different directions! Indiana had lost seven straight and we had won seven straight to start the season. Since we were unbeaten, every team we played wanted to be the first to beat Detroit. Phoenix came out strong, playing inspired basketball through the first three periods, but Joe Dumars and I combined for 61 points and we pulled away in the fourth quarter. The streak was now at eight and we were starting to get national attention.

Eight of our first ten games were on the road, and we were dead tired going into the next game against the Houston Rockets. We desperately wanted to keep the streak intact. The best start in the history of the franchise had been in 1970-71 when the Pistons with Dave Bing and a rookie named Bob Lanier started 9-0. For the first time, Chuck talked about being a part of history and setting a record. Never before had we really talked about records; we thought only about winning. We scored 40 points in the third quarter and led by three going into the fourth, but then we hit a brick wall. We ran out of gas in the fourth and Houston won to end the streak.

Now it was time to head back to Detroit for a couple days of rest before we ended the toughest stretch of the season with one more road game at Charlotte. Dick Harter has done an outstanding job with the Hornets. Not too much is expected of expansion teams in the first couple seasons, but Charlotte already had some success in the early part of the season.

I have mixed emotions when we play Charlotte because they have several people whom I consider very good friends. Dick Harter, Kelly Tripucka, Ralph Lewis and Earl Cureton all were in Detroit, and I enjoyed each of their friendships and still do today. One of the distinct advantages of playing in the NBA is the lasting friendships which develop over the years.

We played in the Charlotte Coliseum for the first time, and I have to admit that not only are the fans knowledgeable, but they became diehard Hornets fans almost immediately. The arena was sold out, and the decibel level was as loud as I have ever heard in any stadium. We didn't play well and I think fatigue became a factor in the second half, but Joe Dumars again bailed us out, scoring 26 points. Adrian had returned

Joe Dumars showing the form that later made
him the MVP in the Championship Series.

after missing three games with his injury, but then James Edwards sprained his ankle in the second quarter.

The road trip was finally over. We had finished it with a respectable 5-1 record and were 9-1 to start the season, but there were no breathers in sight. We now had to play the New York Knicks, followed by a rematch with the NBA Champion Lakers to be shown on national television.

With little time to prepare for New York's full-court press, we came home the day before Thanksgiving to play the Knicks. Over the last couple seasons under coach Rick Pitino the Knicks have played an up-tempo game, trying to force the opponents into turnovers with their full-court trapping defense. Unfortunately, on this night the strategy worked to perfection against us. Although we stayed close the first half, the Knicks made a big run late in the third quarter from which we were never able to recover. In addition, they made nine out of sixteen three-point field goals that really hurt us when we tried to rally.

It was by far our poorest performance of the year so far, but in an 82-game season you're going to have nights like that. You have to forget them immediately without letting the poor play carry over into the next game. This was especially true for us now, since we were playing the Lakers Thanksgiving weekend in a nationally televised game.

We took Thanksgiving Day off and used it to get reacquainted with our families, but after this brief break it was back to work preparing to play the Lakers. There was a lot of pre-game hype for the contest, which was being billed as Game Eight of the NBA Finals. Everyone in the media was promoting it as our revenge game, and maybe it was in a small way. None of us could forget it was the Lakers wearing the championship rings, and even a victory now would be small consolation for what had happened in June. Nevertheless, we wanted it badly to establish the fact that we were legitimate contenders for the title. Since the Lakers had beaten us twice during the last regular season, we wanted to change that trend too.

After our morning shoot-around, CBS Sports taped an interview with Magic Johnson and me. It was the first time I had seen Magic since summer, and we had a few laughs, talked about old times, then went home to rest before the game. Fortunately, we're both able to recognize the fine line between business and pleasure and not cross it at inappropriate times. When the referees throw the ball up, Magic and I are all business, but off the court we're the best of friends.

It was a long afternoon since the game wasn't to begin until 8:30 p.m. The crowd got into it early and it was exciting right from the start. Although it wasn't the best game either of us played by a long shot, it was very competitive. We led most of the way, but could never pull away decisively. They pulled to within two points late in the game after a couple of Magic free throws, but the biggest play of the game followed when Dennis Rodman grabbed an offensive rebound and hit Laimbeer for an assist. The Lakers missed a couple three-pointers to end the game and we escaped with the win.

If either team was trying to stake their claim as the team to beat for the title, I don't think either of us succeeded. Sure, we won, but I don't think we sent much of a message to the Lakers. The only thing we proved is that we're two pretty evenly matched teams.

The first month of the season was to end with a home-and-home series against the struggling Indiana Pacers. George Irvine was now coaching Indiana; they were playing better and injuries were starting to take their toll on us. James Edwards was still out, Joe Dumars missed the trip to Indiana because of a sprained ankle suffered in the Lakers game, and Rick Mahorn was down with the flu. We knew we were in for a tough time against the Pacers.

It was close through three, and we had forged ahead by five going into the fourth quarter when the bottom dropped out. We couldn't buy a basket for the first six minutes of the period, and the Pacers moved out to a big lead. We made a valiant comeback effort, only to fall short at the end.

With their win, the Pacers came into The Palace the next night full of confidence. We came out trying to bury them early, and although we were up by 10 at the end of the first quarter, Indiana hung close and stayed with us the rest of the game. When Reggie Miller hit a three-pointer with 30 seconds left they pulled to within one, but I made a six-footer with no time left on the 24-second clock and we hung on to win 114-111.

Although we finished November with an 11-3 mark and Chuck Daly was named coach of the month, we weren't all that happy with our play. Since our 8-0 start, we were only 3-3. Part of the reason we weren't playing as well the last half of the month was the changing of player rotations we were forced into on defense because of the injuries to Dumars, Dantley, and Edwards. We were also tired. Twelve of our first 17 games were on the road, and we couldn't look forward to being home for any length of time until December 22. We were also getting accustomed to playing in The Palace. It was a big change from the Silverdome, and we knew eventually this wonderful arena would give us a tremendous home-court advantage, but we had to get a couple of months playing there under our belts first.

"The Worm" takes the elevator to the top floor for an offensive put-back.

BAD BOYS

4 = DECEMBER

ON THE
ROAD AGAIN. AT CERTAIN
times in the season it seems as if I've
never done anything but live out of a suitcase, and this was one of those times. We
were heading for Washington, which at
least allows us to be able to eat dinner at
A.D.'s mom's house. Adrian, Joe D., Darryl
Dawkins, John Salley, and I piled into a
couple of cabs, eagerly anticipating a good
home-cooked meal and a place to relax
other than our hotel rooms. Besides, Mrs.
Dantley makes the best home-made bis-
cuits I've ever tasted (no offense, Mom).

This was our first trip to D.C. since
eliminating the Bullets in the playoffs last

spring. They had forced us into a tough five-game series, including a Game Five which Chuck has said made him more nervous than any other game in his career. That series made us that much tougher the rest of the way. We played the best half of basketball we had played to that point, taking a 61-41 lead into the locker room at halftime. Even though we had the big lead, we all knew Washington was going to make a comeback in the second half. They cut the lead to seven points going into the fourth quarter and were in a position to win. Bernard King played the best basketball I had ever seen him play since his severe knee injury a couple of years ago. You really have to respect a guy like Bernard, who, even though he's missed so much time because of injuries, never quits. Although he scored 37 points, we held off the Bullets in the final quarter and won 120-114.

This wasn't your everyday, run-of-the-mill road trip. After playing in Washington on Friday, December 2, our next game was Sunday night in New Jersey. Under normal circumstances, spending a Saturday night in New Jersey sounds about as exciting as watching somebody get a haircut. But I've learned that if I'm ever looking for something to do, I always look no farther than John Salley. John's always got places to go and people to see. This trip was no different, because John happens to be good friends with Eddie Murphy. We went to Eddie's house, the other end of which must be in a different zip code. I'm a big fan of his, and this was the first time I had ever seen him other than in a public appearance.

As it turned out, he claimed to be a decent chess player, so I challenged him to a game. Even though I hadn't played in a while, I managed to beat him—no joke! He's one of the best comedians in the world, and every time you see him he's laughing and joking, so I was surprised to discover he also has a serious side, and is really just a nice guy.

Over the last several seasons we've had good success against the Nets, and this time was no different. Salley played one of his best games of the season, scoring 19 points and leading a balanced attack. Not bad, another win on the road, two for two on the current trip, and 8-2 on the road for the season. A big reason for this success was our playoff experience last spring. Any time the game was close or on the line, our guys refused to get rattled and stayed very much under control, still playing our game. Next stop, and last on the trip, Milwaukee.

In my first seven seasons in the league, one of the most difficult places to win was the MECCA in Milwaukee. The Bucks have always been good, but they also played in an arena that intimidated the opposing team. Not only was the MECCA one of the oldest arenas in the NBA, it was also one of the smallest. The Milwaukee franchise realized this and built a new stadium right next door to the old one—the Bradley Center. I was looking forward to playing in the new building because we rarely had success in the old one.

The Bucks had become one of the surprises of the young season. Most people had written them off at the beginning of the year, saying they were too old and needed to make major changes. But Terry Cummings was having his best year as a pro and they were playing well as a team. Whenever you're on the road, the last game of the trip is called the getaway game because you leave for home immediately afterward. We must have been thinking about that the second half. Although we led by one point at halftime, we got blown out of the new arena in the third and fourth quarters. Milwaukee put on a clinic and handed us our worst defeat of the season, 109-84. We started to notice for the first time with the Milwaukee game something that was to become increasingly obvious as the season progressed: when a team had us beat, they didn't want to just beat us, they wanted to really rub it in our face. The positive note after this game was that we had won two out of three on the road, and we were going home for three of our next four games.

The next night we came home to play Chicago for the second time. Including the playoffs, we were on a four-game winning streak against the Bulls. While we had been having good success against Michael Jordan, our key weapon was A.D., because Chicago is one of the few teams in the league that still covers Dantley with one man instead of double-teaming. All we've had to do is get the ball to Adrian and let him go to work. This game was no different, as he led us to another win, scoring 31 points including 14 in the fourth quarter. Defensively against Jordan, we may have done our best job ever. For the first time in 75 games, he scored less than 20 points thanks to three guys named Dumars, Johnson, and Rodman. After trailing for most of the

Bill Bonds of WXYZ-TV being
escorted off the floor by Piston Girls

first half, we outscored Chicago in each of the final three periods and won by 13, 102-89.

When we arrived in Atlanta for our next game, many of the Hawk players and coaches were talking about how physical our team was and expressing concern over the possibility of injuries to their team. There's always been a big rivalry between Detroit and Atlanta, perhaps even bigger than Detroit-Boston, and with the off-season trades for Reggie Theus and Moses Malone, many preseason predictions had Atlanta winning the Central Division. To this point in the season they hadn't lived up to the expectations, and they were starting to feel the pressure. Detroit coming to town was the biggest game of the season for them so far, and we all knew it would be very physical.

Both teams shot poorly the whole game, neither one even managing to shoot 40 percent from the floor. Joe Dumars was fouled by Glenn Rivers, and another fight almost erupted because Bill Laimbeer went to Joe's defense. Even though he was hurting the rest of the game, Joe led us with 24 points as we won 92-82. It was important for us to beat Atlanta the first couple of times because we didn't want them to get a lot of confidence against us. Even though they weren't playing up to their preseason hype yet, we knew they'd be heard from before the end of the year.

Now we were 15-4 and playing well together, but I was struggling with my shooting. I'm not really sure what the problem was, but against Atlanta I had made only 5 of 19 field goal attempts, and with that performance my overall shooting percentage had slipped to just 43 percent. I came out early to The Palace the next day because I wanted to work on my mechanics and try to get my shot back before the Sixers game. We needed a strong effort because at the time the Sixers were leading the Atlantic Division. Fortunately, my discipline paid off as I had my best shooting night of the season. I think this was the first game we really felt at home at The Palace. I scored 37 points, the season's high for me, but more importantly I hit 16 of 22 field goals and we defeated Philadelphia, 106-100.

We looked forward to a couple days off before our next game, which we really needed. We had just come off a stretch of four games in five nights and the team was a little tired, and also we were about to face two leading Central Division rivals, Milwaukee and Cleveland. Milwaukee was one of the surprise teams in the league, establishing itself as a legitimate contender, and Cleveland was probably playing the best basketball in the NBA.

First up was Milwaukee in The Palace. They led at halftime 65-58, but then we made a big third-quarter rally. We moved in front by seven points late in the period, but then everything broke down. Ricky Pierce scored 10 points in the final two minutes and we found ourselves down by one at the end of three quarters. The Bucks pulled away in the fourth quarter and beat us for the second straight time, 119-110.

Our prospects for the immediate future didn't seem much brighter, since we left for Cleveland right after the Milwaukee game. Although they had been beaten by the Lakers at home two nights earlier, Cleveland coach Lenny Wilkens blamed the loss on the fact that they were preparing for the Pistons. They must have prepared well. They scored 40 points in the first quarter and totally dominated us the rest of the way, beating us 119-98. Amazingly, the game wasn't even as close as the final score indicated, and it gave the Cavs plenty of confidence which helped them the rest of the season as we battled each other for the Central Division crown. It was time for the Detroit Pistons to regroup, because Cleveland was starting to look like they would run away with it. Fortunately, our next two games were at home against expansion teams.

Of the two new teams, Charlotte was playing better than Miami. They had veteran players who knew what it took to win, and under Coach Dick Harter they had progressed well as a team. This was the third matchup, and the first two had been close. Actually, I'm glad we only play Charlotte four times, be-

DECEMBER

73

cause if we played them six like the other teams in the division, they'd probably win a couple. This game was close like the others and we couldn't manage to pull away. Although we turned the ball over 27 times, we won 100-91.

Originally, we weren't scheduled to play the Miami Heat until February 1, but since The Palace had a chance to book Neil Diamond, the game was switched to December 20. This worked out well for us, because without the change we would have played only one game in the next 10 days. That's bad, because a team tends to get stale over a stretch like that. It's nice to rest and have a chance to get healthy again, but with only practice, and without the motivation and excitement provided by games, you lose the edge.

The next game was Homecoming for Ron Rothstein, the new coach of Miami. As an assistant coach in Detroit, he had been highly regarded by players, coaches, and fans. He was like Buddy Ryan, Mike Ditka's assistant when the Bears won the Super Bowl, before he went to the head coaching job at Philadelphia. Ronnie had been a key part of our success over the last two seasons and deserves much of the credit because of his outstanding pre-game scouting reports and his ability to dissect opponents' offenses and defenses.

The two expansion teams had taken different approaches in selecting players to build their new franchises. While the Hornets went for veterans, Miami has a roster built around rookies and second-year players. Even though we won 116-100, the highlight of the night came after the final horn when a bunch of our guys almost dumped a cooler of Gatorade on Ronnie's head. At the last minute, since he was wearing a nice suit, we decided to spare him the expense of a dry-cleaning bill.

After being thoroughly embarrassed by the New York Knicks earlier in the season at home, we were really looking forward to the rematch. New York during the Christmas holidays is a great place to visit, but all I wanted to do was get in and out of town as quickly as possible. In every NBA city there are rabid fans whose whole world revolves around the fortunes of their team, and New York is especially bad in that regard. By December the Knicks had established themselves as one of the premier teams in the league, holding down the top spot in the Atlantic Division usually occupied by the Celtics, or occasionally the Sixers.

After the morning shoot-around in Madison Square Garden, I returned to my hotel room. I usually have the hotel operator screen my calls, but before I had a chance to call the front desk, the phone rang and some guy said that if I played that night against the Knicks, he was going to kill me. At first I didn't take it too seriously, but the more I thought about it, the more I started to worry. Unfortunately, this has happened to me about a half dozen times in my career, so at least I knew what to do—I called league security, and they took appropriate measures.

This was a big game for both teams, and we knew it would be intense and physical. It was close all the way, but we were in a position to win, leading 85-82, when we let the lead and the game slip away. Mark Jackson hit a jump hook shot with 32 seconds left and the Knicks had beaten us again, 88-85. The only other thing I can say about the death threat is that when you walk out on the court, you try to block everything but the game from your mind. Does it affect you? Of course, and I shot just 5 for 18 from the field, but I'd say it was more because of their tough defense than because I had trouble concentrating.

Even though we lost to New York, we were all looking forward to spending a few days at home over Christmas. Chuck didn't want to give us too much time off, so we practiced on December 23, working on our biggest problem: offensive production. For some reason, we seemed to have difficulty scoring

Rick Mahorn displays the intensity that helped the Pistons to the 1989 NBA Championship.

all season long, although we had established ourselves as one of the best defensive teams in the league.

Being home for the holidays gave us all a chance to go Christmas shopping. Like a lot of other people, I always wait until the last minute, but it's a little more difficult for me because I can't go to a shopping mall without being swamped by people wanting my autograph. I try to wear some kind of disguise when I go out, like sunglasses and a hat, but it usually doesn't help. Going out to buy a simple present for my wife usually turns into a couple-hour excursion.

With three days off, I was anxious to stay home and be with my family since we had been away for such a long time. I will admit, however, that I sneaked into The Palace a couple of times to practice my jump shot. On December 27, the day before the Phoenix game, I got another death threat, this time from Chuck Daly. He ran us so hard I think he was trying to kill us, making sure we ran off our Christmas dinners and were ready for the Suns. I haven't run that much since I was in high school at Westchester St. Joseph's.

Phoenix is a greatly improved team with a couple of exciting players in Tom Chambers and Kevin Johnson. They had just beaten the Lakers, so we knew what they were capable of doing. Johnson is one of the quickest players in the league, and it was going to be my job to chase him around all night. We led most of the game, thanks to a big edge at the free-throw line, won the game 106-100, and started preparing for another tough Western Conference opponent, Houston.

The Rockets have probably the premier center in the NBA. Akeem "The Dream" Olajuwon is big, strong, can score and rebound with the best, and creates problems for any team he faces. Fortunately, we have Rick Mahorn, one of the best post-up defensive players in the league. There were at least four confrontations between the two, but Akeem was in foul trouble most of the game and Rick held him to just 14 points. Both Joe Dumars and I had big offensive games, but Rick was the real star and we beat Houston 95-83. Two months of the season were history, and so was 1988. Our team made a New Year's Resolution: we were going to win the NBA Championship.

MARK AGUIRRE

POSITION: Forward
HEIGHT: 6'6"
WEIGHT: 232 Pounds
COLLEGE: DePaul '82
HIGH SCHOOL: Chicago Westinghouse, Illinois
BIRTHDATE: 12-10-59
BIRTHPLACE: Chicago, Illinois
WHEN DRAFTED: First Round (1st Overall)
HOW ACQUIRED: From Dallas in Exchange for Adrian Dantley, and Detroit's Number One Draft Choice in 1991
PRO EXPERIENCE: Eight Years
MARITAL STATUS: Married (Angela)
RESIDENCE: Bloomfield Hills, MI

AGUIRRE	G	GS	MIN	FG	FGA	PCT	FG	FGA	PCT	FT	FTA	PCT	OFF	DEF	TOT	AST	PF	BLK	PTS	AVG
				FIELD GOALS			**3-POINT FG**			**FREE THROWS**			**REBOUNDS**							
Through 4/23 (Tot)	80	76	2597	586	1270	.461	51	174	.293	288	393	.733	146	240	386	278	229	36	1511	18.9
Through 4/23 (Det)	36	32	1068	213	441	.483	22	75	.293	110	149	.738	56	95	151	89	101	7	558	15.5
Playoffs	17	17	462	89	182	.489	8	29	.276	28	38	.737	26	49	75	28	38	3	214	12.6

	MIN	REB	AST	ST	TO	BL	PTS	MIN	REB	AST	STL	TO	BLK	PTS	REB	AST	PF	STL	TO	BLK	PTS
	SINGLE GAME HIGHS							**AVERAGE PER GAME**							**AVERAGE PER 48 MINUTES**						
Through 4/23 (Tot)	46	11	17	3	7	3	41	32.5	4.8	3.5	0.56	2.6	0.45	18.9	7.1	5.1	4.2	0.83	3.8	0.67	27.9
Through 4/23 (Det)	46	11	7	3	5	2	31	29.7	4.2	2.5	0.44	1.9	0.19	15.5	6.8	4.0	4.5	0.72	3.1	0.31	25.1
Playoffs	36	10	4	2	4	1	25	27.2	4.4	1.6	0.47	1.2	0.18	12.6	7.8	2.9	3.9	0.83	2.1	0.31	22.2

THIS SEASON: Acquired from the Dallas Mavericks on Feb. 15 in the NBA's biggest trade of the season...While acquiring Aguirre, the Pistons sent Adrian Dantley and Detroit's number-one draft choice in 1991 to the Mavericks...With Aguirre, the Pistons were 31-6, including a 29-4 mark when he was in the starting lineup...For the first time in his NBA career, he averaged less than 20 points per game...Entered the season with a career scoring average of 24.9 points per game, but in 1988-89 he averaged just 18.9 points per game...With the Pistons, he finished the season averaging 15.5 points per game...Scored better than double figures in 31 of 36 games...Had his Pistons' high of 31 points versus the New Jersey Nets on Feb. 25...Scored 20 points or better in nine games with Detroit...Grabbed a season's high of 11 rebounds versus the Milwaukee Bucks on April 9...All-time leading scorer in Dallas Maverick's history, averaged 21.6 points per game in 44 games this season with the Mavs...

Vinnie Johnson driving to the basket

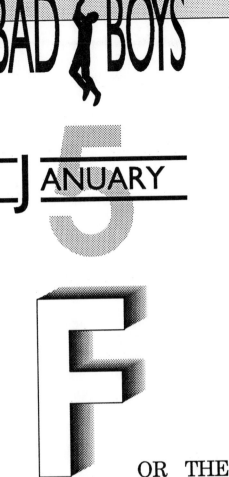

BAD BOYS

JANUARY 5

OR THE
LAST TWO SEASONS, OUR
team has enjoyed a luxury not shared by
any other team in the league: our own
private jet, Roundball One. Owner Bill
Davidson bought the plane prior to the 1987
campaign, and part of our success, at least,
must be attributed to the fact that we no
longer fly commercially. It may not seem
like a big deal, but it's a great advantage
when we play games back-to-back. If we
play away on a Tuesday night, for example,
and then at The Palace on Wednesday,
we're in our own beds late Tuesday night
rather than in a hotel facing an early wake-
up call and getting back to Detroit only

hours before game time. Basketball's an emotional sport, and most of us can't sleep after a game anyway, so spending the hours of restlessness traveling home rather than watching TV in a hotel room makes a big difference. Adrian Dantley said early last year that the use of the plane would add a couple of years to his career, and I hope that's true for all of us.

I guess we really didn't know how much we appreciated Roundball One until we lost it. It was out of service in early January, and we had to travel to Atlanta for our first game of the new year on a scheduled airline. The game was January 3, and because we left the day before, we had to miss all the football bowl games which were played on Monday. I have to say it was nice to mix with the crowds again, though, walking through airport terminals and signing autographs. People haven't seen us much at Detroit Metro airport lately, and everyone was very friendly.

During our last road game against New York we seemed uptight, but on the way to Atlanta we were relaxed and confident. We've had good success against the Hawks in the Omni, and having won there once already and playing them again at The Palace three days later, the pressure was on them. Our only distraction was that the NBA Rumor Mill, which is never silent for long, was working overtime, and this time it concerned us. Stories out of Indianapolis had Dick Versace, our top assistant, going to Indiana as the new head coach of the Pacers.

Atlanta-Detroit games are usually low scoring, defensive contests, but this one was anything but typical. We were leading 38-34 after the first quarter, and it was still close at the half, but the Hawks got hot and killed us in the third period. Moses Malone played one of his best games ever against the Pistons (28 points, 22 rebounds, 5 blocked shots), and Atlanta won the game 124-103.

The rumors turned out to be correct, and Dick Versace became the new head coach of the Pacers. We were definitely going to miss him, but the more immediate problem was finding a replacement. Ironically, our two straight games with Atlanta resulted in Chuck hiring one of their assistant coaches, Brendan Suhr. I don't think Atlanta was too happy about Brendan leaving the Hawks, because they wouldn't permit him to sit on our bench for the next two games, including the first one which was against the Hawks.

With their easy victory in the first game, the Hawks were full of confidence when they came to Detroit. We had been preparing intensely for two days, however, and it paid off. We shot well and absolutely destroyed them in the third quarter, leading by as many as 27 points. Combined with a strong defensive effort, we had little trouble disposing of Atlanta, 111-88.

The next night it was Dick Versace's Indiana Pacers, on the road. Since he had just left the Pistons, no one knew better than he what we did both offensively and defensively. But the Pacers are a funny team. Against us, they always seem to crank their game up a notch and play with terrific intensity, and then they go out the next night, play indifferently, and lose to somebody they should beat. As a pro, you have to strive above all to play with consistency and with the same level of intensity each night. If you don't, you can get beat on any given night, and you're going to lose a lot of games you should win.

With the coaching change, the Pacers came into our game with a new attitude. The night before, they had beaten the Clippers by 30 points, and they were ready to do the same thing to the Pistons. I know Dick was excited about playing us. He wanted this game badly, and he had his team playing well right out of the gate. They took it to us early, and we never recovered, losing 113-99. This was our second loss to a team we thought would be lucky to win 30 games all year. It wasn't one of the high points of the season.

The Knicks were coming to town again. We hadn't beaten them in our first two meetings, and I guess you could say at that point they definitely had our number. They cause us plenty of trouble, especially when they get the ball to Patrick Ewing in the low post. We have to double team him, but when we do that he dishes it back outside to a guard or forward who shoots a three-pointer, a weapon they've used very effectively this season.

We were in control most of the game, but once again we couldn't deliver the knockout punch. For the second straight time at The Palace, the three-point shot destroyed us. The Knicks made 9 of 16 threes and outscored us in the fourth quarter 27-16. They started to get the feeling they were invincible against us, which we really didn't mind, because when you're overconfident you make mistakes and you lose.

Losing the game was bad enough, but we received even worse news afterwards. Late in the game, Joe Dumars was called for a foul after attempting a steal from Gerald Wilkins, and he came running down the court holding his left hand. It didn't seem to be anything too serious when Chuck took him out of the game, but our trainer, Mike Abdenour, and Dr. Ben Paolucci had serious looks of concern on their faces. An hour after the game we got the bad news: X-rays showed a broken left hand and Joe would be out five to six weeks. We were already without one starter because of Rick Mahorn's back problems, and now we would be missing another for an extended length of time. I don't think there's a team in the league that can win consistently with two starters out of the lineup. The next few weeks were going to be critical if we had any hope of challenging for the division title.

For the first time in four years, the Pistons had to play without Joe Dumars. In many ways, Joe may be our most valuable player. He has been the most underrated player in the league by the media, though not by the other players, who all realize how good he is. He's not only a standout on defense, he can also score big when we need it, as he's shown again and again this season. We've been called the deepest team in the league because of the number of quality players who can step in and make a good contribution. The next few weeks would put that theory to the test, as Vinnie would be called on to play a lot of minutes with Joe injured. He had been struggling offensively, and now we really needed to get him going.

We had lost three of our last four games, and a lot of people were asking what was wrong with the Pistons. But even with those losses we were off to the best start in the history of the franchise, so my answer would have been, "Nothing." The injuries weren't helping things much, but we still felt we were one of the best teams in the league. One of the problems was the red-hot Cleveland Cavaliers, who were off to a 25-6 start and were getting all the attention in the Central Division. In a way, that was fine with us, because media attention can distract you from your primary purpose of winning basketball games.

With only one day to prepare for our next game against Washington, Chuck knew the whole rotation of our players had to change drastically. He told me I'd better be ready to play 40 minutes a night for the next four to five weeks, and I told him I could handle it. The Bullets weren't playing too well and we finally had a game where it didn't seem impossible to score. The Teacher, Adrian Dantley, had his best scoring game of the season in a 119-103 victory. He always seems to have good games against the Bullets because he's playing against his hometown team. It's the same for me when we play the Bulls. Although I don't always have good games against Chicago, I play harder because I know all my family and friends are watching.

A Sunday afternoon in Milwaukee had us playing the hottest team in the league. Earlier in the season the Bucks were being called one of the surprises, but with the talent they have, no one should have been surprised. With Cleveland, New York, and Detroit, Milwaukee had established itself as one of the top four teams in the Eastern Conference, and the realization that we had a combined 0-6 record against the other three didn't do much for our confidence. Injuries are part of the game, and we couldn't use that as an excuse. If we were going to contend for the Championship, we had to beat the best teams in our conference, beginning with this game in Milwaukee.

We led for the first three quarters, but one of the toughest things to do in the NBA is hold a lead on the road when the home crowd gets into the act. When the fans get caught up in the excitement and help trigger a comeback, the momentum swings to the home team. At the end of the third quarter, I was really tired and Chuck took me out to give me a rest. We were down a guard because of the injury to Joe, and in the next few minutes Michael Williams showed us why he's a rookie. As a point guard, one of your most important responsibilities is to control the tempo of the game.

Isiah relaxes for a moment before getting back into action.

Michael hasn't had a lot of experience in pressure situations, because Vinnie, Joe, and I have always been in at crunch time. The Bucks took control of the tempo at the beginning of the fourth quarter and turned the game into a track meet. They outscored us 42-26 in the last period and won 120-112. Although they turned it around in the fourth quarter, an incredible discrepancy at the foul line didn't help our situation. Milwaukee shot 25 more free throws than we did, so even though we outscored them from the field, we lost. Our reputation as the "Bad Boys" was really hurting us on the road, because officials seemed to be anticipating calls rather than waiting for the play to be completed.

Our first three-game homestand of the season awaited us at The Palace, starting with the Celtics. The Detroit-Boston games have evolved into one of the biggest rivalries in the NBA, and when we play the Celtics there's not a lot of love lost. After we knocked them out of the playoffs last year, there was a subtle shift in the way the two teams perceive each other. Before, we had always considered playing the Celtics one of the biggest games of the season, while for them it was just another game. That hasn't been completely reversed, but it's certainly true that every Pistons game is extremely important to the Celtics.

For the first time I can ever remember, we were playing Boston Bird-less. Earlier in the season when we had beaten Boston, Larry Bird played with painful bone spurs in both feet, and after the game he decided to have surgery which left him out for the season. But I have a hard time feeling sorry for a team that's handed us so many whippings during my eight years in the league. And they still had Robert Parish and Kevin McHale, two of the best low-post scorers in the league.

Boston came out with a lot of intensity and played tough defense. Nothing we tried worked and Chuck wasn't at all happy with our effort, to say the least. Trailing 53-42 at halftime, he absolutely exploded in the locker room. Chuck's not normally a screamer, but this time he made an exception and they must have heard him in the cheap seats. He's usually under control and has a subtle way of getting his point across. If you're playing hard and losing, he won't holler at you because he knows you're putting forth your best effort, but if you're not giving it all you've got, watch out. He really gave us hell at halftime, and his tirade got us going in the second half. We outscored Boston by 20 points and allowed them just 34 second-half points to win 96-87.

The win over the Celtics was a good way to start the homestand, and on paper at least, the next two against New Jersey and Indiana should have been easier. We didn't play well against the Nets and in fact with eight minutes left we only led by two, but Dennis Rodman grabbed a bunch of key rebounds and we won 103-90. We had been looking forward to the rematch with the Pacers ever since they had beaten us the week before. We outscored them 19-0 the first six minutes of the second quarter, took a 26-point lead, and it was all but over. Final score: 132-99. Not a bad homestand. We went 3-0, and it was time to look ahead to the Boston Celtics in the Garden and another nationally televised game on CBS.

This was Super Bowl Sunday, and apparently the Celtics hadn't lost on a Super Bowl Sunday in quite a while, so the papers were making a big deal about their streak. Earlier in the week when we beat them, we were able to effectively stop Parish and McHale, but not this time. Both of them killed us inside and we lost 112-99. Most of the guys are serious football fans so there was a lot of interest in the San Francisco-Cincinnati game, but since we were still without Roundball One and had to take a commercial flight, we missed most of the game. We did catch the exciting finish, however, and saw the 49ers win.

Our thoughts quickly returned to basketball. For the first time, we were five games behind Cleveland and in danger of getting so far out of it we wouldn't be able to make a run for the Central Division title. Fortunately, we had another three-game homestand so we could try to make up a little ground while we waited for everyone to get healthy.

We started the stretch at home against the Golden State Warriors. The Warriors are coached by Don Nelson, who was at Milwaukee when they won the Central Division year after year. Nelly has one of the most creative minds in basketball and always has competitive teams. Not many people realize he's the guy who virtually wrote the book on the zone defense. A zone, of course, is illegal in the NBA, but his teams always play near that fine line between legal and illegal. He's always had great defensive teams and this year's was no exception. When I say he has a creative mind, I'm not kidding, because for most of the season he's been winning games with four guards and a center.

We made it look easy at the beginning, leading by as much as 18 in the first quarter, and still holding a 10-point lead at halftime. Even midway through the fourth, things seemed to be under control with a seven-point lead. But Don Nelson-coached teams never quit, and just like that they reeled off eight straight points and we were down by one. We seesawed back and forth for a couple minutes and still found ourselves down by one point with 30 seconds left, 104-103. Although I love to be in these situations, where one shot can win the game, this time I was angry because we had blown our lead and the game shouldn't even have been close. During the timeout, Chuck set up a pick and roll play, but it broke down and I found myself with the ball and with only one man to beat. The problem was it happened to be Manute Bol, at 7-foot-6, the tallest player and best shot blocker in the league. With the game clock running down, I saw Manute coming at me and said, "Uh-oh." For the first time in my life, I wished I were 10 feet tall because I just wanted to dunk the ball on Manute. I threw it up with a prayer, and when I released it I knew I had a nice touch on it, but I didn't think it would bank in because it was so high. Fortunately, I got a lucky bounce and the shot went in.

If we had lost that game, I'm sure it would have really hurt us psychologically. It was bad enough as it was, because even though we were 26-12, we were stagnant and not improving as a basketball team. I remember picking up the newspapers the next day and seeing that Chuck had said the same thing. He said we weren't playing well, and it had nothing to do with the plays we were running, but rather with an attitude of selfishness. This wasn't the direction we wanted to be going with a big game against Cleveland next on the schedule.

If there was any one game this season which really enhanced our reputation as the "Bad Boys" of the league, it was the Cleveland game. They led the division and were coming into our house to play the so-called defending champs, who were playing like anything but champions. Things didn't get any better for us during the first half of the game, and we trailed Cleveland 48-39.

When Larry Nance hit a jump shot to put Cleveland up by 16 early in the second half, Bill Laimbeer and Brad Daugherty got tangled up under the basket. After they exchanged elbows, they

Two Pistons' fans display their favorite Bad Boys.

began throwing punches and probably for the first time in his career, Laimbeer actually hit someone with a punch. Although he's been in his share of shoving matches, somehow Bill has always been able to hold back and not throw punches. But not this time. He hit Daugherty square on the jaw and really hurt him. I was near Brad and could see his eyes glass over, so I yelled at Cleveland coach Lenny Wilkins, but fortunately it turned out not to be a serious injury. Both players were ejected and the game turned into a physical war. We trailed by as many as 17 points, cut the deficit to 13 at the end of the third quarter, then held them scoreless for over seven minutes, tying the game with three minutes left.

With 13 seconds left, we were down 80-79, so for the second straight game the winner was going to be decided on the last shot, and again I was the one who was supposed to be taking it. James Edwards screened for me and I was open on the baseline for a jumper. The play was run to perfection, but this time I didn't make the shot. It's great to be a hero and sink the game winner, but more importantly to me, I feel I'm strong enough to take the heat when I miss the last shot. I do know that I'm the one who wants to take that shot, make or miss.

With the fight in the Cleveland game, Laimbeer, "Bad Boy Number 1", was facing a stiff fine. But the next day we found out he was not only going to be fined but also suspended for a game. We couldn't believe it. Among other things, Bill had the fourth longest consecutive game playing streak in NBA history at 685 games. I talked to him that night and really felt bad because there were a lot of nights over the last eight seasons when he probably shouldn't have played but did because the streak meant so much to him. It was a shame it had to end this way.

Every night before home games in The Palace, Bill and I would sit in the sauna for a few minutes talking about our game plan for the night. It was strange not to have him there. When we go out for pre-game warm-ups, Bill is always the first one on the floor and I'm right behind him. This was the first time in eight years it didn't happen that way. Sacramento was playing well, but with Bill out we didn't want to have a close game going down to the wire. We had probably our best half of the season, outscoring the Kings 64-36 in the first two quarters, then winning easily 122-97.

All season long our team has generated as much or more attention off the court as on, with the fines, suspensions, coaching changes, and trade rumors. After the Sacramento game, trade rumors were flying everywhere in the country. They started in Detroit and Dallas with talk of a blockbuster Adrian Dantley for Mark Aguirre deal. Rumors are part of life in the NBA and you never know how much truth there is to them. I will say that of all the trades allegedly going to occur, about 99 percent of them never materialize.

Mark Aguirre has been a very close friend of mine since about the age of 10 when we were both growing up in Chicago. We've always stayed in touch since our grade school days. When the rumors were flying fast and furious, he called me up to see what I knew. It was no secret at the time that Mark wasn't real happy in Dallas. I told him I really didn't know much, that our whole team had been involved in trade rumors at one time or another, and that it was just a fact of life in the NBA. A couple years ago, everyone had me going to Houston for Ralph Sampson. I think the real reason the rumors started is that we weren't playing good basketball, even though we had a decent record. The proposed Aguirre-Dantley deal became such a national story that it distracted everyone on the team.

Last year we had beaten Chicago four of five times in the Stadium, and already had opened with a win there in our first game this season. You just don't expect to have that kind of success in one team's building, especially against the Bulls and Michael Jordan. We had beaten them four straight times, and although none of the games had really even been close, this game was close from start to finish. Without Joe Dumars in the lineup, Dennis Rodman had to defend Jordan most of the game. The fourth quarter is usually Michael's time to win the game, but Dennis kept him under control, and in fact fouled him out when he took a charge. We went into overtime, which is our time, and outscored Chicago by six to win 104-98.

Now we were playing better basketball, and we got the added good news that Roundball One was back in service to take us to Philadelphia for our next game with the Sixers. It's hard to believe, but we've had even more success in Philadelphia than in Chicago and have won six straight against the Sixers. Despite all the rumors, Dantley was unbelievable and had probably his best shooting game as a Detroit Piston. Although he wouldn't admit it, the trade rumors were making him play better basketball. He scored 33 points and we had another road win over the Sixers, 124-106.

Next it was the Bulls for the second time in a week, and another game on national television. The pre-game hype focused on our dominance of the Bulls over the last year and a half, and we had to guard against overconfidence. Nothing will beat you quicker in this league than taking another team for granted. It was an early afternoon game and we came out sluggish. Chuck called a timeout early and asked us if we wanted to embarrass ourselves in front of a national audience. We made a strong showing in the second quarter and then played the Bulls even the rest of the way. It was our fourth straight win and we were starting to feel good about ourselves again. The trade rumors had subsided and the whole team was playing with confidence.

With just one game left before the All-Star Game, we really

wanted to take a five-game winning streak into the break. The only thing standing in our way was the Milwaukee Bucks, and we still had not beaten them or any of the other top three teams in the Eastern Conference. Against Milwaukee, Cleveland, and New York, we had a dismal 0-8 record, and if we wanted to think of ourselves as one of the best teams in the league, we knew we'd damn well better start beating our toughest competition. Milwaukee is a big and physical team, which causes us problems, especially in the backcourt since we have small guards by NBA standards.

We held the Bucks to just 37 points in the first half and controlled the game throughout. One of the keys to our 107-96 victory was Joe Dumars. It tells you something about Joe not only as a player but as a person when you realize he returned from his hand injury two weeks early. Most guys in the league would have waited until after the All-Star break, giving them an extra couple days off, especially since his first game back was against one of the most physical teams in the league. And if they played at all, most guys would have played tentatively, but not Joe D. It's too bad he was hurt and missed 12 games, because there's no question in my mind that he would have made the All-Star team if he had been healthy.

34
FENNIS
DEMBO

POSITION: Forward-Guard
HEIGHT: 6'8"
WEIGHT: 215 Pounds
COLLEGE: Wyoming, '88
HIGH SCHOOL: Fox Tech High School, San Antonio, TX
BIRTHDATE: 01-24-66
BIRTHPLACE: Mobile, Alabama
WHEN DRAFTED: Second Round (30th Overall) Detroit
HOW ACQUIRED: College Draft
PRO EXPERIENCE: One Year
MARITAL STATUS: Married (Dorthea)
RESIDENCE: San Antonio, TX

DEMBO	G	GS	MIN	FIELD GOALS FG	FGA	PCT	3-POINT FG FG	FGA	PCT	FREE THROWS FT	FTA	PCT	REBOUNDS OFF	DEF	TOT	AST	PF	BLK	PTS	AVG
Through 4/23	31	0	74	14	42	.333	0	4	.000	8	10	.800	8	15	23	5	15	0	36	1.2
Playoffs	2	0	4	1	1	1.000	0	0	----	0	0	----	0	0	0	0	1	0	2	1.0

	SINGLE GAME HIGHS MIN	REB	AST	ST	TO	BL	PTS	AVERAGE PER GAME MIN	REB	AST	STL	TO	BLK	PTS	AVERAGE PER 48 MINUTES REB	AST	PF	STL	TO	BLK	PTS
Through 4/23	7	5	2	1	1	0	8	2.4	0.7	0.2	0.03	0.2	0.00	1.2	14.9	3.2	9.7	0.65	4.5	0.00	23.4
Playoffs	2	0	0	0	1	0	2	2.0	0.0	0.0	0.00	0.5	0.00	1.0	0.0	0.0	12.0	0.00	12.0	0.00	24.0

LAST SEASON: The Pistons' 1988 top draft choice (30th overall) from Wyoming had to make the big adjustment from college small forward to NBA big guard...Played in a total of just 31 games with all but one of the remaining games being DNPs due to Coach's Decision...He missed the Atlanta game on January 3 due to a sore back...Of his 31 appearances, he scored in 13 games...Scored his career high of 8 points at Cleveland on December 15 when he connected on 4-4 field goals...Although he was primarily used at the big guard position, he did see limited action at small forward...Joined fellow rookie Michael Williams as the only Pistons' player not to shoot better than 40 percent from the field...His 31 games played were by far the lowest total of any Pistons' player who was on the roster from the start of the season...

Bad Boys: the view from above

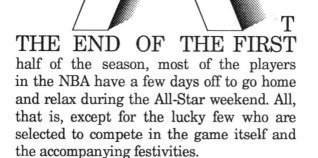

THE ALL-STAR WEEKEND AND THE LAKERS GAME

AT THE END OF THE FIRST half of the season, most of the players in the NBA have a few days off to go home and relax during the All-Star weekend. All, that is, except for the lucky few who are selected to compete in the game itself and the accompanying festivities.

I have to admit that when Mark Price of Cleveland passed me in the balloting for a starting position on the Eastern Conference squad, I thought if I didn't make the team it wouldn't be too bad and I could enjoy the days off. But let's face it—the ultimate honor an NBA player can receive is to be named to the All-Star team, even though it's a hectic three days.

Before everyone left town and went their separate ways, Chuck had us practice on Thursday. Afterwards, I met with the staff of Channel 4 in Detroit because they were going to do an "On the Road With Isiah" feature over the next week, which included the All-Star Game. Since I am a part-time reporter for Channel 4 and had done television work the previous summer, it would be an easy feature. I spent the rest of Thursday night making airline and hotel arrangements for my mother so she could attend the game in Houston. The All-Star weekend is always one of the highlights of the year.

On Friday morning, Lynn and I left for Houston on Roundball One. For the first time in the last six All-Star games, our PR Director Matt Dobek wasn't making the trip. I felt real uncomfortable about this, because the weekend often turns into total chaos, and Matt's the guy who keeps everything under control when everyone starts making unreasonable demands on my personal time. Not only was I missing Matt, but also absent from the game for the first time were my two best friends in the league, Earvin (Johnson) and Mark (Aguirre). Earvin was hurt in the last game before the break and was staying home to rest. I called Mark to see if he could come down to Houston, since it wasn't that far from Dallas, but he wanted to avoid the media as much as possible because of all the trade rumors. It really bothered me that neither one was in Houston, and that basketball had imposed on our friendship. Sometimes it just doesn't seem fair that the game ends up coming between us, but that's exactly what happened.

The lobby of the hotel at All-Star headquarters was a total madhouse. Between television cameras, reporters, and autograph seekers, it seemed like there were 5,000 people all trying to talk to me at once, and I was still trying to arrange my mother's room so she wouldn't have any problems when she checked in. I'm president of the NBA Players' Association, so the first thing I had to do was go to a meeting discussing union concerns. This was followed by a press conference attended by all the All-Stars, which lasted for almost two hours. Towards the end, Rimas Kurtinaitis, the Russian player selected to compete in the three-point shootout, said the reason the Russians beat the Americans in the Olympic Games was because the United States had too many blacks. Phil Jasner of the *Philadelphia*

Daily News asked me my reaction to this statement. Over the years, I've had my share of controversy, and I do my best to stay away from it. All I said was, "It's a good thing he's in America, because you can say whatever you want here."

We had nothing else scheduled for Friday, so I went back to my room. Warren Moon, the quarterback of the Houston Oilers, was having a party that night, but it had already been a hectic day and I knew there would be two more of the same, so Lynn and I decided just to go out for a quiet dinner. We were sitting at the table when I spotted Major Jones across the room, and without thinking, I hollered, "Heat it up, Maje." The people in the restaurant looked at me like I was nuts, but Major knew what I was talking about. He had played for us in 1984-85, the season the roof collapsed at the Silverdome and we had to move downtown to the Joe Louis Arena. There we used the Red Wings' dressing room, and Major practically lived in the sauna, and that's what we yelled at each other all the time. I hadn't seen him in a couple of years, and we reminisced about the old days when Brook Steppe, Dan Roundfield, and Kent Benson were on the team. We didn't have one of the best teams in the league then, but we sure had plenty of fun together.

The East All-Stars practiced early Saturday morning. I left my room to catch the elevator, and as the door opened, there stood Brad Daugherty, Larry Nance, and Mark Price. Nance said, "Where are the Bad Boys now?" I think he was only kidding, but I wished Laimbeer and Mahorn were with me.

After practice, I left to shoot a Toyota commercial, so I had to miss the three-point shootout, the Legends' game, and the slam-dunk competition. The shoot lasted about four hours, and I had to hurry back to make the Schick sponsors party on Saturday night. Schick throws this bash every year for all their corporate personnel and clients, and for the last four years they've asked Earvin and me to make appearances and sign autographs. Since they're an NBA sponsor and in return I get some extra All-Star Game tickets, I've always been happy to participate in the festivities. This year Earvin wasn't there, so I had to carry the show without him. Way to go, Magic! Many of the NBA Legends, from the game earlier in the day, were in the crowd, however.

Rick Barry was among those at the party, and he was the guy I was most impressed with. He was with his kids, taking pic-

Isiah soars to the basket

tures and getting autographs, and he asked me for mine! I couldn't believe it. I had idolized him as a kid, and was ready to ask for his autograph when he asked me first, on behalf of his kids. Usually, a guy of his stature wouldn't be caught dead asking for an autograph, even if it was for his son. That's what impressed me; Rick Barry was just being a father. That's the kind of father I want to be as my son grows up.

I hadn't had much of a chance to see my mother the whole weekend. The week before Houston, she kept saying over and over, "Junior, I ain't never been to Houston, and I can't wait to get there." Well, when she got there, she stayed in her hotel room the whole weekend, doing nothing but ordering room service and sleeping. She told me this was a perfect vacation for her, away from everyone in Chicago for a couple days.

The final event on Saturday night was the All-Star Banquet, when all the players are introduced. Even though it was my eighth All-Star Game, I still get goose bumps when they talk about me. It doesn't really dawn on you that all those nice things they're saying are actually about you, until you walk out on the stage and everyone's applauding. It made me feel very special seeing all the people who have been so supportive through the years, helping me become someone who's more than just a basketball player. I knew I had made them feel proud just by their reaction.

Comedian Jay Leno was the entertainment. Frank Layden, one of the funniest coaches in basketball and the president of the Utah Jazz, and I went on stage and did a couple of funny skits with Jay before he took the show over. It's amazing how many celebrities show up at affairs like this. I've always loved music, and over the years I've become a big fan of Patti Labelle. Well, at the banquet she came up to me and asked me for my autograph. I absolutely froze. I thought, "Oh my God, this is Patti Labelle in the flesh, and she's actually talking to me." It's funny. No matter how other people may perceive me, my reactions when I meet somebody famous are just the same as anyone else's would be.

That was enough excitement for one day, so I headed back to the hotel. The next morning Karl Malone and I had to go over early to hype the game for CBS. Lenny Wilkens coached the Eastern Conference team and just told us to play hard every minute we were in the game. I had been telling the press all weekend I didn't think the game would be as exciting or well-played as previous games. The fans come to a game like this to see spectacular plays. It's Showtime for the individual players, and that's fine because that's what the fans pay to see. But without Magic running the offense for the West, there wasn't going to be the run-and-gun shootout everyone had become accustomed to. In the last couple of games, Magic and I had just forced the ball up the court as quickly as possible, which usually produced a lot of exciting plays. Not so this year. In fact, the whole weekend may have disappointed some fans, because Larry Bird wasn't in the three-point shootout, Michael Jordan and Dominique Wilkins weren't in the slam-dunk contest, and Earvin didn't play in the game.

The game itself was a contrast in styles. While the East was trying to make the difficult plays and create excitement, the West concentrated on sound, fundamental basketball. That's why our East team got killed. Even though we are fierce rivals, Michael Jordan and I made a couple of great plays together, and I think we were both happy about that. In the locker room afterwards, there must have been 400 reporters, with no exaggera-

Are these the Bad Boys?

tion. As I was giving interviews, I looked across the room and saw my mother standing there! I asked her what in the world she was doing in the men's locker room. She said, "Junior, you knew they couldn't keep me out of here."

Now it was time to return to the real world of the NBA regular season, with our first stop in Los Angeles to play the Lakers. I went to L.A. right from Houston, and thought I could get a couple hours of sleep before the team arrived. As soon as I lay down, Bill Laimbeer called on the telephone to congratulate me on my play in the All-Star Game. I took the phone off the hook and lay back down for all of 15 minutes before Mike Abdenour was knocking on my door telling me the bus was ready to leave for practice. So much for getting some rest.

Chuck ran us as hard as he did in the first practice after Christmas, but it was good for us because we knew we had to be ready for the Lakers' running game. This was the first time back to The Forum since Game Seven of the Finals, and we knew how important it was psychologically. We wanted to sweep the series the same way the Lakers had done against us the year before.

With Magic out, the Lakers didn't push the ball up the court as quickly, and they played more of a half-court game. The way Kareem played, the reports of his game slipping are premature. He scored 23 points and had his sky hook in rare form, but we led most of the way and held off a late charge, defeating them 111-103. The winning streak was at six straight and our confidence level was building.

The Lakers game was played on Valentine's Day, and after the game Earvin had a party and invited all our players and coaching staff. I saw Eddie Murphy again, but this time it was a more public setting. He had his bodyguards around him and seemed like a different person. We talked awhile, but he seemed uncomfortable. I've now seen him in public and in private, and they appear to be two different worlds. This was a typical la-la land party with movie stars everywhere. I felt like staying longer, but I knew I'd better get back to the hotel because I had an early meeting, practice, and a plane to catch.

February 15, 1989. It'll be a day long remembered by Pistons' fans. For me it started early, as I had two meetings scheduled, one with a group of people from Walt Disney, and then another with Touchstone Pictures. After my playing career is over, I think I might have an interest in acting, and this was a good chance to meet some people and talk about the movie business. In fact, there's a movie being made about my mother right now. I guess the meeting could be called exploratory. It was a good way of expressing ourselves to each other.

After the meeting I went back to the hotel to get ready for practice. As I was walking through the lobby, the camera crew from Channel 4 stopped me to ask what I thought about the trade. I had no idea what they were talking about, and my first thought was that I had been traded. "You haven't heard?" they said. They turned the cameras on and told me that Adrian Dantley had been traded for Mark Aguirre.

4

JOE DUMARS

POSITION: Guard
HEIGHT: 6'3"
WEIGHT: 195 Pounds
COLLEGE: McNeese State '85 (Business Management Major)
HIGH SCHOOL: Natchitoches-Central (LA)
BIRTHDATE: 05-23-63
BIRTHPLACE: Natchitoches, LA
WHEN DRAFTED: First Round (18th Overall) Detroit, 1985
HOW ACQUIRED: College Draft
PRO EXPERIENCE: Four Years
MARITAL STATUS: Single
RESIDENCE: Lake Charles, LA

			FIELD GOALS			3-POINT FG			FREE THROWS			REBOUNDS							
DUMARS	G	GS	MIN	FG	FGA	PCT	FG	FGA	PCT	FT	FTA	PCT	OFF	DEF	TOT	AST	PF	BLK	PTS	AVG
Through 4/23	69	67	2408	456	903	.505	14	29	.483	260	306	.850	57	115	172	390	103	5	1186	17.2
Playoffs	17	17	620	106	233	.455	1	12	.083	87	101	.861	11	33	44	96	31	1	300	17.6

	SINGLE GAME HIGHS						AVERAGE PER GAME							AVERAGE PER 48 MINUTES					
	MIN	REB	AST	ST	TO	BL	PTS	MIN	REB	AST	STL	TO	BLK	PTS	REB	AST	PF	STL	TO	BLK	PTS
Through 4/23	49	6	13	3	8	2	42	34.9	2.5	5.7	0.91	2.6	0.07	17.2	3.4	7.8	2.1	1.26	3.5	0.10	23.6
Playoffs	41	5	10	2	3	1	33	36.5	2.6	5.6	0.71	1.8	0.06	17.6	3.4	7.4	2.4	0.93	2.4	0.08	23.2

THIS SEASON: Had his best season as a pro in his fourth campaign...Every year in the league he has improved his scoring average...In his rookie season he averaged 9.4 points per game...Improved to 11.8 points per game in his second season then 14.1 points per game last year...Then this season, he averaged 17.2 points per game, 5.7 assists while shooting 50 percent from the field and 85 percent from the free-throw line, all career bests...Had his best game as a pro in the Pistons' Central Division clinching game at Cleveland on April 12...In that game against the Cavs, he scored 42 points (18-26 FGs), including 24 points in the third quarter, which tied the all-time club record...In that decisive third quarter, he scored 17 straight points which was the second highest consecutive point total ever by a Pistons' player...He scored less than double figures in just 10 of the 69 games he played...For the first time in his career, he had a serious injury which sidelined him for an extended period of time...Broke his left hand versus the New York Knicks on January 12 and had surgery two days later...He missed 12 straight games, although he did return from the injury in just three weeks...Had been expected to be sidelined from five to six weeks...Has seen even more action at point guard this season, even while playing with Isiah who has moved to shooting guard in some situations...Has been acclaimed as one of the game's top defensive guards...His assists total increased dramatically over the final 10 games of the season when he averaged 10.0 assists during that time...Scored 20 or more points in 27 games...Often regarded as one of the games most complete guards, received increased attention this season for his offensive explosions...

Mark Aguirre, after the trade was announced, telling a friend, "I'm glad to be a Piston."

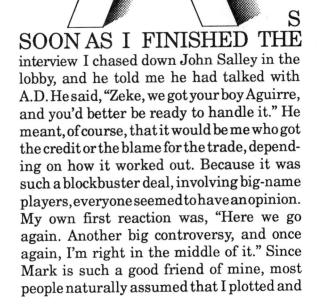

BAD BOYS

THE 7 RADE

As SOON AS I FINISHED THE interview I chased down John Salley in the lobby, and he told me he had talked with A.D. He said, "Zeke, we got your boy Aguirre, and you'd better be ready to handle it." He meant, of course, that it would be me who got the credit or the blame for the trade, depending on how it worked out. Because it was such a blockbuster deal, involving big-name players, everyone seemed to have an opinion. My own first reaction was, "Here we go again. Another big controversy, and once again, I'm right in the middle of it." Since Mark is such a good friend of mine, most people naturally assumed that I plotted and manipulated behind the scenes to pull it off, and if it didn't work out, I was going to take a lot of heat. My second reaction was a selfish one. I was concerned about how the fans would treat me. I have really busted my butt for the Detroit Pistons ever since I came here, and I certainly wasn't going to be happy if everyone started booing.

In analyzing the trade, I looked only at the positive effects it would have on our team, and I came up with five immediately. First, Mark is younger; second, he's a better post-up player; third, he's more of an outside threat and can shoot three-pointers; fourth, the addition of Aguirre would open up the offense for both Laimbeer and Dumars; and fifth, Rick Mahorn would become more of a threat at the opposite forward position. I started getting excited about the possibilities and the new ways we could utilize the potential that already existed. I knew my big role would be in helping to get Mark acclimated to his new team.

As usual, my phone was ringing off the hook, but I wasn't answering. I knew all the calls were from reporters trying to get my reaction to the trade. We had a practice scheduled at Loyola Marymount before we headed to Sacramento that night, and on the way to the school the team bus was unusually quiet. We had just won six straight and were playing well, and normally there would have been a lot of laughing, joking, and kidding around, but not today with the bombshell that had just been dropped. For the first time I can remember, there was complete silence on the team bus. By unspoken agreement, every player has his own seat, and Bill Laimbeer always sits right behind me about in the middle of the bus. He leaned over and said, "Junior, no matter what happens, I'm in this with you." I appreciated that.

We got to practice and Mark hadn't arrived. We were told he'd meet the team at the airport and fly with us to Sacramento that night. We had a good practice and then once again had to face the inevitable horde of interviewers wanting to know about the trade.

Even though we were on the West Coast, word had filtered back from Detroit that there was a lot of negative reaction to the trade, and that we had made a big mistake. I thought everyone was reacting emotionally, because there's no doubt A. D. was a very popular player, and I was getting a little angry about the media circus the road trip was turning into. No one questioned

Mark's talent, but a lot of people felt the balance and chemistry on the team had been upset. Nevertheless, I was sure that in time, everyone would realize this had been an excellent trade, and I wasn't at all worried about the chemistry. That was something I could control to a great extent. The important thing is to have talent, and like I said, there's no question that Mark is a very talented player. All we had to do to prove that this was a good trade was to keep winning.

After the interviews, we hustled back to the hotel to make it to the airport on time. Mark was already on the plane waiting for us, and all the players greeted him cordially. A lot of guys asked him about Dallas and the problems he was having there, and Mark told them he wanted to put all that behind him and concentrate on the future as a member of the Detroit Pistons. I knew the burden of making the transition as smooth as possible was going to fall on my shoulders. Chuck is very good at getting new players involved in our offense. He'd take certain aspects of Mark's game and make them fit our style of play, and there wouldn't be any problem on the court. Off the court was a different story. I needed not only to make Mark feel accepted, but also to make sure the other players accepted him. Our team is a closely knit family. We all care for each other as individuals and that has a lot to do with our success. Mark had to become just one of the guys.

To make the adjustment, five of us had a little meeting that night. Rick Mahorn, Bill Laimbeer, Vinnie Johnson, and I, in my opinion, are the four strongest personalities on the team. Each of us, in his own way, is outspoken. We had dinner in the hotel with Mark to let him know the ground rules. Since I had asked everybody to get together, I thought I ought to start.

I said, "Mark, welcome to the Pistons. Here's what's expected of you. First, you have to learn what it means to be a Piston. One thing it means is playing hard every minute of the game you're on the court. There are no nights off on this team. Second, your game won't be evaluated on the basis of how may points you score. On this team, every player has a role which best helps the total team effort, and every player is expected to accept that role. That's how we win. You were the star in Dallas. Here in Detroit, our ninth man on the squad is as popular as you were in Dallas. When the Pistons win, we're all stars."

THE TRADE

"We're totally honest with each other. We don't lie. We demand certain things on the court, and if those demands are not met, someone's going to be on your ass. But it's important that you not take it personally, because off the court the relationship will be different."

The other three guys, in different ways, each made excellent contributions in letting Mark know what was expected of him and making him feel part of the team. Laimbeer was next. If you know anything at all about Bill, you know he doesn't mince words. He gets right to the point without sparing feelings, no matter how brutal it may sound.

Laimbeer said, "The only reason I like you is you're a friend of Isiah's. If you weren't Isiah's friend, I wouldn't even talk to you. All the things I heard and read about you have been bad. I really don't care if they're true or not. Isiah said to give you a chance, so I'm giving you a chance."

Mahorn said, "On the court, we don't let each other down. We always take care of each other. I never want to be embarrassed out there, and you'll have as much to do with that as I will. Everyone knows you're a great offensive player, but I don't really care. Defense wins games and we are an outstanding defensive team. If you get beat by your man, don't worry because I'll be there to help out. But if I get beat and you're not there to help me, that's it for you. I guarantee you I'll be hollering at Chuck to get you out of the game."

Vinnie said, "The most important thing for you to understand is that we have a lot of guys who can play. Backing you up is the best defensive player in the game, Dennis Rodman, and at the end of the game, Chuck goes with defense. You're going to be put in the same spot I'm in on many nights. There's games when I'm on a roll and can't miss a shot, but in the last couple minutes Chuck brings in Joe Dumars for me regardless. I can't get mad because Joe's a better defensive player than I am. The same thing is going to happen to you. In the fourth quarter, you may not miss a shot, but Chuck's going with Rodman in the last couple minutes because defense is going to win that game. Just remember, it's nothing personal, it's just how we win."

Mark listened well. He let it all sink in for a few moments, then said, "I know you've heard a lot about me, but no matter what you've heard, I want you to know I'm here for one reason, and that's to win a championship. I promise you I will do anything to win. Isiah's known me since we were kids, and he knows what I'm all about. I'm glad you're giving me a chance, because that's all I need."

The next day we had a shoot-around and Mark couldn't believe all the media attention our team was getting. I told him that was normal for us, because we were the Bad Boys and he just added to that reputation. We ran a few plays so if Mark got in the game against Sacramento he'd at least know what was going on. As it turned out, Adrian didn't report to Dallas, so league rules forbade Aguirre to play for us that night. It didn't really matter, as Rodman started at small forward and we played terrific defense, holding the Kings to just 37 percent field goal shooting and winning our seventh straight game, 95-84.

Mark's first full practice with his new team was the next day in San Francisco, and I had been trying to prepare him for the experience. I told him it would be rough, and if he wasn't ready, he'd get killed. I don't think he believed me. All he said was, "Yeah, yeah, I'll be ready. I can handle anything they throw at me." Well, he had never been guarded by Dennis Rodman. Dennis didn't even allow him to get a shot off, let alone make one. Then when Mark tried to drive the lane, he got flattened by Rick Mahorn. I said, "Welcome to the Detroit Pistons." By the end of practice, he was beaten up pretty badly, and I had to laugh. He couldn't say I didn't warn him.

We all knew that eventually Mark would be our team's starting small forward, but in the first few games Chuck decided to bring him in off the bench. In our next game, against Golden State, Rodman started and played probably the best game of his career, with 32 points and 21 rebounds. Laimbeer almost duplicated his effort with 32 points and 15 boards, and it was a good thing because none of the three guards, Joe, Vinnie, or I, could shoot straight. We had a chance to win in overtime, but they called a breakaway foul on Mark which not only gave them the free throw, but possession as well, and we lost 121-119. There would have been no overtime if our guards had been shooting well.

Our road trip ended with a rare Monday afternoon game in Denver, and again I couldn't shoot the ball, although Vinnie and Joe made some shots. Denver led by 16 at the half, and to our

THE TRADE

credit, we never gave up. We made a big comeback and in fact took the lead late in the game, but it was too little too late, and we lost another squeaker, 103-101.

At last it was time to go home. Mark was disappointed because we had lost the first two games he had played with us, but I tried to explain that this was a major transition, and besides, the two games we lost were on the road and to very good teams.

Portland was first up at The Palace, and I was nervous about how the fans would accept Mark, because Adrian had been very popular and successful in Detroit. I was also more than a little concerned about how they would greet me, since I was largely perceived as the guy who engineered the trade. Ken Calvert, our public address announcer, introduced Mark first and he received a standing ovation. Never had I fully appreciated as I did at that moment how great Detroit fans really are. What they were saying was, "The trade is history. Whatever we may have thought about it, it's over. We're all behind you."

The first game back from a long road trip is almost like another road game. You come home from the airport, get a little rest, and have to go right back out there again. We were up to it, though, playing great defense and holding Portland to just 60 points through the first three quarters, and winning handily, 105-94.

Up to this point, Mark really hadn't had much of a chance to learn our offense, because we were playing games and didn't have any practice time. No matter how much film you look at, the quickest and most effective way to learn our plays and what we like to do offensively and defensively is to practice with the other players. After the Portland game, we had a couple days off and the practice time benefited Mark tremendously.

Earlier that week, the Pacers had waived John Long, who for my first five years in Detroit had been a valuable player for the Pistons, and who was now on the verge of seeing his NBA career come to an end. Our offensive attack depends on our three-guard rotation, and Chuck realized that if anything happened to Joe, Vinnie, or me, he needed an established NBA player to step in. It was a logical choice to sign John once he cleared waivers, and this was a great opportunity for him to play for a winning team. He had been with the Pistons during the down years, and now he's getting a chance to share in some of our success. Unfortunately, we had to release a player on our roster to make room for John. The most logical choice was Darryl Dawkins, because all our big men were playing well and we really couldn't afford the luxury of a fourth center. I know it was a tough decision for the coaching staff to release Darryl, but we had to do it to get the additional insurance for the backcourt.

After we had seen him in a couple of games, we noticed that Mark wasn't in very good shape. It was hard to believe, but any time Chuck played him for an extended period of time, he'd get winded and have to come out. He found out in a real hurry how tough

Mark Aguirre reacts to a Detroit rally in his first home game at The Palace.

our practices are, and if he was going to make a contribution, he was going to have to lose some weight and get into shape. He started running extra windsprints after practice and began watching his diet.

After a couple hard days of practice, Mark was much more comfortable with our system for our next game with New Jersey, and we saw for the first time what he's really capable of. He's one of the most explosive scorers in the league, and he demonstrated that against the Nets, scoring 31 points in just 26 minutes. I had never realized how big a three-point threat he was, but New Jersey found out quickly, and we had an easy win on the road, 113-95. Then, just when we thought we were all healthy and ready to make a run at Cleveland, John Salley went down with an ankle injury and was going to be out for an extended period of time.

The next night, at home against the Clippers, Chuck decided this was a great opportunity to make a lineup change and move

Mark in as a starter. Dennis Rodman did a great job as a starter, but he's even more valuable to our team coming off the bench. The Clippers had been a disappointment all season, and we wanted to jump on them early and not give them any hope of an upset. We led by 16 points after the first quarter and were never seriously challenged. We won 110-98 and got ready for a big showdown in Cleveland with the division-leading Cavaliers.

We lost to Cleveland for the third straight time, 115-99, but even though the final score was lopsided, we had a chance to win the game with four minutes left. At this point in the season, we were still learning a lot about Cleveland. They had come from out of nowhere, and our guys still didn't know what their players' tendencies were. Cleveland had never been a rival or a threat to us the way Atlanta, Boston, or even Chicago has over the last couple years. They were the new kid on the block, and we made excuses for our three losses by saying we didn't know enough about them. We decided that night that things were going to change. We were going to learn, and learn fast. Starting now.

53

JAMES EDWARDS

POSITION: Center
HEIGHT: 7'1"
WEIGHT: 263 Pounds
COLLEGE: Washington, '77
HIGH SCHOOL: Roosevelt, Seattle, WA
BIRTHDATE: 11-22-55
BIRTHPLACE: Seattle, WA
WHEN DRAFTED: Third Round (46th Pick), Los Angeles 1977
HOW ACQUIRED: From Phoenix Suns in Exchange for Ron Moore and Detroit's Second-Round Draft Choice in 1991
PRO EXPERIENCE: Twelve Years
MARITAL STATUS: Single
RESIDENCE: Phoenix, AZ

EDWARDS	G	GS	MIN	FG	FGA	PCT	FG	FGA	PCT	FT	FTA	PCT	OFF	DEF	TOT	AST	PF	BLK	PTS	AVG
				FIELD GOALS			**3-POINT FG**			**FREE THROWS**			**REBOUNDS**							
Through 4/23	76	1	1254	211	422	.500	0	2	.000	133	194	.686	68	163	231	49	226	31	555	7.3
Playoffs	17	0	317	40	85	.471	0	1	.000	40	51	.784	11	25	36	12	53	8	120	7.1

	MIN	REB	AST	ST	TO	BL	PTS	MIN	REB	AST	STL	TO	BLK	PTS	REB	AST	PF	STL	TO	BLK	PTS
	SINGLE GAME HIGHS							**AVERAGE PER GAME**							**AVERAGE PER 48 MINUTES**						
Through 4/23	35	9	3	2	5	4	18	16.5	3.0	0.6	0.14	0.9	0.41	7.3	8.8	1.9	8.7	0.42	2.8	1.19	21.2
Playoffs	32	4	2	1	3	2	15	18.6	2.1	0.7	0.06	0.9	0.47	7.1	5.5	1.8	8.0	0.15	2.3	1.21	18.2

THIS SEASON: For the first time in his NBA career, he did not average in double figures...Averaged better than double figures in each of his first 11 seasons in the NBA and entered the season with a career scoring average of 15.0 points per game...But, in 1988-89, he averaged just 7.3 points per game...Scored in double figures in 25 games...Was averaging 11 points per game after the first 10 games of the season before he was injured...Sprained his left ankle on Nov. 22 in a game at Charlotte and missed the next five games, then struggled upon his return...His season high was 18 points, which he recorded twice during the season...Did not have a game of double figures in rebounding...Played in a total of 76 games in his first full season with the Pistons, including one game as a starter (versus Sacramento on January 29)...

Fans of the Bad Boys wear their feelings on their sleeves—and everywhere else.

MARCH MADNESS

I N EARLY
MARCH, WE WERE FIVE
games behind the Cleveland Cavaliers,
and if we were going to make a run at the
division title, the next two weeks would be
critical. They would make or break our
season and determine whether we would
be a contender or whether we would fade
and finish second or even third in the
division. The schedule made it even more
difficult, because we were to play 17
games in the 31 days, averaging more
than one game every two nights. We were
feeling the pressure for the first time.

Because the season is so long, it's easy for
any team to get bored, and when boredom

sets in, you get complacent. Complacency became Public Enemy Number One for us in early March. We were determined to push ourselves with playoff intensity in every game in order to challenge Cleveland. This meant every minute, every possession, each of the five guys on the floor was going to play with a determined attitude and push himself to the limit.

Our first test was the Utah Jazz, the team leading the Midwest Division. We won that game because of something that happened in 1981-82, my rookie year. The Pistons' management had decided to trade Greg Kelser, who starred at Michigan State with Magic Johnson, to Seattle for a relatively unknown kid named Vinnie Johnson. Over the years, I've seen Vinnie have some incredible games, but never anything like what he did to the Jazz on March 1 at The Palace. The Microwave heated it up in the second quarter and scored 19 consecutive points to close out the first half, a team record which may never be broken. We've got four or five explosive scorers, any one of whom can carry the whole team for a long stretch when he gets hot. We're smart enough to recognize when a guy's on a roll, and when that happens, we make sure he gets the ball. That's what happened in the second quarter with Vinnie. He wound up with 34 points and we won, 96-85. The hand injury to Joe Dumars may have been a blessing in disguise because Vinnie played himself into great shape in his absence.

On Friday, the Cavaliers were coming to town. It's hard to think of any game in March as a must-win situation, but they had just beaten us on Tuesday in Cleveland, and if we entertained any hopes of winning the division, we absolutely had to have this game. We had an additional motivation as well. The day before, Rod Thorn of the NBA fined Rick Mahorn $5,000 for what he called a flagrant elbow against Cleveland's Mark Price. Every player on our team thought that was an excessive fine for a play in which a foul was not even called. I think we took the attitude that it was the Pistons against the world, and that attitude carried over into the game.

The game itself had more sideshows than a circus. In addition to Mahorn's fine, the hotel the Cavs were staying at had had a bomb scare and Cleveland coach Lenny Wilkens had received a death threat. Nor was it an artistic game. Tempers were short from the beginning and the refs didn't want to hear about it.

There were four technicals called against our team, and Chuck Daly had two of them. The score was close in the middle of the third quarter when Chuck was ejected, handing over the reins to Brendan Suhr who did an outstanding job the rest of the way. In the first three losses against Cleveland, Brad Daugherty had done a great job in dominating Laimbeer, but Bill is such a competitive guy I think he took this game as a personal challenge. He scored 24 points, grabbed 14 rebounds, and we took our first game from the Cavs 96-90. A few days later, the NBA began an investigation into reports that Chuck had been in contact with the bench during the game, an infraction of league rules, and they apparently found him guilty because they fined him $1,500.

Even though I've vacationed in Florida several times, I had never been to Miami, so I was looking forward to our next game. Though they're an expansion team, the Heat had already beaten a few pretty good teams in their own arena, and it wasn't hard to figure out why. When guys from Chicago, Detroit, and Cleveland get down there in the sunshine and get a respite from the cold midwestern winter, they look at it as a mini-vacation, and basketball is sometimes the furthest thing from their minds. We didn't want that to happen to us. Laimbeer hit almost every shot he took right from the opening tip, and our nine-point lead at the end of the first quarter turned out to be the margin of victory, 109-100.

We had to play Denver the next night in Detroit, and the Nuggets are not someone you want to face in the second of back-to-back games. Doug Moe, their coach, plays a passing game which is difficult to defend against because basically what they do is pass and screen for 48 minutes. And we were already tired because we didn't get in from Miami until two in the morning.

Early in the game, my legs were tired, and chasing Michael Adams around didn't help things any. I was in early foul trouble and Chuck had to put me on the bench in the first quarter. I came back in the second only to pick up my third foul immediately, and I sat out the rest of the half. In the third quarter, I got whistled for my fourth and had to sit down again. Finally in the fourth quarter, with the game still in doubt, Chuck put me in with about 10 minutes to play. I was really well rested, and when Denver cut the lead to four points with eight minutes left, Chuck called timeout and I knew it was time for me to take over. I felt good, my jump shot started connecting, and I scored 15 points in the last 10 minutes. Rick Mahorn had his best game of the season, scoring 19 points to go with his 19 rebounds. I don't think many people realize how valuable Horn is to our team. Over the last couple years, when we've played well, as often as not it's because Rick has been playing well. Because his reputation precedes him, most people don't give him credit. Sure, he's one of our intimidators, but he's also one of our best defensive players. We beat the Nuggets 129-112, but we all knew the game was a lot closer than the final score indicated.

For the first time since the Aguirre trade, we felt we were making significant improvement. Against Seattle we had our best half of the season, scoring 65 points and taking a 21-point halftime lead against the Sonics. Our confidence level was higher than it had ever been. Earlier when we were winning, we always felt kind of like we were living on the edge, but not any more. We expected to win, and we were winning convincingly.

Rolling Stone magazine had been traveling around with us for a couple of weeks, working on a Bad Boys cover story that they planned to run during the playoffs. After the Seattle game, Chuck gave us the day off and a bunch of us had to do a photo shoot for the magazine. They wanted to do something wild and out of the ordinary, so they rented a couple of Harleys, dressed Mark and me in leather jackets, and added sunglasses and handcuffs to complete the "Bad Boys" image. It was a good diversion from practice for a change.

We had another five-game winning streak going, and we were really feeling good about ourselves. Philadelphia was next on the schedule, and although we had won seven straight games in the Spectrum, we knew it was only a matter of time until they beat us in their own gym. For pure excitement, this was one of the best games of the season, and I honestly don't think the Sixers could play much better than they did in this game. We led by one point going into the fourth quarter.

When a game is on the line, I feel it's my responsibility as team captain to step in and take charge. I made my first shot in the fourth quarter, and I told Vinnie I was starting to feel like I couldn't miss. My teammates began looking for me, and I was making every shot I took. There's a phenomenon that sometimes happens in sports called a "zone of altered consciousness" in which an athlete seems unstoppable. It doesn't happen too often, but when someone like a tennis player or basketball player is in the zone he soars in a rhythm all his own, almost oblivious to his surroundings. It's like he's outside his body, watching himself perform, knowing every move he makes and every shot he takes can't miss. It's a moment every athlete lives for, and one which makes the thousands of grueling hours of practice worthwhile. That's the way I felt in the fourth quarter against the Sixers. I could see things happening on the court before the plays developed, and I was counting my three-pointers before they left my hands. I scored 24 points in the quarter, which I later found out was a Pistons' regular-season record. But what was even more important was that we won the game, 111-106. In the locker room afterwards, everyone was comparing my performance to Game Six of the 1988 NBA Finals, but there was no comparison as far as I was concerned, because this time we won.

The Washington Bullets, whom we had eliminated in the first round of the playoffs each of the last two seasons, were one of the hottest teams in the league when they visited The Palace on March 12. They were battling Boston for the eighth and final playoff spot in the Eastern Conference, and had had the night before the game off while we were winning at Philadelphia. It was a tough and physical game, and a couple of fights nearly erupted in the third quarter. Washington led most of the way, but we took control at the beginning of the fourth quarter.

Laimbeer is one of those players who keeps track of his stats during every game, and though I didn't know it, he was closing in on 10,000 career points, a major accomplishment for any NBA player. He had 22 in the game when Washington called timeout, and he told me he needed two more for his 10,000th career point. With 40 seconds left, I spotted him cherry-picking at the other end of the floor, and I threw the ball the length of the court. He sunk a 20-foot jump shot for our team's last basket of the game, and we won 110-104.

Our next game was against the Pacers, a team which had made major changes since we had last played them. The guys who always gave us the most trouble had been traded in the last few weeks, including Herb Williams, Wayman Tisdale, and John Long, who of course was now with us. The Pacers had already beaten us twice in their own building, but were having an otherwise disappointing season. The game turned into a real shootout and even though we scored 67 points in the first half, we only led by five at halftime, and Indiana in fact took the lead in the third quarter. Vinnie, Joe, and I combined for 82 points and we finally won in Indianapolis, 129-117.

Our winning streak reached eight games, and even more encouraging was the fact that our guards were shooting better, which opened up our entire offense. Other teams have to respect our jump shots and come out to get us, which allows us to pass to our big men open under the basket. Plus, Mark was effective inside, posting up, and creating easy opportunities. We were all getting better shots, like open jumpers for the guards from 10-12 feet rather than 18-20. Everyone thinks of Mark as a scorer rather than a good passer, but he was developing an uncanny ability to hit the open man when he got double-teamed.

The eight straight victories tied our longest winning streak of the season, and we were coming home to play the Celtics in The Palace on St. Patrick's Day. They're still a scary team, and the Ed Pinckney/Joe Kleine trade was a flat-out steal for them. They now have four seven-footers, and since they have so many guys who can rebound and score in the paint, they can control the tempo of the game. On the other hand, since we're smaller and quicker, we should be able to run against them. Come playoff time, if they dominate the boards and control the tempo, they'll cause us real problems even if Larry Bird is not back. But the luck of the Irish wasn't with the Celtics on St. Patrick's Day, and our guards continued to shoot well. Vinnie had 30 points in just 23 minutes and our winning streak was now at nine games.

Our improved performance on the road was now to be put to the test with trips to Milwaukee and Atlanta. Sometimes scheduling has as much to do with a defeat as the opponent, and I think this is what happened in Milwaukee. We were supposed to leave on Roundball One after the Boston game, but bad weather forced us to lay over in Detroit until the morning of the game, while the Bucks didn't play the night before and were well rested. This isn't to say that they wouldn't have won anyway, but at the beginning of the second half, our bodies hit the wall, like a marathon runner at the twentieth mile. We had stayed close, but in the third quarter Milwaukee ran by us like we were standing still, closing us out 117-100 and ending our winning streak at

James Edwards skies for two more.

eight games. It was to be our only loss in an otherwise
phenomenal month in which we posted a record-shattering 16-1
mark.

The Hawks came into their game against us playing with confidence. They had just beaten the Lakers in the Forum and were
now looking to make a run at both Cleveland and Detroit. What
had all the ingredients of being a great game, however, turned
into a blowout. I had been hitting my jump shot with consistency,
and I had plenty of opportunities in the first quarter, propelling
us to a 17-point lead. They kept coming back, and even got to

MARCH   MADNESS

within six in the third period, but when a team gets so far behind, it takes everything out of them just to get back to even. After their last run, we took the game over and weren't threatened again on our way to a 110-95 victory and the start of a new winning streak.

Our next two games were at home and against San Antonio and New Jersey, teams that would not be making the playoffs. You want to take a big lead early against these teams, because the longer you let them hang close, the more their confidence level increases. We rolled to a big halftime lead against the Spurs, played good defense, won 115-94, and got even more good news when we heard that Philadelphia had beaten Cleveland.

In just over three weeks, the Pistons had made up five games against Cleveland and were now tied for the lead in the Central Division. We actually had a better winning percentage, because we were a game ahead in the all-important loss column, with a record of 47-17 compared to their 48-18. We both knew that neither club was going to go away and hide and that we would be in a dogfight the rest of the way. New York and the Lakers had struggled earlier in the month and had slipped in the race for the league's overall best record, which determines home-court advantage throughout the playoffs. The Pistons and the Cavaliers now had the additional incentive of not only winning the Central Division, but of being the best team in pro basketball.

Friday night we took care of business against New Jersey. Joe Dumars was incredible. Everyone on our team realizes he is capable of single-handedly taking the game over, which he did against the Nets, scoring 35 points. He scored at will and we were on another roll, with our third straight win. Charlotte made it four in a row, and it was also our fourth in a row over the Hornets. Coach Dick Harter had them playing hard, but our overall depth was too much for them, and we returned to The Palace for the long awaited showdown with Dallas.

PLAYER PROFILE

15

VINNIE JOHNSON

POSITION: Guard
HEIGHT: 6'2"
WEIGHT: 200 pounds
COLLEGE: Baylor '79 (Education Major)
HIGH SCHOOL: Brooklyn (NY) F. D. Roosevelt
BIRTHDATE: 09-01-56
BIRTHPLACE: Brooklyn, NY
WHEN DRAFTED: First Round (7th Overall)
Seattle, 1979
HOW ACQUIRED: In Exchange for Greg Kelser,
Nov. 21, 1981
PRO EXPERIENCE: Ten Years
NICKNAME: V.J.
MARITAL STATUS: Single
RESIDENCE: Southfield, MI

JOHNSON				FIELD GOALS			3-POINT FG			FREE THROWS			REBOUNDS							
	G	GS	MIN	FG	FGA	PCT	FG	FGA	PCT	FT	FTA	PCT	OFF	DEF	TOT	AST	PF	BLK	PTS	AVG
Through 4/23	82	21	2073	462	996	.464	13	44	.295	193	263	.734	109	146	255	242	155	17	1130	13.8
Playoffs	17	0	372	91	200	.455	10	24	.417	47	62	.758	16	29	45	43	32	3	239	14.1

	SINGLE GAME HIGHS						AVERAGE PER GAME							AVERAGE PER 48 MINUTES					
	MIN	REB	AST	ST	TO	BL	PTS	MIN	REB	AST	STL	TO	BLK	PTS	REB	AST	PF	STL	TO	BLK	PTS
Through 4/23	46	8	10	5	5	2	34	25.3	3.1	3.0	0.90	1.3	0.21	13.8	5.9	5.6	3.6	1.71	2.4	0.39	26.2
Playoffs	29	6	5	2	5	1	25	21.9	2.6	2.5	0.24	1.2	0.18	14.1	5.8	5.5	4.1	0.52	2.7	0.39	30.8

THIS SEASON: After struggling during the early portion of the season, he returned to his old form and had an outstanding final three quarters of the season...Averaged less than double figures through the first 23 games, but then finished the season averaging 13.8 points per game...Over the final 59 games, he averaged 15.8 points per game...For the seventh straight campaign, he averaged better than double figures...Scored better than double figures in 56 games...Joined Dennis Rodman as the only Pistons' players to play in every game...Started 21 games for the season, replacing either Dumars or Thomas...in those contests, the Pistons were 16-5...Had one of the best performances of his career versus Utah on March 1 when he finished with 34 points...In that game he set the all-time Pistons' consecutive points scored record with 19 straight points to end the first half versus Utah...For the most part, he continued in his familiar role as the Pistons third guard in Coach Chuck Daly's three guard rotation... ,

Halftime entertainment at The Palace

BAD BOYS

DALLAS AND THE FINAL WEST COAST ROAD TRIP

9

UZZ, BUZZ, BUZZ. IT SEEMED like the only topic of conversation in town was the Dallas game and A.D.'s homecoming at The Palace. It was definitely the toughest ticket in town. In the past, it would have been just another big game between two perennial powerhouses, but this was a down year for Dallas, and they had not adjusted to the trade nearly as quickly and effectively as we had. There had also been a lot of publicity about the fact that Adrian didn't report on time, choosing to wait and talk with the Dallas owner first.

I had been getting sick and tired of reading for the past two weeks about how I en-

123

gineered the trade for Mark Aguirre. If this is Isiah's team, like everyone seems to think it is, then yes, I made the trade. I also drafted Joe Dumars, Dennis Rodman, and John Salley, and I traded for Bill Laimbeer, Vinnie Johnson, and James Edwards. I deserve all the credit for the Pistons' success over the last two or three years, and all the blame for our struggles in the early '80's. As flattering as this may sound, however, the truth is that I'm only one small part of a large organization. Jack McCloskey, also one part of that organization, happens to be one of the smartest general managers in the NBA and he does his homework. He had dissected this move and looked at it from every angle for months, then got the input of the coaching staff before he decided to pull the trigger. Isiah Thomas was never approached by anyone in the Detroit Pistons' organization regarding the trade. Sure, Mark and I talked during the time rumors were circulating about the possibility of his coming to Detroit, but that was the extent of it.

Anytime we play a "big" game, it never seems to live up to its advance billing. With all the hype surrounding this Detroit-Dallas game, you'd have thought we were playing for the NBA Championship. The game itself was horrible. We came out flat, and Dallas couldn't miss. We were lucky to trail by only seven points at the end of the first quarter, but that's one thing about our team: even when we're playing poorly, we somehow manage to stay close enough to give ourselves a chance. We may not win, but we're not going to get blown out, especially at home. Our defensive intensity picked up in the second quarter, and the Mavericks started having trouble scoring. We slowly started grinding it out, though nothing came easy the whole night. We tied it up at halftime, and held them to just 31 points in the second half to win 90-77. But as far as big games go, this one was a dud.

Before, during, and after the game there was some tension in our locker room. Mark has a lot of respect for Adrian, but he wants to beat him every chance he gets, and the reporters were trying to make a big deal of the Aguirre-Dantley matchup. Every game was now critical to us, and we didn't need anything to distract us. All we wanted to do was win. I was relieved when we did, and nothing controversial happened. Mark acted like a real pro throughout the whole ordeal. It's funny, but if I had believed everything I read about him while he was in Dallas, I'd have thought he was some kind of wild and crazy lunatic. But I knew better. Mark was courteous and handled his responsibilities properly and professionally. I figured if he could make it through this ordeal, he could make it through anything with the Pistons.

We reached an important milestone with the victory over Dallas: our third straight 50-win season. It was getting to be routine, but in my early years with Detroit it seemed like an impossible goal. We now upped the ante and set our sights on winning 60 games, which only seven franchises in the history of the NBA have achieved.

The most critical road trip of the season was next on the schedule. We were in good shape in the divisional race because Cleveland had lost the night we beat Dallas, and we were heading west with a three-game lead in the loss column. The four-game trip, against the Jazz, the Sonics, the Clippers, and the Blazers, would go a long way in determining not only the division winner but also the best record in the league. Usually when you go on the road, you're looking for a split, but we were starting to think like K. C. Jones and the Celtics of old when

Laimbeer acknowledges Boobirds after fouling out on the road.

they won 60 games year in and year out. When he took Boston on a four-game trip and was asked how many they had to win, K.C. would say, "I don't know. I guess I'd settle for four."

You always want the first game on any trip, and this time it happened to be our toughest of the four. Utah was leading the Midwest Division, and it turned out to be probably our hardest game, both physically and mentally, of the season to that point. Utah and Detroit have the numbers one and two defenses in the league, and when Karl Malone is your small forward, you know you're intimidating. We had more physical contact in this game than any other. If you went into the lane, you paid the price. Their fans were in a frenzy at the start of the game, and before we knew what happened, I looked up at the clock and the score was 10-0 Utah with five minutes left in the period. Given the way the first seven minutes went, it was remarkable we hadn't been completely blown away, and we felt it was a major accomplishment to come back to 19-14 at the end of the first quarter.

In the second quarter, we knew that any bad pass, any missed shot, and any missed free throw could wind up costing us the game. That's big-time pressure, given the importance to us of winning, and we concentrated like never before. Chuck got ejected, which seemed awfully unfair to us in such a big game, but those are the breaks. We kept scrapping and narrowing the gap, and finally late in the fourth quarter Laimbeer made a couple of free throws to give us a three-point lead. Utah called timeout, needing a three-pointer just to tie, and we talked about fouling them before they could get a shot off. That's risky, because if you do it and they somehow shoot a triple and make it, it can be a four-point play and you've lost the game. On the other hand, if you foul them, even if they make the two free throws, you've got the ball and the game.

On their last play, John Stockton was dribbling out top and Thurl Bailey set a screen. I switched with Rick Mahorn, who didn't think Stockton had a chance of making the shot. He knew he'd be too late if he tried to foul him, so he let him have it, with results that were devastating to us but sent the Utah crowd into hysteria. We struggled back to the huddle totally exhausted, feeling like we had lost the game even though the score was tied 88-88 at the end of regulation. If either team had the advantage now, it had to be the Jazz. They got a big lift from the last shot, we were playing without our coach, and were on the road and were tired. It was after midnight Detroit time, and our bodies hadn't had a chance to adjust to the two-hour time difference in Salt Lake City.

Surprisingly, the team's mood was upbeat in the huddle before the overtime. It was time to take care of business. Malone had fouled out, and that took away a big weapon for them. With eight seconds left, the score was still tied, but we had the ball. This is the kind of situation I love to be in. I love the challenge of having to make the last shot to win the game, and I'm strong enough to take the criticism if I miss it. I knew the play was coming to me and I wanted to end this war once and for all. The play worked perfectly, and I had an open jump shot from about 15 feet. I had a great look at the basket, and when I released the ball, I was sure it was going in. As the buzzer went off, the ball went in, but then popped out. The game was in a second overtime and both teams were emotionally drained. We had played a full game and an overtime, and neither team had scored 100 points.

Back at the bench, I told the guys that we had come too far to let this game slip away. Utah plays basically six players and we're nine deep, and it was our depth and determination that won this game for us, although the fact that three of their players had fouled out certainly helped. Joe Dumars made two free throws to put us ahead by four points with three seconds to go, and we all breathed a huge sigh of relief when the final seconds ticked off and we escaped with a 108-104 victory. Although no one said it, we all knew that losing this game would have been devastating.

In some NBA cities, and Salt Lake City is one of them, the team hotel is close enough to walk to the arena. I walked back with Mark, making plans to go out to dinner, but once inside the hotel I barely had the energy to make it to my room. I collapsed on the bed and never even bothered to call Mark. I was so totally exhausted and emotionally drained I couldn't even fall asleep. I remember looking at the clock at 6:00 a.m. and I still hadn't slept a wink.

We were looking forward to the trip to Seattle, because it was Final Four weekend, and besides all the normal excitement, we

Bill Davidson (left), owner of the NBA Champion Detroit Pistons, and Bo Schembechler, Athletic Director of the University of Michigan, home of the 1989 NCAA Champion Wolverines, helped bring basketball immortality to the State of Michigan in 1989.

had the additional thrill of watching the University of Michigan compete for the national championship. The only other sports story in Michigan to rival the Dantley/Aguirre trade and the Pistons' success was the fact that assistant coach Steve Fisher had brought the Wolverines all the way to the Final Four after head coach Bill Frieder's resignation. The college basketball coaches were holding their convention in our hotel, and the lobby was a real circus, making it almost impossible to get an elevator. It was a who's who of the college basketball world, and with the normal autograph seekers, it reminded me of an NBA All-Star weekend. You can't beat the excitement in the air at events like this.

The coaching staff cancelled practice because we needed the rest after the physical game against Utah, so I had a treatment for my Achilles tendon which was bothering me. You try to keep injuries like this quiet in this league so the other team doesn't find out and try to exploit your weakness. It didn't seem like the injury was too serious, and I made sure no one knew about it.

That night I wanted to get plenty of rest for the Sonics game, so I just ordered a hot fudge sundae and relaxed. At about 10:30 p.m., Bill Frieder called and wanted to see me. I don't know him real well, but he had been taking a lot of heat for leaving Michigan, and I could tell he was a little upset, as I think anyone in his situation would be. After talking with him for a while, I realized he desperately wanted his old team to win the title. He might easily have adopted a sour grapes kind of attitude, maybe even hoping to have them knocked out of it, but not Bill Frieder, and to me that showed a lot of class. I remember playing for the national championship at Indiana in 1981, and it was one of the proudest moments of my life.

It was tough to get a ticket to the Final Four in the Kingdome, but it was even tougher for our game because we played in the Coliseum, which only seats about 14,000. The frenzied crowd was quieted in a hurry by Mark who was on fire and couldn't miss as we shot out to an early 10-point lead. I can't explain what happened after that, or the change that came over the whole Seattle team, but I know there was nothing we could do about it. The Sonics went from 10 points down in the first quarter to a 23-point halftime lead. Usually our team can weather a storm, but this was more like a hurricane or tornado. They made every play and every shot and were up 69-46 at the intermission.

In the locker room, the first thing I said was, "If any of you guys quit, I'm personally going to kick your butt." And I meant it. A good basketball team, which we were, doesn't get blown out like that. Our comeback in the second half started slowly. We were still having trouble offensively, but on defense we were swarming. Every pass, every shot Seattle attempted was difficult because of our tenacity. This was the hardest and toughest defense we played all season. We outscored them by 16 points in the third quarter, and now we had a shot at winning, but too often, when you dig such a deep hole, you can't make the final push over the top to get the lead.

Normally in trying to overcome such a huge deficit, you're fast breaking because you have to score points in a hurry, but we ran one play throughout the second half, called the 15-play, which is a screen and roll. They couldn't stop it, and with our intense defense, they couldn't score either. I don't know where all our energy came from, but Seattle only scored 15 points in the fourth quarter and didn't make a field goal in the last 10 minutes of the game. With just over a minute left, we took the lead, and then I made a jumper with the shot clock running out. Seattle had no timeouts left and had to try a desperation three-pointer just to tie. Fortunately, this time our opponent missed the last shot and we won 111-108. The win was the greatest comeback I've ever been involved in with the Pistons. It was a tough loss for Seattle, blowing a 23-point lead, and it may have haunted them later in the year when they lost an

In 1989, the Pistons' first year in their new home,
The Palace sold out every home game.

even bigger game. In Game Four of the Western Conference
Semifinals, they had a 29-point lead in the first half against the
Lakers, and wound up losing the game and being eliminated
from the playoffs.

This was one hell of a way to start an important road trip,
with victories over the two toughest teams you have to face.
They were two of the hardest but most rewarding wins of the
season, and they told us not only how good we were, but how
much better we could be. With these two games, we served
notice to the rest of the league. We were determined and would
stop at nothing to win it all.

The so-called easy game of the trip was next, in Los Angeles
against the Clippers, who were ailing because of the serious injury to Danny Manning. Yet we couldn't take them lightly because a few weeks earlier they had beaten the probably
overconfident Cleveland Cavaliers. We controlled the tempo of
the game from the start, and the Clippers never really challenged us. Over the past couple summers, I've become good
friends with Gary Grant, the former Michigan star now with
the Clippers. I think he was especially pumped up playing

against me, because he was outstanding with 17 points, 17 assists, and four steals. We won anyway, 117-101, our eighth straight win, which, combined with the earlier nine-game streak made us 17-1 in the last 18 games.

Now we already had a successful road trip, but we still wanted the last one. Life on the road was starting to wear us down, and it felt like we had been gone a month rather than a week. I've never been on a team that has won a game in Portland's Memorial Coliseum, but we did our best to motivate ourselves anyway.

The night before the game, Michigan and Seton Hall were playing for the national championship. It was a great game to watch, and I was glad to see Michigan win, but I had mixed emotions. Watching Rumeal Robinson sink the two free throws, and seeing the Michigan players celebrate, all I could think about was our loss to the Lakers in Game Seven. No matter how well you play, you need some breaks along the way to win a championship. This year Michigan got them, and last year the Lakers got them and we didn't. All I could think about watching Michigan was, "We're doing our part. We're playing as well as we can. This year I hope we get the breaks."

Against the Trailblazers, somehow we managed to take a 10-point lead into the locker room at halftime, but sitting around and looking at the faces, you could see that there was nothing left in our guys. I know my legs were gone, and so were probably everybody else's. There was no energy left. We were a step slow on every play and Portland scored 71 points in the second half. I'm not using this as an excuse, but for the third time, I think the schedule beat us more than the opponent. I think this happens to us less frequently than it does to other teams, and our record bears this out. Tough schedules are a fact of life in the NBA, and everyone at some point has to play four games in five nights. But like earlier losses at Houston and Milwaukee, I think with one more day of rest our chances of winning would have been greatly improved.

Finally, we were going home. We arrived in Detroit at seven in the morning and had a day off before back-to-back games with Chicago, which gave us time to do a little thinking about the race. You always wonder what the other team is thinking. I'm sure Cleveland had to think we'd do no better than split on

DALLAS AND THE FINAL WEST COAST ROAD TRIP

the road, and hoped we would win only one. They had to be nervous now. The race was indeed going to go down to the wire, as everyone knew it would. Even though we were home, we were still looking at our own turn for four games in five nights followed by a big game with Cleveland and then a road game in New York. It would probably all be decided in the next week. We had played 71 games and lost only 18 of them, but in the next seven, we'd be rolling the dice for the whole season. In 1987, when the Tigers were in the race for the American League East title, their whole season came down to a weekend series with Toronto, and our situation was virtually identical. This puts a lot of pressure on a team, but we could take the heat. We were in the kitchen and weren't about to leave.

40

BILL LAIMBEER

POSITION: Center
HEIGHT: 6'11"
WEIGHT: 245 Pounds
COLLEGE: Notre Dame (Degree in Economics)
HIGH SCHOOL: Palos Verdes, CA
BIRTHDATE: 05-19-57
BIRTHPLACE: Boston, MA
WHEN DRAFTED: Third Round (65th Overall) Cleveland, 1979
HOW ACQUIRED: From Cleveland with Kenny Carr for Phil Hubbard, Paul Mokeski, 1982 First Round Draft Choice, 1982 Second Round Draft Choice
PRO EXPERIENCE: Nine Years
NICKNAME: Lambs
MARITAL STATUS: Married (Chris)
CHILDREN: Eric William and Kerriann
RESIDENCE: Orchard Lake, MI

LAIMBEER	G	GS	MIN	FIELD GOALS FG	FGA	PCT	3-POINT FG FG	FGA	PCT	FREE THROWS FT	FTA	PCT	REBOUNDS OFF	DEF	TOT	AST	PF	BLK	PTS	AVG
Through 4/23	81	81	2640	449	900	.499	30	86	.349	178	212	.840	138	638	776	177	259	100	1106	13.7
Playoffs	17	17	497	66	142	.465	15	42	.357	25	31	.806	26	114	140	31	55	8	172	10.1

	SINGLE GAME HIGHS							AVERAGE PER GAME						AVERAGE PER 48 MINUTES						
	MIN	REB	AST	ST	TO	BL	PTS	MIN	REB	AST	STL	TO	BLK	PTS	REB	AST	PF	STL	TO	BLK	PTS
Through 4/23	45	22	7	4	5	6	32	32.6	9.6	2.2	0.63	1.6	1.23	13.7	14.1	3.2	4.7	0.93	2.3	1.82	20.1
Playoffs	43	17	6	1	4	2	19	29.2	8.2	1.8	0.35	1.1	0.47	10.1	13.5	3.0	5.3	0.58	1.8	0.77	16.6

THIS SEASON: Had his Iron Man streak snapped at 685 straight games played which is the fourth longest in NBA history...The streak came to a halt due to a league-imposed, one-game suspension for fighting with Cleveland's Brad Daugherty on January 27...Was forced to sit out the Sacramento game on January 29...Averaged just 9.6 rebounds per game...Had averaged better than double figures in rebounding during each of the previous six straight seasons...In fact, during one stretch of the season, he lost the team's rebounding lead during the middle portion of the season...But, for the seventh straight season, he was the Pistons' top rebounder...Twice during the year, he grabbed 9 defensive rebounds in a quarter, which is a Pistons' record...Had 30 games of double figures in points and rebounds...Entered the season with 33 career three-pointers, but this season he connected on 30-85 on triples...Scored his season high of 32 points at Golden State on February 18...His 32.7 minutes per game represented his lowest minutes played average since he's been with the Pistons...His season's high in rebounds was 22 on April 6 versus Chicago, including 16 in the second half...For the fourth time in the last six seasons, he shot better than 50 percent from the field...Also, for the fourth straight season, he shot better than 80 percent from the free-throw line after struggling from the charity stripe through the first half of the season...

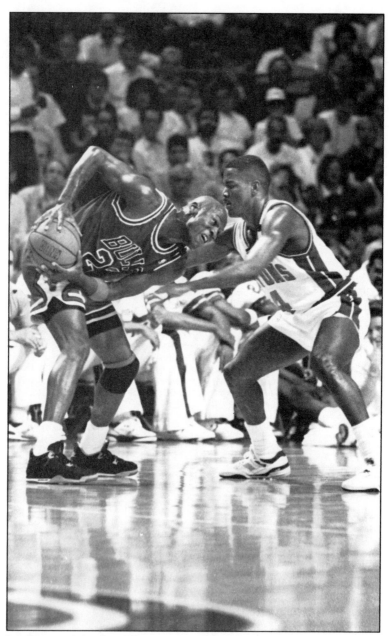

Joe Dumars defending Chicago's Michael Jordan

BAD BOYS

CENTRAL DIVISION CHAMPS 10

COMING HOME OFF A TOUGH WEST coast road trip is difficult because the first game you play at home is almost like another road game. The reason is simple: you get so used to living out of a suitcase that when you get back to Detroit, at first it seems just like another stop on the road. And in this case we were to be home for only one game, because we had a home-and-home series with the Bulls.

Chicago coach Doug Collins had moved Michael Jordan to point guard, and the Bulls became one of the hottest teams in the league, with Jordan averaging a triple-double in points, assists, and rebounds since being put in the new position. We did not have time to prepare for Jordan playing the point, and the responsibility for trying to contain him fell on the shoulders of Joe Dumars.

In the past, when Jordan was playing shooting guard, we could give Joe plenty of help by double teaming him. Once the Bulls gave Jordan the ball, I was the designated player who ran directly at him and double teamed, so he would have to pass the ball. Our team's attitude was that we'd make the other four guys beat us, not Michael Jordan alone. Now at point guard, Jordan always has the basketball, and he can see the entire floor with the ball in his hand. When he's constantly handling the basketball, he's difficult to trap because it's much easier for him to read the defense. He always has me in his view now, and with his great dribbling skills he can create opportunities for his teammates.

On Thursday, our game plan didn't work very well in the first half of the first game. Jordan scored 20 points, and the Bulls led by five at the intermission. At halftime, Joe and I talked about the problems we were having trying to contain Jordan. Chuck decided it was time to adjust and have Joe play Jordan straight up in the second half. I know from personal experience that trying to penetrate against a team that plays a straight man-to-man is very difficult. You have to dribble through literally nine guys, because your four teammates become a decoy for the defensive team. In the third quarter, we played outstanding defense for the entire quarter, and that really made the difference in the game. I know Chuck Daly would like that type of defensive effort in all four quarters, but we didn't respond in the first 24 minutes of the game. We also outscored the Bulls in the third quarter, 29-16, and went on to win the game, 115-108. Our victory gave us eight straight wins over the Bulls since they beat us in the second game of the 1988 playoffs.

We left for Chicago right after the game, and because the Bulls didn't want us to have an advantage, they got a charter back home the same night. Their management must have decided that the second game was a big one and the additional cost was not important if it helped them win. Because the first game had not been a blowout, the Bulls were pulling out all the stops to beat us in the rematch. If we had had a lopsided victory on Thursday at The Palace, I'm sure their coaches would have decided to rest their key players on Friday. But the entire game had been close, and they had been in a position to win even in the late stages of the game. Both teams expended an enormous amount of energy. On the second night of back-to-back games, the depth of your team becomes a key factor in deciding the outcome. If that was going to be the case in the second game against the Bulls, then I liked our chances.

This was our sixth and final game against the Bulls this season, and without a doubt it would be our toughest. Since we were 5-0 against them, they desperately needed to beat us at least once. If they were going to meet us in the playoffs, they needed to prove to themselves that they could beat the Detroit Pistons. From our viewpoint, it seemed virtually impossible to beat the Bulls three straight times in Chicago in the same season. The odds had to favor Chicago.

The Chicago Stadium was rocking as usual and our team was ready for the challenge. We played very well in the early stages of the game, and I liked our chances because there was no big emotional outburst from the Bulls' players at the start of the game. With about four minutes left in the first quarter, I thought we were about ready to break the game open, but what happened on the next play changed the rest of our season.

For whatever reason, every time we played Chicago this season, Bill Cartwright and I had confrontations. Now, Cartwright's a guy who can get banged an entire game by Rick Mahorn and Bill Laimbeer and nothing ever happens, but for some reason I was different. In the first five games, Cartwright had cut me twice and we nearly came to blows in two other instances. I needed four stitches just above my left eye the first time, and the second time I had seven stitches above my right eye. I'm not saying his flying elbows were intentional, but I was tired of being the guy catching them in the head.

Cartwright caught the ball in the low post and turned toward the basket attempting to shoot. I decided to sneak up and try to strip the ball away from him. I stole the ball, and, as he was following through, I saw him take a roundhouse swing at me followed by a left punch to the back of my head.

Now, I have played basketball for 24 years, and I know the difference between a basketball reaction and a physically violent reaction. There is no question in my mind that Bill Cartwright intentionally tried to hurt me. Yes, I retaliated, and yes, I was wrong. I landed several punches on Cartwright's face for all the previous aggravation he had caused me. The incident wasn't caused by this one confrontation alone—it was the culmination of all the previous provocations. Our entire team came off the bench, and for a few minutes we had a scary situation with several players wildly throwing punches. Laimbeer and Mahorn came to the rescue and I'm glad they did. Otherwise, I probably would have gotten killed.

One of the reasons we are such a close-knit group is because, right or wrong, we support each other. The Detroit Pistons are a team in the deepest meaning of the word. We always stand up for each other and live or die with each other. That may be the single most important reason we are so successful. Our opponents play a 12-man team, not a group of individuals.

Any player who comes off the bench during a fight is automatically fined, and guys like Mahorn and Laimbeer realized the consequences, but were more worried about me. That's why they are great teammates. But fighting does not have a place in our game, and it is very poor sportsmanship. I had asked the league earlier in the year to look into the previous confrontations between Bill Cartwright and me. But they had done nothing, so I finally decided to take the situation into my own hands. That was not the right thing to do, and I sincerely regret my actions.

After all the players had been separated, there was no question in my mind that I would be ejected, but I knew for damn sure that if I was going, so was Cartwright. It was not a fair trade-off, but I still liked our team's chances. The NBA's Bad Boys always respond positively when there is a fight. There were still four minutes left in the first quarter, and both Cartwright and I were done for the rest of the game.

The Chicago Stadium is one of the oldest buildings in the league, and there aren't any television sets in the locker rooms like there are in The Palace. I couldn't watch or listen to the rest of the game, but my family was there so they took turns giving me updates.

Once I had settled down after all the commotion from the fight, I realized that my left hand was really starting to bother me. Like most people, I really hate the cold and ice, but because of the throbbing pain I told the ball boy to get me an ice pack. By then, I knew there was definitely something wrong. The Chicago Bulls' team doctor wanted to look at my hand, but I was afraid he was going to tell me something I didn't want to hear, so I wouldn't let him. To this day, I'm not sure how I hurt my hand, but I don't think it happened when I hit Cartwright. To the best of my recollection, it probably happened when I tried to break my fall after Cartwright hit me.

At halftime, we were leading by 11 points. Our trainer, Mike Abdenour, looked at my hand and didn't like what he saw. There was concern something might be seriously wrong with it.

In the second half, Vinnie Johnson stepped in my place. He scored a total of 30 points in the game, 25 in the second half. We were up by 17 points in the third quarter, withstood the fourth quarter rally by the Bulls, and finally won the game, 114-112, in overtime. After beating the Bulls, we finished with a perfect 6-0 record against them for the season.

For the five-game stretch that would decide our season, we were already 2-0, but there was a major concern regarding my hand, with a strong possibility that the injury might keep me out of action for an extended period of time. Since the first quarter, I had kept ice on it and there still was no relief. When we returned to Detroit at 2:00 a.m., I immediately went to Harper-Grace Hospital. One of the security guards came up to me and asked if I was the dummy who hit people on the head. I came pretty close to hitting him on the head with my one good hand. As I told Mike Abdenour, the worst thing about being a so-called celebrity is that people think they can say absolutely anything to you. You might expect a hostile fan in Chicago, Boston, or Los Angeles to say something like that, but not someone in Detroit. I'm sure the security guard meant no harm, but it definitely was the wrong thing to say.

Dr. Eugene Horrell met us at the hospital to examine me. A couple of years ago when I needed surgery on my thumb, he performed the operation and he's an excellent physician. The first thing he did was pinch my hand, and I damn near jumped through the roof. Even without X-rays he knew it was broken, and although he told me it was, I kept trying to convince myself it didn't hurt and wasn't broken. Sure enough, though, the X-rays confirmed that it was.

Dr. Horrell said he was putting a cast on my left hand and I

The Number One cheerleader getting the crowd into it.

was going to be out 6-8 weeks. I said, "You can put a cast on my hand, but I'm playing against Cleveland on Wednesday." He pinched my hand again and it hurt even more than the first time. Mike and Dr. Horrell said that if everything went according to plan, I would be able to return by the second round of the playoffs.

Because I have worked so hard for so long, I was determined that an injury was not going to stop me from playing for a championship. I finally convinced them to put just a splint on my hand to see how it would react. It was 4 a.m. when I finally made it

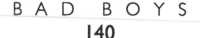

home. I told my wife, Lynn, what the situation was and she looked at it positively. She said it could be a blessing in disguise because, knowing our team, we would only come even closer together.

In the morning, I turned on the radio and the first thing I heard the deejay say was, "Bad news for Pistons fans, Isiah's out for the season." That was the end of listening to the radio. And I definitely wasn't going to read the newspapers.

During the afternoon, Brendan Suhr, Matt Dobek, and a friend of mine, Emmett Denha, came by to visit. We had a few laughs and even looked at the tape of the game. I really did get some good swings in at Cartwright, but in my opinion he started the fight.

I was trying to convince myself that my hand was feeling better, even though it really wasn't. I took the splint off it to see what kind of damage I had done. After one day, I wasn't sure when I would again be able to play because it had swollen tremendously.

Then, later in the day, Tom Wilson from the Pistons' office called me with more bad news. Rod Thorn from the league office had suspended me for two games and fined me $5,000. Of all the fights that took place over the past few years, I was the first player to draw a two-game suspension. The league was saying this was the worst fight of the season. I totally disagree, but the league office did what it thought it had to do, and I had no choice but to accept the fine and suspension.

On Sunday night, we were playing the Milwaukee Bucks. NBA rules dictate that a suspended player is not allowed in the arena during his team's game. One of the most difficult things for me to do was watch my teammates play. I sat home watching the game on television and noticed that every player raised his game to another level. The Bucks had won four of the first five games against us this season, but our starters carried the load. All five scored in double figures and we beat the Bucks, 100-91. Our winning streak was now at three games, and with two more wins we could all but eliminate Cleveland from the race.

When a player gets injured, what he dreads more than anything is the "boot." By using a combination of pressurized ice and water, this instrument helps reduce swelling. If I was going to be able to play after the two-game suspension, I needed to keep my hand in the boot almost constantly until game time on Wednesday. But that's not an easy thing to do, because your hand can get frostbitten. During the day Monday, I stayed in the Pistons' training room getting treatment. Then, about an hour before game time, I went home but took the boot with me. For the second straight night, I had to sit in front of the television and watch the Pistons play.

In this five-game stretch, the Bullets were the team that really worried me. Washington was playing for its playoff life, fighting for the eighth and final spot in the Eastern Conference. The Bullets also just happened to have won 15 of their last 16 games at home. It was our fourth game in five nights and I'm sure our guys were tired. Both Joe Dumars and Bill Laimbeer were hurting, so I knew this was not going to be an easy game for us by any means.

Every time we visit other NBA cities, we really enjoy reading the newspapers because the stories are usually outrageous. Two days earlier, in the Washington Post, Jeff Malone of the Bullets said his team needed to bring its boxing gloves to the arena on Monday night because the Detroit Pistons were coming to town. That was not a wise thing to say, because it only motivated our players. Then, just prior to the opening tip-off, the Bullets decided to make a big deal of introducing their starting lineup. They had spotlight introductions as if this were the game of the century. It was as if Washington was saying, "We're going to party on the Pistons." That too was not a wise thing to do.

Sure enough, our team came out very inspired and simply blew the Bullets out of their own gym. We led by 14 points after one quarter, 17 points at halftime and won the game 124-100. It was maybe our most impressive win of the season. Because our team has so many weapons and has such a diversified style, it's difficult for any team to defend us.

For the second straight game, a Piston player from the past really helped contribute to our win. John Long is living a dream right now. When I first came to the Pistons, John was one of the top scorers on the team. He played at Romulus High School, then at the University of Detroit, and then was a solid NBA player with the Pistons. After eight years, the Pistons decided to trade John away. And for two seasons with Indiana, he made Detroit pay for that trade. Fortunately, back in February the Pacers decided that John was not a part of their future and agreed to waive him. Chuck Daly and Jack McCloskey realized you can always use a veteran player with experience during the playoffs, and we signed him for the remainder of the season. For the first month, John was used in a very limited role because we were playing just three guards—Joe, Vinnie, and me. With my suspension over the last two games, John basically became the third guard and he helped contribute to both wins.

Our team was now on an emotional high. In the biggest stretch of the season we were 4-0, but the most important game of the season to this point was next. The Cavaliers knew that if they had any hope of winning the Central Division, they had to beat us in our gym or the race was over.

Over my first eight years in the league, I probably learned the most from competing against the Boston Celtics. The Celtics play a better mental game than any other team in the league, and what they do is trick you. Sure, they're a very good basketball team, but they use all the tricks they can to distract their opponents. I decided I was going to borrow a page from Larry Bird's book of tricks that he had used against us and many others over the years.

In January of last year, we were chasing the Celtics for the best record in the Eastern Conference and the home-court advantage in the playoffs. I remember picking up a newspaper in the middle of January and Bird said, "Detroit might as well forget about the race because I can't see anyone but Boston and the Lakers in the Finals." Right after that, a Boston writer came up to me and asked what I thought of Bird's comment and I said, "It's interesting that Bird has Detroit on his mind already and it's only January." Cleveland was in store for some of the same treatment.

This was the biggest game that most of the Cleveland players had ever played in the NBA. Although the Cleveland players were keeping quiet, both Lenny Wilkens and Wayne Embry, the coach and the general manager of the Cavaliers, were very vocal. They said I should not be allowed to play. Both of them thought I should be suspended for games that I was physically able to play, which meant that the suspension would have taken effect after the Milwaukee and Washington games. But there was a precedent for this situation. Back in 1987, when Robert Parish hit Bill

CENTRAL DIVISION CHAMPS

Laimbeer several times, the league suspended him for one game. Our contention was that Parish wouldn't have played anyway because he had a severely sprained ankle, and should have been suspended for the following game. According to league rules, however, you are suspended for the next game whether you are able to play or not. Cleveland did not have a valid argument in stating that I should not be allowed to play.

Even though my hand was going to hinder my effectiveness, I wanted to give our team an emotional lift. I couldn't participate for a very long period of time, but Joe and Vinnie might need a break for a couple of minutes and at least I could give the team that. If I made any contribution, it was going to be a plus. In addition to that, I was not going to allow Bill Cartwright or anybody else the satisfaction of knowing that they kept me out of a game.

With so much at stake for our team, this was one of the most intense games we played all season. In the first quarter, we led by seven points, and starting the second, Chuck put me in the lineup. I was having trouble going to my left and in some ways I may have hurt the team, but both Joe and Vinnie needed some rest. Cleveland took a one-point lead with four and a half minutes left in the second quarter, but that was their only lead of the game. In the final two minutes of the first half, the contest was decided—we outscored Cleveland 10-2, bringing our lead at halftime to 10 points. The Cavaliers never recovered from then on. We increased the lead to 19 points in the third quarter, and we even led by more than 20 points in the fourth quarter. Vinnie scored 23 points in the first half and led our team with 31 for the game. With our 107-95 win, we now led Cleveland by four games in the loss column.

In the locker room after the game, I made one of those statements usually made by someone from the Celtics. I said, "Cleveland should start resting their guys because this race is over." I knew the race was not over, but I wanted the Cavaliers to think it was.

We finished the most important stretch of the season with a 5-0 record. We were very close to clinching the division and the home-court advantage throughout the playoffs.

Up to this point, we had beaten every team in the league at least one time, with the exception of the New York Knicks. We headed for the Big Apple determined to change that. I am a big soap opera fan, and some day when my playing career is over, I may consider acting and the soaps may be a direction I look in. One of my favorite soap operas is "One Life To Live." The cast from the show invited me to the set to watch a taping when I was in New York, but I didn't get there early enough so we went out to dinner instead.

The next day, we had a shoot-around in Madison Square Garden before the game that night. After the practice, Laimbeer and Mahorn had to make a delivery to the league office. They had a plaque engraved for Rod Thorn, who levies all of the fines against our team. The plaque said Rod's office was paid for by their fines. At least Mahorn and Laimbeer have a sense of humor. Apparently, most of the people in the NBA offices thought the plaque was funny too.

Isiah in his first game back after his hand injury, watches the Pistons' decisive victory over Cleveland on April 12.

This was going to be our final opportunity to beat the Knicks this season. If we didn't do it and met them later in the playoffs, they obviously would have a big mental edge. In each of our first three games against New York, we controlled the tempo for a large portion of the game, only to lose the lead in the fourth quarter and ultimately the game. But this was the first time we were playing the Knicks since the trade, and we knew if we could beat their trapping defense, we had the game. I play an important role in beating the trap, but because I was playing with one hand it was mainly going to be up to Joe and Vinnie.

For the fourth straight time we controlled the tempo, and with just over a minute left in the game, we led by one point. But Patrick Ewing scored a big basket, and then the Knicks stole the ball and went on to win. For the second straight game, I didn't score, although my hand was starting to feel better. Even though we lost again and the Knicks swept the season series, I knew we were better than the Knicks. If we played them in the playoffs with all our people, I liked our chances.

With the addition of the expansion teams this season, we only play teams in the Atlantic Division four times except for the Washington Bullets, whom we play five times because of divisional imbalances. After our blowout victory earlier in the week at Washington, the Bullets really needed this win to make the playoffs. But we were playing for the best record in the league, so we were pretty motivated ourselves, and our magic number to cinch the division was down to two. Earlier in the day, Cleveland had beaten Chicago, so we could only reduce the number to one game. Steve Colter scored 27 points for the Bullets, many of the baskets against me, but we still won the game 104-98. With the magic number at one, we traveled to Cleveland to try to finish off the Cavaliers on Tuesday night.

All the pressure was now on Cleveland. When we had last left Cleveland, the Cavs had beaten us three straight and led us by five games, and now the situation was reversed. On the day of the game, the Cleveland newspapers were filled with statements from the Cavalier players. They all talked about how they dominated us in their building and that there was going to be no celebration in the Richfield Coliseum.

But we approached it just like we did any other game. On the team bus to the arena, Laimbeer, Dumars, and I all agreed that this game was not going to be close. Either our team was going to get blown out, or Cleveland was going to get blown out. Our attitude was that even if we lose, we'll clinch at home against Indiana the next night, so let's just go out and have fun. Too often there is so much pressure that you don't allow yourself to play your best basketball. We decided, if you're open, shoot, and if you miss, it's no big deal.

In the first quarter, the problem for Cleveland was that we didn't miss as we jumped out to a 12-0 lead. For the third straight game I didn't start, and sitting there on the bench I watched our team pick apart the Cleveland defense. On the road it's very difficult to sustain a big lead against a good basketball team. At some point in the game, you are very conscious of the other team making a big run at you, and that's just what happened. The lead started slipping away in the second quarter, and by halftime Cleveland had cut the deficit to just four points. But again, all the pressure was on them, so there was not a real big concern like there would be under normal circumstances.

At the start of the third quarter, Cleveland scored the first basket and cut our lead to two points, but then Joe Dumars took over. It was as if Joe had his hand in the basket. He reminded me of myself when I get that certain feeling. It's difficult to explain what happens exactly, but your rhythm becomes perfect and every move you make is done before anyone can make a reaction. Joe scored the next 17 straight points of the third quarter, and Cleveland was not only through for the night, they were through for the season. The race was over. It was the Joe Dumars Show and I really enjoyed watching it. Every player on our team was looking for Joe, and he made every basket from every distance. I guess Cleveland was hoping for him to go cold, but he never did. He finished the quarter with 24 points, tying a Pistons' record. My pre-game prediction that the game would be lopsided proved true, as we won 118-102 and clinched both the Central Division and the best record in the NBA.

After the game, there was no celebration. Our only goal was to win the championship and this game was just a step in that direction, although it was an important step, since it guaranteed us home-court advantage throughout the playoffs. No matter what our other accomplishments were, we all felt that without the championship, the season would be a failure. That's a pretty strong statement, but it's true.

The win over Cleveland was our 60th victory of the season. We had put ourselves in a select group of teams. I remember a few years ago, actually each of my first seven years in the league, looking at the NBA standings in the newspaper. Our team would have maybe 44 or 45 wins, and I'd think we were doing all right. Then I'd look at the Atlantic or Pacific Division and wonder what it felt like to be the Lakers or the Celtics with 60 wins. I must say it feels pretty good to have everyone else wish they were in your position.

A couple of seasons ago at the All-Star Game, I was in the locker room talking with Kevin McHale. We had just won four of five games and I felt good about the way our team was playing. It was the second week in February, and the last time we had played the Celtics was the first week of January. McHale said to me, "Damn, Zeke, you know we ain't lost in a month. In fact, the last team to beat us was you guys." I sat there for a minute and wondered how it would feel not to lose a game for a month. Now I understand what McHale was talking about and it feels great. It just took our basketball team a lot longer to experience such long stretches of success.

But, the thing I'm most proud of in our team, and I emphasize the word team, is that we won 60 games with everyone contributing. There was not a group of three or four guys who carried the load. People may say that I'm stubborn and that I do look at the statistics. If you go strictly by my stats over the last two seasons, you would think I had the two worst years of my professional career. But the Detroit Pistons have enjoyed the two most successful seasons in the franchise's history during those two years. The concept of not rewarding an individual for his personal statistics but rather rewarding him for the success of the team is very important.

Again, the case in point is the Boston Celtics. Cedric Maxwell started at power forward and the Celtics won the NBA Championship. Because that team was so successful, it was very easy to bring McHale off the bench. Over the last two seasons, the players on our team have been rewarded with new contracts because our basketball team has been winning.

Our unselfish attitude has been the reason behind everyone being happy. From Bill Davidson and Jack McCloskey and all the front office people, down to the coaches and players, winning has made our entire organization one happy unit. If you compare the level of talent on our team to other teams that have won 60 games, I'm not sure we could compete. But from a team standpoint, we not only could compete with all those other 60-win teams, but I would venture to say we would be very successful. In the future, I honestly believe other teams in the NBA will use the formula of creating a team with unselfish individuals rather than just gathering a group of talented players. You definitely need talent to win, but you need a cross-section of talent with your unselfish players. As long as statistics control the negotiations of player contracts, then management will be pro statistics in most organizations.

The motivation factor for the final three games of the regular season was not very high. We now would finish at home as we prepared for the playoffs, but the final three games really were of no consequence. It was time for Chuck to start resting some of the guys, but play them enough to keep them in game condition.

The first of the final three games at home was against Dick Versace's Indiana Pacers. Chuck finally moved me back into the starting lineup and I was beginning to feel more comfortable. I was playing with a protective glove and my hand's range of motion had improved. We beat the Pacers pretty easily, 115-105, and set a new team record with our 19th straight home-court win. The Palace had become a tremendous advantage as we continued to play more games. We had been successful in the Silverdome, but our 35 victories in The Palace was another team record.

Our next game was the first in a five-game series against the Philadelphia 76ers, who still had not beaten us this season. In fact, we were looking for another five-game series sweep like we had against Washington. The night before the first game, the Sixers had clinched the seventh playoff berth and could not move up or down entering the playoffs. In the first round of the playoffs, Philadelphia would play New York, regardless of the outcome of the rest of the regular season.

We won the last four games against Philadelphia, and the final game seemed more like an exhibition contest with both coaches substituting freely. Our starters had a big third quarter and we swept the series, beating the Sixers in the final game, 100-91.

If we won our final game of the regular season in 1988-89, against the Atlanta Hawks, the Detroit Pistons would record the eighth most successful season in the history of the NBA. The Hawks came into the game as the league's hottest team with a nine-game winning streak. From a playoff standpoint, if both teams were to advance past the first round, we would meet in the Eastern Conference Semi-finals. With all this in mind, I thought the game would be very competitive, but that wasn't the case. Atlanta did stay close for a half, but in the third quarter we opened up a big lead and defeated the Hawks, 99-81.

Prior to our game with the Hawks, the Boston Celtics defeated Charlotte and qualified for the eighth and final playoff spot in the Eastern Conference. Our first-round opponent would now be our old nemesis, the Boston Celtics.

Finally, the regular season was over. The NBA season is very long and it's difficult to stay focused from start to finish. It's easy

CENTRAL DIVISION CHAMPS

to lose concentration and that eventually costs you wins. I think the single motivating factor was our entire team's recollection of last year's Game Seven of the NBA Finals. No home team has ever lost a Game Seven of the Finals. At the start, there was one goal to accomplish in the regular season, and that was to have the best record in the NBA, assuring us of the home-court edge. Obviously, if we did that there would be other accomplishments along the way. And there were, like the Central Division title and a 60-win season.

Even though our regular season was very successful, our entire season would be judged on our playoff performance. If somehow the Boston Celtics eliminated us in the first round, it would be a long, disappointing summer. Anything less than an NBA Championship for the Detroit Pistons would be a disappointment. Getting to the NBA Finals last year and not winning the title, especially after coming so close, made our team put all the pressure on ourselves. Entering the playoffs, we knew what type of effort was needed and the Detroit Pistons were ready for the challenge that lay ahead.

25

JOHN LONG

POSITION: Guard
HEIGHT: 6'5"
WEIGHT: 195 Pounds
COLLEGE: Detroit '78
HIGH SCHOOL: Romulus, MI
BIRTHDATE: 08-25-56
BIRTHPLACE: Detroit, MI
WHEN DRAFTED: Detroit Second Round (29th Overall)
HOW ACQUIRED: Signed as Free Agent after Waived by Indiana
PRO EXPERIENCE: Eleven Years
MARITAL STATUS: Married (Karen)
RESIDENCE: Southfield, MI

			FIELD GOALS			3-POINT FG			FREE THROWS			REBOUNDS						
LONG	G	GS	MIN	FG	FGA	PCT	FG	FGA	PCT	FT	FTA	PCT	OFF	DEF	TOT	AST	PF	BLK	PTS	AVG
Through 4/23 (Tot)	68	1	919	147	359	.409	8	20	.400	70	76	.921	18	59	77	80	84	3	372	5.5
Through 4/23 (Det)	24	0	152	19	40	.475	0	0	----	11	13	.846	2	9	11	15	16	2	49	2.0
Playoffs	4	0	8	1	1	1.000	0	0	----	3	3	1.000	0	0	0	0	0	0	5	1.3

	SINGLE GAME HIGHS						AVERAGE PER GAME							AVERAGE PER 48 MINUTES					
	MIN	REB	AST	ST	TO	BL	PTS	MIN	REB	AST	STL	TO	BLK	PTS	REB	AST	PF	STL	TO	BLK	PTS
Through 4/23 (Tot)	36	6	5	4	3	1	25	13.5	1.1	1.2	0.43	0.8	0.04	5.5	4.0	4.2	4.4	1.51	3.0	0.16	19.4
Through 4/23 (Det)	25	2	4	0	2	1	17	6.3	0.5	0.6	0.00	0.4	0.08	2.0	3.5	4.7	5.1	0.00	2.8	0.63	15.5
Playoffs	3	0	0	0	0	0	3	2.0	0.0	0.0	0.00	0.0	0.00	1.3	0.0	0.0	0.0	0.00	0.0	0.00	30.0

THIS SEASON: After starting the season with the Indiana Pacers then later waived, he was signed to a contract for the remainder of the season on February 23 by the Pistons...Returned to the team that he spent his first eight seasons in the NBA with...Ranks fifth on the all-time Pistons' scoring list...Averaged 7.3 points per game with the Pacers this season in 44 games...With Detroit this season, he played in 24 games and averaged 2.0 points per game...But, did make key contributions in a two-game stretch with the absence of Isiah Thomas...First, versus Milwaukee on April 9, he scored 9 points in 18 minutes of action...Then, the next night in Washington, he scored a Pistons' high 17 points connecting on 6-7 field goals in his longest stint this season with the Pistons (25 minutes)...Was a member of the Pistons during the lean years, now returns during the most successful season in Detroit...Only player to be a member of a 60-win Pistons' team and a 60-loss Pistons' team...

Bill Laimbeer stretches out Kevin McHale's jersey (accidentally, of course).

BAD BOYS

FIRST ROUND PLAYOFFS

DETROIT VERSUS BOSTON

THE BEST WEEK OF PRACTICE FOR our basketball team is always the week prior to our first playoff game. There is a very simple reason for this: our team has an entire week to concentrate on a single opponent. Since we were meeting Boston in the playoffs for the third straight year, we weren't exactly unfamiliar with their style of play.

With the series scheduled to start on Friday, we had Monday off, but I went to The Palace to work out anyway. For the past two weeks since I broke my hand, my stamina has not been very good. In game situations, you think you're in shape until you go up and down the court a few times and realize you aren't.

I also went to the doctor to experiment with a brace on my hand, but we couldn't come up with anything that gave my hand the proper amount of support and still allowed me freedom of movement on the court with my left hand. I was very concerned, because this could have been the first playoff series I was healthy for since 1985. What I needed to do was find out what I could and could not do, then adjust my game accordingly. Back in 1986 we were eliminated in the first round of the playoffs against the Atlanta Hawks, and in that series I played with a seriously injured left thumb, which later required off-season surgery. I felt then that I was reasonably effective because I was able to determine how best to use the hand. This was a similar situation.

I have a gymnasium built in my house so I'm able to work out while at home with my family, and I found that whereas I was able to shoot well and dribble with either hand, the range of motion with my left hand was limited. I figured I would have the most problems on defense, but good coaching says you're supposed to move your feet and not reach for the ball; if I did that I wouldn't have any difficulty.

On Tuesday we had one of the hardest practices of the entire year, including training camp. It was geared to improving our stamina and directing our attention toward the Celtics. The coaching staff did an excellent job of breaking down films of each player on the Celtics' team and their individual moves, and they also had each offensive and defensive set the Celtics used. Each player on our team received a tape which we took home and watched that evening. In terms of preparation, we knew exactly what Boston would do both on offense and defense. This was the fourth Detroit-Boston playoff series in the last five years, and nothing had changed much during that time. We knew Robert Parish and Kevin McHale would get the ball down low and post-up.

Wednesday was another hard day of practice, and then Thursday was a lighter workout as we fine-tuned our preparation for the Celtics. I made a final visit to Dr. Horrell for another examination on my broken left hand, and he told me that nothing had changed. I guess no news was good news. He said the hand wasn't any worse, but it wasn't any better either, so I figured I was as ready as I'd ever be for the first game.

For some reason I was nervous. Despite having played in hundreds of basketball games, I still get butterflies in my stomach before certain games. As I was driving to The Palace, everything we had gone through in last year's playoffs came back into my mind. It all hit me at once, and I couldn't believe it. From almost losing to the Bullets, to beating Chicago and Boston, to the NBA Finals against the Lakers—all of this was fresh in my mind, as if it had happened the day before. I broke down and began to cry. I didn't want to see the same thing happen this year. I was well aware of how difficult it would be to make it back to the Finals, and that the 82-game regular season schedule was only a prelude. The playoffs are what it's all about, and the first team standing in our way was the Boston Celtics, a team with an incredible tradition. They know what it takes to win, but thanks to our experience last year, the Detroit Pistons know too.

I arrived at the arena a couple of hours before game time and did some early shooting, again testing the left hand. While it wasn't perfect, it was feeling the best it had since the fight with Bill Cartwright.

The game began, and just a minute into it I made my first jump shot. I said to myself, "Junior, this might be your night." Well, although it really wasn't my night, it was a good night for our team. We seesawed back and forth in the early going, and held a slim 27-25 lead at the end of the first quarter, but I felt the tempo was in our favor.

When Dennis Rodman and John Salley are active on defense, denying the ball inside and blocking shots, they're very intimidating, especially at The Palace. In the second quarter, they blocked seven shots between them, including five by John, and we held the Celtics to just 10 points, tying an all-time NBA playoff record. At halftime we led 48-35, mostly because of those two guys and Joe Dumars, who had scored 16 points by intermission. We stayed in control the rest of the way and had our first win of the playoffs, beating Boston 101-91.

The way we won reminded me of the Philadelphia 76ers when they won the NBA Championship in 1983. They had plenty of depth like we do, but what they did in just about every game was turn up the defensive intensity and smother the opposition. Even

Mark Aguirre, Vinnie Johnson, and Isiah watch first-round playoff action.

though they might not play consistently on offense night after night, they made it almost impossible for the other team to score a lot of points against them. There were never any easy baskets scored against that Sixers team, and in our first playoff win we were playing the same kind of defense.

Even though we won, I felt that Chuck and the guys on the team had lost confidence in me. I guess they thought my hand was really limiting my effectiveness, and so they didn't look to me as one of the main options on offense. That was strictly my opinion, because no coach or player said anything to me about it, but I could tell they were not very confident about my abilities. As a player, I know which plays I can make and which ones I can't make. It really bothered me inside, having my teammates and coaches losing confidence. There is no question they had reason to doubt how effective I could be, but because I am the team captain, they should be able to point to me as a stabilizing factor. This was a first for me, and I was going to do my damnedest to change their attitude.

At practice on Saturday, I had another brace made up for my left hand. I wished that I could do away with the thing, but if I was ever hit hard on that hand without it, it would be a major-league problem.

The next game with Boston was scheduled for Sunday at three-thirty, because it was to be televised by CBS. A Pistons-Celtics matchup usually makes for good ratings for the networks. In this case it was a wise choice, because Game Two proved to be outstanding.

After their loss in the first game, the Celtics honestly believed they could win the second game. They felt if they didn't have any offensive lulls, they could steal one in our gym.

We again controlled the pace at the beginning of the game, but the Celtic players are familiar with our offensive sets and they know how to defend our plays. If we're not making our shots, their chances of winning increase dramatically. In any series, both teams make adjustments based on what happened in the previous game. For the most part, the team that loses the first game usually makes more drastic changes simply because if they don't, they're likely to lose again. And if Boston lost the second game, they knew they'd have little chance of winning the series.

Strategy became very important to both teams, but it still came down to those players on the court deciding the outcome. For a long stretch in the second and third quarters, the Celtics couldn't miss, and in fact we trailed by nine points in the middle of the third quarter. All season, our team had worked on gaining the home-court advantage in the playoffs. Now, playing just our second game, we were in danger of losing this home-court edge.

One of the biggest assets our basketball team has is a strong willingness to compete. The Boston Celtics have players just like that in Dennis Johnson, Robert Parish, and Kevin McHale. Those guys have been there before in tough situations and have been successful. During this game's third quarter, our team was so bad offensively that our only hope of winning was going to be a great defensive effort.

Even though we were down by nine points, Chuck went to a defensive lineup with Rodman and Salley. Baskets were not coming easily for either team, but we needed to shut down the Celtics almost completely and take them out of sync.

For the first time since breaking my hand, the team looked to me to score, and I felt ready for the challenge. I certainly did not want to let my teammates down at this point in the season—especially when I was feeling as though they'd lost confidence in my abilities. Toward the end of the third quarter, we started our uphill climb. I scored 14 points during the third quarter, which helped put us in a position to win the game.

FIRST ROUND PLAYOFFS: DETROIT VERSUS BOSTON

Again we made a strong defensive push against the Celtics. In Game One, they only scored 10 points during the second quarter. This time our strong effort on the defensive end came during the last quarter, when the Celtics scored just 13 points. Although this game was hardly an artistic win, we beat Boston 102-95 and needed just one more win to eliminate our perennial challenger.

My family from Chicago had all come to town to watch the second game and help celebrate my birthday. I'm sure that if we'd lost, there would not have been much of a celebration, but since we were leading the series 2-0, I was able to relax and enjoy myself. My mother had been in town for Game One, but had not felt well enough to attend the game and had watched it on television instead. Fortunately, this time she was able to see the second game of the series in person, and then enjoy my birthday party.

Two inventive fans trying to be noticed by the CBS cameraman. At least they made it in this book.

On Monday morning we practiced and then prepared for our five o'clock flight to Boston for Game Three of the series. That night, Joe Dumars and I both had a taste for Italian food, and we settled on a place called Luccia's. The restaurant was not within walking distance of our hotel, so we grabbed a cab. We had only one problem—the cab driver didn't know how to get to the restaurant. Most players on our team realize we're not exactly well-liked in Boston, so ordinarily we'd never think of asking a Bostonian for any type of assistance. But the cab driver pulled over at a corner, and Joe asked a small group of people for directions to the restaurant.

In previous years, I'm sure we would have received nothing but aggravation in this same situation. Based on previous experience, I was half expecting them to curse us out instead of offering to help us find the restaurant. But that was not the case this time. All three people walked up to the cab and asked for autographs. I was in shock, because I'm never asked for an autograph when we are in Boston. We seemed to be witnessing a serious Bostonian attitude change. The best was yet to come, however, at the restaurant, where the restaurant owner paid for our dinners and even wished us luck in the game against the Celtics! That marks a tremendous change in attitude, because for as long as I can remember, in Boston we've always been the hated Detroit Pistons.

After dinner, both Joe and I went back to our hotel rooms to spend a quiet evening preparing for the Celtic game the following night. Trying to keep an upcoming game off your mind is very difficult. As players, we become consumed by the game all too often, so that everything else going on becomes secondary. I was able to stop thinking about the game for at least an hour, while I watched an episode of "Columbo" on television. That show, along with "Mission Impossible," "A Different World," and "The Cosby Show," are the television programs I never miss, whether I'm at home or on the road.

On Tuesday, game day, I called home. My wife, Lynn, gave Joshua the telephone, and he kept saying, "Da, da." I can't even explain the way I felt after he said that—the only way you would understand is if you have kids of your own.

The big story in Boston prior to Game Three was whether Larry Bird would play. He had been given the go-ahead to practice, and there was a good chance he would play in the game.

Traditionally, in the first round of the playoffs, Game Three is always ugly. When a team is down by two games and just trying to survive, it does not make for a game with any flow or continuity. Chuck's philosophy in games like that is to hang around, hang around, and steal the game at the end. In the first playoff series we won back in 1985, we swept the New Jersey Nets with just that style of play. After going up by two games, the third game in New Jersey was ugly, but somehow we hung around and managed to steal the game at the end.

Joe Dumars probably has been our Most Valuable Player this season. In Game Three against Boston, he had 12 points in the first quarter and we survived an emotional start by the Celtics. The game remained close throughout the first half. In the second quarter, however, Ed Pinckney went up for a shot and I was able to get my right hand on the ball. I refused to let go, and when

Pinckney ripped the ball away, I felt something tear in my shoulder.

These playoffs were really getting to me. I already had a broken hand, and now I knew there was something wrong with my right shoulder. I didn't tell our trainer or doctor there was a problem, though, because I had decided I was going to play through the pain. That's not always the right thing to do; if you're injured, you can sometimes hurt the team more by insisting on playing, but I thought the team could use my leadership if we were going to beat the Celtics.

At halftime, I honestly thought something good had to happen to our team. I was right, because the bench was absolutely incredible during the second half. That just might be the best single attribute of our team: we have 10 guys who can really play the game. We wear teams down because of this great depth. Entering the fourth quarter, we trailed by just two points. I was extremely tired, and I knew the Celtics had to be exhausted too.

Dick Motta, who coached the Dallas Mavericks and who is now the color commentator for our televised games, has a theory that nothing can replace fresh legs. In the fourth quarter, we had fresh legs in John Salley and Dennis Rodman, and those two guys made it nearly impossible for Boston to score during the quarter. For the third straight game, we shut down the Celtics' offense almost completely, giving us a series sweep. However, the final score of 100-85 was not indicative of how close Game Three had been.

The entire Boston series was a showcase for Dennis Rodman. After what the two of us went through regarding the "Larry Bird incident" a few seasons ago, I'm amazed at how mature the Worm is now. Not only has Dennis developed as a player, as we all knew he would, but he has really matured as an individual. Dennis can handle the most difficult of situations now, something that was not easy for him to do when he was a rookie.

After the game, I was sitting in the training room waiting for another evaluation of yet another injury. Dr. Paolucci was honest with me and said I might have a torn rotator cuff. Now, I had no idea what a rotator cuff was, but I knew Jim McMahon of the Chicago Bears had torn one. In fact, McMahon was out for the entire season because of his injury. Although I did not know much about my injury, I told Dr. Paolucci it was probably just a

Pistons' shot blocker par excellence, John Salley, almost gets another against the Celtics' Robert Parish

"The Worm" goes high to snag a rebound against Boston's Mark Acres.

strain or a sprain. I'd made a big commitment to win the championship, and I knew that if I could just stay healthy, we'd be in good shape for the rest of the playoffs.

Since we'd swept the Celtics, I was going to have an extended period of time to rest, maybe as much as eight days. In the training room after the Boston series, we also devised another brace for my left hand that would allow me greater freedom of motion. Too often when I went to my left hand, I didn't have a feel for the basketball. That's a big part of my game—going to my right or to my left with the ability to score the basket or make the pass from either side. But now I was having some difficulty finishing the play.

FIRST ROUND PLAYOFFS: DETROIT VERSUS BOSTON

Each player on our team has agreed not to drink alcohol during the playoffs. If a player is caught drinking any form of alcohol, he receives a $100 fine per offense. After the final Boston game, most of the guys went to the bar across the street from our hotel, but, true to form, no one drank while at the club. I couldn't go with the other players because my shoulder injury was causing severe pain.

Back in my hotel room, I tried to order a hot fudge sundae. There was no answer from the room service people, so I called the front desk. I was told that the kitchen had to be closed once a year for inventory, and there would be no room service available for 24 hours. I said to myself, "This is not my day." I took the ice off my shoulder and tried to get some range of motion. That was not a wise decision, however, because the pain became even more severe. Needless to say, I had a very difficult time sleeping that night.

The next morning was a travel day back to Detroit, and Chuck cancelled practice. During the flight home, George Gervin's name was brought up. All the guys sitting in the front section of the plane were reminiscing about the "Ice Man." It seemed like each story was better than the last. I was fortunate to have played against George Gervin, and he truly was a legend. Offensively, George was so creative that you had to admire his special moves. After Roundball One landed, I followed Dr. Paolucci because I had an appointment with Dr. Robert Teitge. For once in my life, I was correct in my injury evaluation. The X-rays revealed a strained ligament, which would keep me out for a week to 10 days. If the doctors were saying a week to 10 days, I figured I'd be back in the lineup in a few days—I'm a quick healer.

With the day off, I could spend some time with my family. It was a nice day, and Joshua, who had never touched dirt or grass before, had his first extended experience playing outdoors. Watching Joshua crawl around, trying to put everything in his mouth, I realized how glad I was that we'd swept the series and gotten this day off. It is very important for me to spend as much time with my family as I can, and I'm grateful for every available opportunity to do so.

RICK MAHORN

POSITION: Forward-Center
HEIGHT: 6'10"
WEIGHT: 255 Pounds
COLLEGE: Hampton Institute '80 (Business Administration Degree)
HIGH SCHOOL: Weaver, CT
BIRTHDATE: 09-21-58
BIRTHPLACE: Hartford, CT
WHEN DRAFTED: Second Round by Washington, 1980
HOW ACQUIRED: From Washington with Mike Gibson in Exchange for Dan Roundfield, June 17, 1985
PRO EXPERIENCE: Nine years
MARITAL STATUS: Single
RESIDENCE: Camp Springs, MD

				FIELD GOALS			3-POINT FG			FREE THROWS			REBOUNDS							
MAHORN	G	GS	MIN	FG	FGA	PCT	FG	FGA	PCT	FT	FTA	PCT	OFF	DEF	TOT	AST	PF	BLK	PTS	AVG
Through 4/23	72	61	1795	203	393	.517	0	2	.000	116	155	.748	141	355	496	59	206	66	522	7.3
Playoffs	17	17	360	40	69	.580	0	0	----	17	26	.654	30	57	87	7	59	13	97	5.7

	SINGLE GAME HIGHS							AVERAGE PER GAME							AVERAGE PER 48 MINUTES					
	MIN	REB	AST	ST	TO	BL	PTS	MIN	REB	AST	STL	TO	BLK	PTS	REB	AST	PF	STL	TO	BLK	PTS
Through 4/23	43	19	4	2	5	4	19	24.9	6.9	0.8	0.56	1.3	0.92	7.3	13.3	1.6	5.5	1.07	2.6	1.76	14.0
Playoffs	35	9	2	2	3	4	17	21.2	5.1	0.4	0.53	0.6	0.76	5.7	11.6	0.9	7.9	1.20	1.5	1.73	12.9

THIS SEASON: Had another strong campaign, starting 61 of the 72 games he played...Did miss 10 games during the season due to lower back strain...But, that injury was not related to the injury which hampered him during all of last year's playoffs and then required off-season back surgery...The surgery which removed a disc did not bother his play the entire season...Did play the final 43 games of the season and entered the playoffs completely healthy...Started the final 33 games of the regular season and during that time, the Pistons were 29-4...Scored in double figures in 20 games...Had 20 games of double figures in rebounds...Had his best game of the season versus Denver on March 6 when he scored a season's high with 19 points and grabbed a season's high 19 rebounds...After not connecting on 50 percent of his shots in his first two seasons in Detroit, he has now connected on better than that mark for two straight seasons...Played an average of 19 minutes per game with the Pistons in his first two seasons, but over the last two years, he's now been an average of 27 minutes...Team's top low-post defensive player...

163

Mark Aguirre driving around Milwaukee's Jack Sikma in the Eastern Conference Semifinals

BAD BOYS

MILWAUKEE: THE EASTERN CONFERENCE SEMIFINALS

WITH OUR THREE-GAME SWEEP of the Celtics in the first round of the playoffs, we had an unexpectedly long layoff before facing either the Atlanta Hawks or the Milwaukee Bucks, who were still engaged in a very physical battle in first-round play. That series went the distance of five games, enabling our team to get healthy before we met the winner.

Even though they had several injured players, the Bucks went into The Omni and defeated the Hawks in the fifth and deciding game. Our series was to begin the next Wednesday in The Palace—giving us a total of eight days off before playing another game.

During the regular season, the league schedule has each team playing games nearly every other day. Now we faced a long stretch before playing again, but that's what happens when you sweep an opponent during the playoffs.

In our case, we were fortunate to have such a reprieve in the schedule because a few of us were pretty banged up. Laimbeer had a bad foot, Dumars was bothered by a groin pull, and of course I needed at least another week before I could enjoy the full range of motion in my left hand. Therefore, it was a time to heal and to prepare for a very physical opponent, which is exactly what we did. Going into the seven-game series against Milwaukee, we were about as healthy as could be expected.

During the layoff, we practiced very hard and Chuck did his best to keep us well-conditioned, using primarily running and jumping drills. Although we did scrimmage among ourselves, there were no real game situations during this period. By "game situations," I mean the tough, physical, hard play that can only be experienced in a playoff game. It's strange, and even funny, to think that basketball has always been called a non-contact sport. Anyone who's played in an NBA playoff game, or even watched one on television, knows better. It's a physical game with plenty of contact. Play against the NBA's so-called Bad Boys—run through a couple of screens set by Rick Mahorn and Bill Laimbeer—and you'll never again say it is a non-contact sport.

I thought our team was reasonably sharp physically as we entered the Milwaukee series. It was hard to gauge where we stood, though, because practice conditioning is so much different than game conditioning. For years, the Boston Celtics would move quickly through the first few rounds of the Eastern Conference Playoffs, then have to wait for their next opponent. The Celtics used these rest periods to their advantage and would typically bury their next opponent in the first game, and more than once that opponent happened to be the Detroit Pistons. I remember going into the Boston Garden and getting destroyed in the first game, because the Celtics knew how important it was not to let your opponent gain any confidence.

We hoped to steal a page from the Celtics' playoff book and put the Bucks away early in the first game of this series. That didn't happen, and in fact the Bucks nearly put us away in the first half. Milwaukee led by 13 points in the second quarter, and we could not have played a more lethargic first half. Our team was nowhere near ready to play, and the Bucks' confidence seemed to increase with every passing minute of the game. Every minor push or shove by Milwaukee seemed to throw our timing off. That's unusual for the Detroit Pistons, because we usually thrive on this type of situation. The pushing and shoving affected us offensively, but our team defense remained outstanding. Throughout the playoffs, our defense kept us in many of the games.

During the second half, our comeback was keyed by the great Piston defense. Milwaukee only scored 32 points in the second half, with just 11 in the fourth quarter. Our offensive output was not very strong during any part of the game, but, as Chuck Daly says, we do hang our hat on defense. We held the Bucks to just 80 points for the game, with the final score of 85-80 attesting to the fact that it wasn't a very artistic win. We'd escaped with a victory in Game One despite our horrible offensive showing.

At practice the next day, the coaches talked about how we needed to contain Ricky Pierce, Jack Sikma, and Larry Krystkowiak. We knew we had to do that, but after the film session I told Joe Dumars our concern should be with our offense. If we could get some fast-break baskets and make our open jump shots, we could make it a little easier on ourselves. Even though we had played poorly in Game One, we had held the Bucks to just 80 points. Any team we faced in the playoffs knew it was going to be very difficult to score 100 points. Now it was up to us to get our offense in gear.

In Game Two, even though our offense did improve, the score was tied at halftime. The Bucks deserve a great deal of credit for their performance in this series, which they began without Terry Cummings or Paul Pressey, two starters who were a big reason for their success during the regular season. They also lost Paul Mokeski to an injury just before the second game. Milwaukee plays with a lot of heart, though, so we knew this would not be a "gimme" by any means.

The game was close in the third quarter, and we led by only seven points going into the final period. It was in the fourth quarter that we received an offensive push from an unlikely source. John Salley had probably been our most consistent player up to this point in the playoffs. While not always scoring many

Isiah and Dennis Rodman gang up against Ricky Pierce in Game Two of the Eastern Conference Semifinals.

points, he had been playing great defense and had been providing rebounding off the bench. With the game still in doubt, Salley looked to carry our offense and hit just about every shot he took. He scored 15 points in the last quarter and finished the game with a career playoff high of 23 points. We scored 37 points in the fourth quarter to win the game 112-92, but the final score didn't reveal how close the game had really been. After the win, we led the series 2-0, with the next two contests scheduled for Milwaukee's Bradley Center.

After the first two games, I knew we were all tired and sore, and if that was the case with the Pistons, I knew the Bucks had to be feeling even more exhausted and beaten up. The Central Division is definitely the "black and blue division" of the NBA. Games are very physical, and each basket comes with a price tag. You just know that every game is going to be a war.

We knew that if we could win the third game, the back-to-back situation of playing on Sunday and on Monday would be a great advantage to our team. Not only were the Bucks shorthanded, but with our overall depth, fatigue would be less of a factor for us.

Usually when I am in Milwaukee, my family makes the short trip from Chicago the night before the game so we can spend some time together. But due to the importance of this playoff game, I told my mother I thought it would be best if everyone stayed in Chicago and watched the game on television. It's not that I didn't want to be with them, but I really wanted to be well-rested the night before this game.

On a Saturday night in another city, I normally would go out to dinner with a few of the other players on the team. But, as is the case in most other NBA cities, the Bad Boys are not really welcome in Milwaukee. Room service is a normal route for me to take, but this time we were staying at a different hotel. After looking at the room service menu, I decided the entree selection was pretty weak, so I didn't order anything.

I tried not to think about eating and went looking for another way to pass the time. Of all the guys on our team, Vinnie Johnson is king of the saunas and steam rooms; he and I decided to check out the hotel's facilities. Usually the two of us, and especially V.J., can last a long time in a steam room, but this was the hottest one I'd ever been in. Vinnie left and I ended up staying for a few more minutes, feeling physically drained. That was it for me, and I went back to my room and fell asleep in a matter of minutes. It was still early in the evening, but since we faced an early afternoon game the next day, I thought it was the best thing to do.

The problem with going to sleep so early is that often I'll wake up in the middle of the night. During the playoffs, I never get much "good sleep"—that doesn't happen until the off season. Playoff basketball consumes your mind, and thinking about an upcoming game can keep you awake most of the night. You consider every single play, all your opponent's moves, every shot. During the course of a sleepless night, I will play the next day's game over and over in my mind. I wish I had a quarter for every time I tossed and turned thinking about a game.

My sleeping habits during the playoffs are best described as "sleep shifts." I sleep for a few hours, stay up for three hours, then try to sleep again. Staring at the alarm clock in a hotel room becomes a nightly ritual. Sometimes, after trying to sleep for a while, I'll try to find something on television that will attract my attention. The remote control is probably a bad invention for those of us constantly on the road. It's almost like a nervous habit to constantly change the channel, since you can do it so easily with a remote. Even if something on one channel begins to hold my interest, I flick the remote button just by force of habit. During the course of a season, I've probably watched small parts of hundreds of movies, having no idea how any of them ended.

I thought Sunday morning would never arrive, but once it did, it seemed like it was game time immediately. Afternoon games in the NBA can be both good and bad. If you win it's great, because you and your teammates have the rest of the evening to savor the victory. If you lose the game, it just makes for another long, sleepless night, because you'll continually think about what you did wrong and what you might have done to win.

For nearly a month and a half, I'd been forced to shoot the basketball with one hand, but in Game Three I could finally squeeze the ball with my left hand again. I'd told Joe Dumars that if we were in good shape going into Game Three, it would be time for Isiah to start playing the way everyone expected him to play. My hand was strong, and this was very important. The key to my game, as I mentioned, is having the ability to go either left or right. Although I am right-handed, I feel very confident going to my left, which makes it difficult for an opponent to defend me. Since breaking my hand, I had been very predictable and easy to guard, because I always went to my right. If I could again penetrate to the basket from either side, it would open the floor for all the other players on my team.

The Milwaukee crowd was really into this game. The Bucks' coach, Del Harris, had billed this series as the Milwaukee Good Guys against Detroit's Bad Boys. Although this really wasn't the case, it did create plenty of extra hype for the fans in Milwaukee. This kind of situation only makes our team play that much harder.

After we scored on the opening possession, the Bucks were dealt a serious blow—one that will affect their team for quite some time. On what seemed to be an innocent play, Larry Krystkowiak made a sharp cut to the basket and was going in for a layup. The next thing I saw was his knee completely buckle beneath him, and it gave me the chills. He was in extreme pain and the injury was very, very serious. That was the end of the season for Larry Krystkowiak, and it was a shame. It just doesn't seem fair for a guy who works that hard to have a season end on a fluke play.

I know the general public thinks most NBA players are over-paid. But here's a guy who, at just 23 years of age, now finds his entire career in jeopardy. NBA players' careers are short to begin with, and one injury can force you to change professions because you can no longer compete at this level. True, the salaries are high, but the career is very short when compared to most professions. Although I personally do not know Larry, you can tell by the way he competes that he has incredible work habits. His injury is very serious, but my impression is he will make it back by sheer determination.

The emotion that had been building during pre-game warmups seemed to drop immediately after this injury. The Bucks were now flat and we knew it was time to take advantage of the situation. After we opened the game with a 14-3 lead, they were forced to play catch-up for the rest of the afternoon. At halftime, with a nine-point lead, Chuck decided to move me to the shooting guard position. Joe Dumars is one of the most ver-

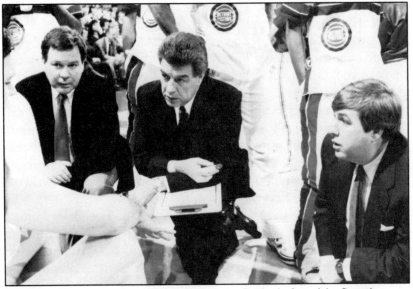

The Pistons' brain trust in a timeout against the Bucks. Left to right: Brendan Malone, Chuck Daly, and Brendan Suhr.

satile guards in the league, and our coaching staff has every confidence in Joe's ability to run the team.

The third quarter saw our best offensive effort in the playoffs to this point. All the players were involved offensively, and I felt very confident about my shooting ability. We scored 38 points in the third quarter, and I was able to score 15 of them. We led the Bucks by 22 points after three quarters and eventually won the game, 110-90. With a 3-0 series lead against the Bucks, it was time to close them out the following night.

Milwaukee's injury situation became even worse. Although Terry Cummings attempted to play in Game Three, he was still severely limited with a bad ankle. By Game Four, the Bucks had five players who were injured and unable to play. They were heavy underdogs, frantically trying to stave off elimination.

Chuck did his best to prevent a decline in our mental attitude and to guard against overconfidence, but he was fighting a losing battle. It was difficult not to feel sorry for the Bucks, and during the first half of Game Four, this was evident by the way we played. But hey, "NBA Action—It's Fantastic! and anything can happen." The Bucks couldn't miss in the first half and found themselves leading by 21 points in the second quarter. So much for feeling sorry for them. We decided they didn't need any sympathy. During the final six minutes of the second quarter, we started our comeback. Our halftime deficit of 10 points was not bad, because considering our play during most of the game, it very easily could have been at least twice as much.

In the third quarter, we scored the first eight points, then continued to climb until we were within one point. Finally, we were back in the game, but although we led by five points going into the fourth quarter, the Bucks were not going to hide. We had several opportunities to put Milwaukee away, but, to their credit, they made the plays to stay close despite being so short-handed. Finally, in the last minute of play, Milwaukee needed a three-point basket to tie the score. Because we had been burned before on this play, we decided to foul Ricky Pierce before he could attempt a three-pointer.

The Bucks were in a difficult situation. They needed to make the first free throw, which they did, but then they had to miss on the second attempt and score on the rebound. Pierce did miss on his second attempt, but the rebound caromed off a couple of

James Edwards looking for the ball against the Bucks' Randy Breuer.

players into the backcourt. Time had expired, and we beat the Bucks 96-94 for a four-game series sweep.

Including the end of the regular season, our winning streak had reached 12 games; we were off to a 7-0 mark in the playoffs. We were about to be tested again, though, because another long layoff loomed on the horizon before the next round would begin.

The winner of the New York Knicks-Chicago Bulls series would play in the Eastern Conference Finals. This was our third consecutive trip to the conference finals, and we knew what to expect. Now we could sit back and be just a bunch of NBA fans, waiting for the winner of this series. However, there was some concern on the part of our coaching staff as they looked ahead to

MILWAUKEE: THE EASTERN CONFERENCE SEMIFINALS

the next series. We had not played well in either of the initial games of the first two rounds, both of which had been played at home in The Palace.

During the regular season, New York was the only team we did not beat at least once. On the other hand, we had defeated the Chicago Bulls in all six meetings, including all three games played in the Chicago Stadium. There were mixed emotions among our players as to which team we wanted to play. Each team presented us with a specific set of problems. Because Chicago led the series 3-2 and was playing at home to close it out, I guess it was best we played the Bulls, only because we had already had enough rest. Realizing how the eight-day layoff had hurt us entering the Milwaukee series, I felt it was time for us to play again.

Michael Jordan had another incredible series against the Knicks, and in Game Six he carried the load again. As a fan, I thought that game was one of the most exciting I have seen in a long, long time. With the Bulls leading by four, Trent Tucker of the Knicks somehow scored on a four-point play late in the game to tie it up. But when you have a Michael Jordan, all you have to do is hand him the ball and ask him to win the game for you. Jordan was fouled, made two free throws, and the Bulls advanced to the Eastern Conference Finals.

Chicago had pulled off two straight upsets in the playoffs, and they were able to win the first game of both series—against Cleveland and New York—on the road. That's a major feat, especially in the playoffs when having the home-court advantage becomes so important. By winning one of the first two in each of those series, the Bulls essentially regained the home-court edge, and in fact those two wins were probably the key to the Bulls winning the two series. So the Chicago Bulls were full of confidence entering Game One of the Eastern Conference Finals against the Pistons.

10

DENNIS RODMAN

POSITION: Forward
HEIGHT: 6'8"
WEIGHT: 210 Pounds
COLLEGE: Southeastern Oklahoma State '86
HIGH SCHOOL: South Oak Cliff HS (TX)
BIRTHDATE: 05-13-61
BIRTHPLACE: Dallas, TX
WHEN DRAFTED: Second Round (27th Overall) Detroit, 1986
HOW ACQUIRED: College Draft
PRO EXPERIENCE: Three years
NICKNAME: Worm
MARITAL STATUS: Single
RESIDENCE: Dallas, TX

				FIELD GOALS			3-POINT FG			FREE THROWS			REBOUNDS							
RODMAN	G	GS	MIN	FG	FGA	PCT	FG	FGA	PCT	FT	FTA	PCT	OFF	DEF	TOT	AST	PF	BLK	PTS	AVG
Through 4/23	82	8	2208	316	531	.595	6	26	.231	97	155	.626	327	445	772	99	292	76	735	9.0
Playoffs	17	0	409	37	70	.529	0	4	.000	24	35	.686	56	114	170	16	58	12	98	5.8

SINGLE GAME HIGHS							AVERAGE PER GAME							AVERAGE PER 48 MINUTES						
	MIN	REB	AST	ST	TO	BL	PTS	MIN	REB	AST	STL	TO	BLK	PTS	REB	AST	PF	STL	TO	BLK	PTS
Through 4/23	45	21	5	3	5	5	32	26.9	9.4	1.2	0.67	1.5	0.93	9.0	16.8	2.2	6.3	1.20	2.7	1.65	16.0
Playoffs	32	19	3	1	4	3	12	24.1	10.0	0.9	0.35	1.4	0.71	5.8	20.0	1.9	6.8	0.70	2.8	1.41	11.5

THIS SEASON: Finished the season as the league's top field-goal percentage shooter connecting on .595 of his attempts, shattering the all-time Pistons' record in the process...Received national acclaim as one of the NBA's top sixth men and one of the league's best defensive players...Should get serious consideration for both post-season honors...Defensively, Coach Chuck Daly used him at four different positions during the season...For the second straight season, he was one of the few NBA players to grab 300 offensive rebounds, and the only non-starter to accomplish that feat...For part of the season, he took over the team lead in rebounding, only to finish second to Laimbeer...Hauled down an average of 9.4 rebounds per game for the season...Improved his free-throw shooting to a career-best 63 percent during the season...Also one of the few NBA players who grabbed more rebounds (772) than he scored points (735)...Went on a rebounding tear over the final 50 games of the season, averaging 11.0 during that time, including 4.4 at the offensive end...Had his best game as a pro in Golden State on February 18 when he scored a career high 32 points and grabbed a career high of 21 rebounds...Had 38 games of double figures in rebounds...Recorded 30 games of double figures in points...Started eight games for the season and during that time the Pistons were 5-3, including a pair of two-point defeats...

"The Microwave" heating it up in Game Two of the Eastern Conference Finals

BAD BOYS

1989 EASTERN CONFERENCE FINALS

WITH ANOTHER LONG LAYOFF, and again not knowing which team we'd be facing in the Finals, we had a difficult time preparing for our next opponent and trying to stay sharp. We knew, of course, it would be either New York or Chicago, but I personally did not want to face the Bulls. I remember telling several people that and they all looked at me like I was crazy. We beat Chicago all six times during the regular season and had had a relatively easy time against them in last year's playoffs. We hadn't beaten New York all year, but the Bulls were putting it all together and playing outstanding basketball at the most opportune time of the year. If I had had a choice, I'd have taken New York, but in the NBA you don't get a choice.

The Bulls were on a roll and playing with confidence, and the longer our layoff dragged on, the more I feared them. I was doing exercises to try to strengthen my hand. If you've ever been in a cast, you know that you not only lose strength, but also the muscle tone in the affected body part. For a basketball player, hand strength is critical, especially in fighting for loose balls.

We were practicing hard, but we just could not duplicate game-type situations, even though we brought in officials to simulate a real game. You need to focus on a specific opponent and their particular style of play, and this we were not able to do. No matter what you do, there's a world of difference between practice and a game. You have to be out there on the court, guarding somebody in a different colored uniform, feeling the adrenaline flowing, the crowd, and the rush of emotions. It just can't be done in practice. There's nothing to match the high you get from competing in a game in front of a national television audience and 20,000 screaming fans.

Michael Jordan is virtually impossible to stop; you hope to slow him down and try to contain him, but that's about it. In the semifinals, the Bulls won the first game in Madison Square Garden and then were able to "hold serve" and win at home to take the series. The good news was we at least knew who we'd be playing; the bad news was we also knew it would be a tough, tough, series. Jordan was playing great, the whole team had a lot of confidence after knocking off Cleveland and New York, and we were coming off a long layoff. Still, most experts predicted we'd win, and in a short series, because of our depth. We knew better.

Before the first game, Jordan made the statement that if the Bulls won the opener, they were going to win the series. I laughed to myself because I knew he had left one crucial thing out of his calculations: experience versus non-experience. This was the Bulls' first appearance in a conference finals matchup, and there's no way he could have known how tough a seven-game series would be.

Game One, The Palace, May 21, 1989. It was not pretty. We came out flat and rapidly progressed from merely horrible to off-the-charts bad. We were stunned. We looked up at the clock in the second quarter, and we were down by 24 points. Hey, wait a minute. This isn't supposed to be happening. This is The Palace. We're the Pistons. We're the team of destiny this year, and we're supposed to meet the Lakers in the Finals. The Bulls, however, seemed to be overlooking those facts. They couldn't miss, and we were having absolutely our worst half of the season. We knew we were in serious trouble, but at least when you get that far behind early, you have a chance to come back, especially if you're playing at home. That's exactly what we did, and we even briefly regained the lead in the middle of the fourth quarter, but we had expended so much energy in trying to catch up we couldn't hold it. The Bulls won 94-88 and had gained the home-court advantage.

I talked earlier about practice and how hard a player has to work in preparing for a game. Sometimes you get the feeling your game has come together because of your work habits and you can do just about anything. That's the way I felt the night before the first game against Chicago. I was in my own gym shooting around and I must have made about 30 or 35 jump shots in a row, and I was bursting with confidence. The next afternoon, I couldn't buy a basket. I even walked up to the rim and offered it $5 if it would let one drop, and it said no.

Chicago coach Doug Collins had decided to have Jordan guard me instead of Joe Dumars. Jordan was smart, because as soon as he saw I was struggling with my jump shot, he backed up and wouldn't allow me to penetrate, which is what I try to do if I'm not hitting from outside. I thought if I couldn't shoot maybe some of the other guys could, but Jordan wouldn't let that happen either. I finished the afternoon shooting 3 for 18, a miserable, miserable performance.

After the game, I went home and didn't know what to do. At least if you lose at night you can go home and go to bed and try to get some sleep, but with an afternoon game you have the rest of the day to sit around and brood. I felt terrible, not only because of the way I played, but because I felt I had let the whole team and the whole organization down. For me, personally, it was by far the lowest point of the season and I felt like the worst person on the face of the earth. I also felt bad because my dream was in jeopardy. We had worked too hard to get to this point, and after just 48 minutes of futility, this series, and therefore the whole

1989   EASTERN   CONFERENCE   FINALS

season, was in danger of slipping away. Everything we fought so hard for, everything we dreamed about, seemed to be vanishing because of one lousy game.

I didn't sleep at all that night. I mean not at all. Players in this league normally have erratic sleeping habits during the season, and I don't get much sleep even under the best of circumstances because of the pressure and stress that builds up inside me. If I get four or five hours in a night, I'm lucky, and mentally I figure that's about the same as 12 hours for a normal person.

Despite the loss, we were all pretty confident before the second game. The Bulls led after the first quarter, but we had tied it by halftime and my jump shot had returned from vacation even though I was still guarded by Jordan. This made him come out and guard me 25 feet from the basket, and when he does that, I'm going inside to see what I can create. The 33 points I scored helped us in a "must-win situation," and we narrowly escaped with a 100-91 victory, with the game once more being much closer than the final score indicated.

Afterwards I replayed the whole game in my mind, running through all the plays we ran both defensively and offensively. After two games, everyone knew the Detroit Pistons were not playing good basketball. That night, I talked to Joe Dumars and told him I didn't think we would win the series because of our talent. I told him I thought we'd win because of our experience. Then it clicked.

It's normal to form opinions, make judgments, and base decisions about the future on your past experience. What I did that night was to go back and relive some of the playoffs I had been involved in, starting with the Knicks in 1984. It was the first playoff series I ever played in, and New York won the first game in our gym. We had led all the way and somehow they stole it from us at the end. We came back to win the second game, but with the series tied 1-1 we knew we had to win one of the next two in Madison Square Garden. We lost the first one and had to win Game Four or our season was over.

Then I thought about the following year when we played Boston. They won the first two in the Garden, but we won the next two in Detroit, and the series went back to Boston tied. We had a chance to win Game Five but we didn't, and the Celtics closed us out in the sixth game. When the series was tied at two games apiece, no one gave us a chance of winning it, even though we had just won two games in a row. Even we ourselves didn't really believe we could do it.

Thinking about these and other playoff experiences, suddenly it all clicked in my mind. The important thing, the way you advance to the next round, is to win the series, not just an individual game. I was letting specific games assume too much importance and losing sight of the big picture. Talking that night about it with Joe, he reminded me that last year every single playoff series the Lakers were in went seven games, and who were the NBA champs? That's right, and the reminder gave me back the right perspective. The funny thing about the Pistons is that we've been so good and lost so seldom this year that when we do lose we sometimes have trouble handling it, and we let it bother us more than it should. But that just goes with the territory. We've been so good for so long that we can't go back to being just average. In 1984, 1985, and 1986, we were an average basketball team, and we never got past the first couple rounds in the playoffs. Now we've set higher standards for ourselves.

After Game Two, I got the impression that the media and the fans were trying to turn this into a Michael versus Isiah series. Whoever scored the most points, his team would win. We weren't about to get caught in that trap. This series was Detroit versus Chicago, nothing more and nothing less. The media hype trying

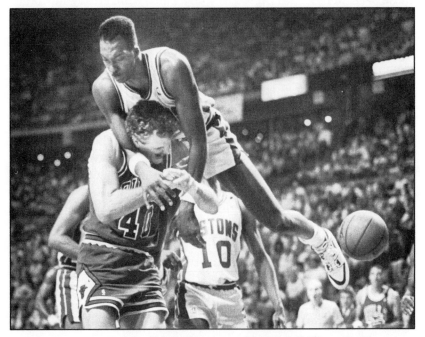

John Salley, airborne against the Bulls' Dave Corzine

to turn it into a personal confrontation played right into Chicago's hands. That, or something close to it, had been the undoing of Cleveland and New York, and they were at home watching the games on television.

Even though we won the second game, I was not a happy camper. In the post-game press conference it almost seemed as if we had lost, because we were capable of playing so much better, and we all knew it. It was too much like my first couple years in the league when I had to score a lot or we lost. We've got too much talent to win the way we won that night. When our points, rebounds, and assists are equally distributed, we're the most dangerous team in the league, but that didn't happen in Game Two.

The third game was more like Piston basketball. It wasn't just Isiah coming down, going one-on-one, and then shooting on every possession. We started moving the basketball, executing, and playing great defense. Overall, it was our best performance in the playoffs, and we had a 14-point lead with seven minutes left in the game. Then, all of a sudden, there was a change in the barometric pressure. You could feel it in the air: there was a tornado coming. We looked up, saw the funnel cloud, and all we could do was run for shelter. As usual, when a tornado hits Chicago Stadium, it was wearing number 23. Jordan took the game over and started scoring at will. I had been running the offense well but not taking that many shots, and in trying to get everyone involved I forgot my most important job, which is controlling the tempo. I couldn't counteract Jordan's offensive explosion because I had more or less taken myself out of the game from a shooting standpoint. Our offense hit the wall. We couldn't score, and I wasn't in a position to take a lot of shots. We finally lost the lead, and the final couple of plays would determine the outcome.

We were tied 97-97, but we had the ball with 28 seconds left. During the timeout Chuck was designing a play, and I don't remember who it was for because all I remember hearing was Laimbeer screaming over the roar of the crowd, "Give the ball to Isiah." Chuck had a puzzled look on his face, but Bill repeated, "Come on. Isiah's the one who got us here, and he'll be the one to win it for us." Chuck said, "But he's got Michael Jordan on him!" Laimbeer replied, "Forget Jordan. We need to win this game, and

Isiah's the one to do it." The whole exchange threw me off a little bit mentally, but I guess I was as ready as anyone.

We inbounded the ball intending to run the shot clock down to three or four seconds, so that if I scored, Chicago would have as little time as possible to retaliate. I was dribbling around the hash mark between the top of the key and mid-court, counting down with the clock...18...16...12...10. With 10 seconds left, I saw Laimbeer moving into position to set the screen, and I thought to myself, "It's too early." But the play was in motion, and as I started to come off the screen I heard a whistle. The only thing I could think of was that Chicago had been called for an illegal defense, so I shot, because if it went in, the basket would count. Instead, I saw the official motion an offensive foul, and I groaned even though I knew it couldn't be on me. They called it on Bill, who throughout the playoffs has always seemed to be in the wrong place at the wrong time in every possible situation. It's not that he's done anything wrong, he's just been in the wrong position. When Larry Krystkowiak was hurt in the Milwaukee series, everyone immediately assumed that Laimbeer had something to do with the injury because he was in the vicinity, but a careful look at the replay proved otherwise. The foul they called on Laimbeer might have been called against any other player in the league, but it just happened to be Bill. When all the fans in an opposing city are screaming obscenities and booing him, Bill just doesn't get many calls to go his way like maybe Jordan or Magic would.

OK, let's talk about officiating. Yes, our team is officiated differently than other teams in the league. They call the game differently when Laimbeer and Mahorn are on the court, and those two guys don't get the same benefit of the doubt that a Karl Malone or an Akeem Olajuwon might. They also blow the whistle differently when Isiah's in the game. He's not allowed to do the things other point guards his size can do. But that's not bad. Once again, it goes with the territory. The Lakers and the Celtics are also officiated differently, so were the Chicago Bears, the Oakland Raiders, and now the San Francisco 49ers. Most winning teams are officiated differently because of their image. It's the price of success. I remember when Detroit was just another team in the NBA, the calls all evened out, and it didn't matter much. Sometimes the calls do go against us, and many times they're very difficult to accept, but I wouldn't want it any other way. When you're good, the officials watch you more closely. Whether that's fair or unfair is not the point; it's a fact of life and as a team you have no choice but to adjust. The Detroit Pistons can't expect to be treated like an ordinary team because they're not ordinary. Sometimes things go our way and sometimes they don't, but that's the price the Pistons pay for being great.

So the call goes against Laimbeer, Jordan scores on the next possession, and the Bulls win 99-97, taking a 2-1 series lead. For the first

Dennis Rodman takes the charge against Michael Jordan.

time in over 10 games, Jordan scored more than 40 points against us. Despite all the defensive players we're able to run at him, he exploited our defense, sparked a fantastic rally, and scored the winning basket with two seconds left. I give him and the Bulls plenty of credit.

We were in trouble, but I always felt we could win the series even if we went down 3-1. There was never any doubt in my mind that we would beat Chicago, but there was plenty of concern over the way we were playing and some of the things we were doing.

After the loss, I felt like I was at the end of my rope. There always comes a time in a person's life, no matter who you are—a basketball player, a corporate executive, a professional, a husband, a wife, it doesn't matter—when you have to ask yourself a question: "Do I stop or do I go on?" I felt at this point that the easy thing to do would be to stop. Sure, I've accomplished a lot of things, and life has been good to me, but my lifetime dream of winning an NBA Championship was slipping away and I wasn't sure if I could do anything about it.

I spent another sleepless night, but ironically it was a productive sleepless night. I stayed awake and did a lot of writing and a lot of soul searching. And I did a lot of thinking about how we could stop Michael Jordan. Mark Aguirre came to my room that night and we talked strategy.

The next morning Mark called me again and I could tell he hadn't slept all night either. He came back to my room and we decided to call Rick Mahorn. Because Horn hadn't played much in the series, he was being whistled for a lot of fouls every time he tried to guard somebody close. We all decided to have breakfast in Horn's room and talk about it.

Then I called Joe Dumars but didn't get an answer, which was strange because he's always in his room when we're on the road, especially at 8 o'clock in the morning. I knew he was in his room, so I went down the hall and knocked on the door. I'll never forget the look on his face. He was wide awake, wearing a long Pistons T-shirt, and he just said grimly, "What you want?" He hadn't slept either, and the three of us joined Horn in his room for breakfast.

Michael Jordan was the only topic of conversation. We had stopped double-teaming him for the first three games of the series because he was playing point guard. Playing him straight up, the Bulls had beaten us two out of three. During the regular season when he was the shooting guard, we always double-teamed him and were able to contain him fairly effectively, having beaten Chicago nine straight times. What we had to do, we decided, was make him think like a point guard. Even though he was playing that position, we felt he was still thinking like a shooting guard, and he was killing us. When you think like a point guard, the most important thing to do is get everyone else involved in the offense, making yourself the last option. We wanted him to think of himself as the last option, because if he kept his "scoring mentality," he'd be virtually impossible to stop. I sometimes lose my concentration and don't react like a true point guard, but we wanted that to happen to Michael as little as possible.

At practice the next day, Joe and I made the suggestion to Chuck that we should go back to double-teaming Jordan. You have to give a lot of credit to Chuck, because here we are down 2-1 in a crucial series and a couple of guards come up to you trying to tell you how to coach. That has to be hard for a coach to swallow, but in this case, to our fortune, the coach happened to be Chuck Daly, whose outstanding gift is his ability to listen. If he feels you're right, he'll go with your idea, and if he doesn't, he won't. In this case, there really wasn't a good reason for him not to go with our suggestion, since he was the one who designed the effective defense against Jordan in the first place, and he readily agreed.

After practice I wanted to be alone. I needed to think about all the things that were going on, so I took a long walk. I walked along Lake Michigan all the way to the campus of Loyola University, lost in my thoughts, and the last thing I wanted to do was talk basketball with anybody. I hadn't read any newspapers or watched TV because I was fed up with basketball and needed to escape for a while.

As I was walking along the beach, with sunglasses and a hat on so people wouldn't recognize me, a woman approached me. "I like your sunglasses," she said simply. I had a strange feeling that something almost supernatural was happening, and what she was really saying was, "Isiah, come over here. Sit down and talk to me." I sat down next to her and we began to talk.

Before I knew it, I found myself sharing some very personal things. I told her that even though I had everything I ever wanted in life, I felt I was at a crossroads, and I really needed help and someone to talk to. I told her about our loss the day before, and a puzzled expression came over her face. She had no idea who I was and didn't care anything about basketball. She said her name was Marlene, she was 67 years old and had three children but had no idea where they were or how to locate them. They never wrote to her, never called, and made no effort to keep in touch. Her husband had divorced her and married a rich woman, and he wouldn't let her use his last name anymore so the kids couldn't reach her. And she was homeless.

Despite all this, she was happy. She had a job, and she loved to come to the beach to watch the children play. By this time, other people had started to crowd around and ask for my autograph, and I was getting annoyed. Marlene looked at me and said, "Isiah, there's something you have to understand. All these people think they know you, and in a way they do. At least they know the public personality. But what they don't understand is that you have no idea who they are."

I had never thought about it that way before. I had always thought I knew my fans and they knew me. I remembered the incident of the security guard at the hospital calling me a "dummy" and I knew Marlene was right. Other people didn't know what went on inside me, and I didn't know what went on inside them. Marlene went on to tell me that the problems I was having with basketball would be soon forgotten. In a couple days, a week, a few months, nobody would remember, and nobody would care. She said, "When I met you, I had no idea who you were, but you seem like a nice young man, and I like your sunglasses." She didn't go to the beach that day to talk to Isiah Thomas. She went to watch the children play.

I felt immensely relieved. She had given me a gift and she didn't even know it. We talked for more than an hour, and I never thought about basketball once. She gave me back my sunglasses and we continued walking along the beach. People continued to come up to me to say hello, but nobody seemed to notice Marlene until I introduced her. When we finally parted, I had a kind of empty feeling inside, but I also felt truly grateful. I'll probably never see her again, but I'll never forget how good she made me feel. If you ever read this, I want to say, "Thank you, Marlene." And I want to add a personal postscript: After that day on the beach, we didn't lose a game the rest of the way.

Before Game Four, Chuck said to me, "Zeke, if we're down 10 points in the first quarter, I'm not taking responsibility for the change in defensive assignments." I said to him, "Coach, I guarantee you the Bulls aren't going to score more than 80 points tonight." I felt a little like Joe Namath predicting a Super Bowl win over the Colts in 1969, because I knew how tough it would be to hold Chicago to that total, but I wanted to show him I had a lot of confidence in our decision. As I was walking off the court with Chuck after we won 86-80, I pointed at the scoreboard, and he flashed me the famous Chuck Daly grin.

Now the series was back to square one. It had turned into a best-of-three series with us holding the home-court advantage

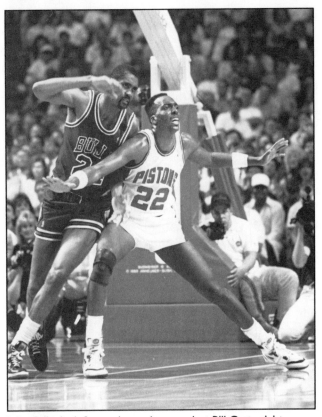

John Salley's defense, shown here against Bill Cartwright, helped the Pistons to a crucial victory in Game Two against Chicago.

because two of the remaining games would be at The Palace. Still, everyone was asking, "What's wrong with the Pistons?" I wasn't worried. Once we were back to even, I knew there was no way we'd lose.

Chicago came out very determined in the first half of Game Five. True to form, we dug an early hole for ourselves and fell behind by eight points in the first quarter. We picked up a little steam in the second quarter to cut the margin to four at halftime, and we led by one point going into the final period, when the Microwave took over. Vinnie Johnson, the "Hoo," went on a scoring explosion, and he did it against Michael Jordan no less. I didn't even come off the bench in the fourth quarter because he was on such a roll. His 16 fourth-quarter points led us to a 94-85 win, and we were one game away from advancing to the Finals for the second year in a row. All the talk after the game was about why Jordan took only eight shots, but to his credit he didn't force the play, and, let's face it, for more than three quarters the Bulls had a chance to win. You can't ask for much more than that in a playoff game on the road.

Heading back to Chicago for Game Six, there was no question in my mind that the series was over, although I knew we were facing a tough game. I knew we'd have to play the best basketball of the series, but deep down inside I knew we would.

Chicago Stadium was rocking. It was loud and noisy, and the crowd was really into the game. The Bulls figured if they could force a seventh game, with Michael Jordan anything could happen. On one of the first plays of the game, there was a mad scramble for a rebound and Scotty Pippen was knocked out cold. They said he was unconscious for a couple minutes and would be out for the remainder of the game, and, as luck would have it, Bill Laimbeer was in the middle of the play. But there was no foul called, and if Bill hit him, you couldn't tell. It might even have been one of the Chicago players. In any case, it was definitely an accident, but it really hurt the Bulls not to have their starting small forward.

I was again connecting with my jump shot on a semi-regular basis, and we managed a two-point lead at halftime. We turned up our defensive intensity a notch in the third quarter and Chicago had trouble scoring. We ended the Bulls' season with a 103-94 win, and now we could turn our attention to the Los Angeles Lakers. Despite all the worrying I had done throughout this series, our team was heading back to the NBA Finals.

I've attended the Finals every year I've been in the league. Usually it's been to watch the Lakers and Celtics play either each other or somebody like Houston or Philadelphia. And every year as one of those teams has won the championship, I've gone into the winners' locker room afterwards. With one exception, it was always the Lakers' or Celtics' locker room. Why did I visit with the winners year after year? Because I wanted to find out the secret of winning. Those teams didn't necessarily win because they had superior talent, they won because they had something the other teams lacked, and I wanted to find out what it was. It was a quest for knowledge, a search for some answers. I discovered that the main reason those teams won was selflessness. The common denominator among all the championship teams and the reason they won all the time was an unselfish style of play.

If you check the record books, you'll find that yes, Bird and Magic are two of the greatest players ever to play the game. Yet compare individual statistics, and you'll see their numbers are not all that much greater than a lot of other players in the league. But then check the number of games Bird and Magic have won during their careers. You'll find that number puts them in a class by themselves, especially in the decade of the 80's.

When I came into the league, I always wanted to do it statistically. I'd set goals of averaging 20-plus points and 10-plus assists per game, and I figured if I could reach those numbers the Pistons would win. But that philosophy only took us so far. We won games, but never a championship. At some point I had to make the decision that a championship was worth sacrificing my personal stats and worth "playing ugly," statistically speaking, if necessary.

I had to figure out what made those guys so special. I had to steal a little from Bird's game, a little from Magic, and even some from Julius Erving, because those were the only three players to lead their teams to championships during the 1980's. Being 6-foot-1, I knew I couldn't dominate or manipulate the game the way they did, so I had to find other ways to control the play. It's been hard, but I've done it. I looked at some of the other point guards my size, guys like Tiny Archibald, Gus Williams, and some of the others, and I stole something from them. I'm not going to tell you in this book what I learned. That is a secret I'm going to die with. Magic didn't tell me, nor did Larry Bird. But I sat there, and I smelled the champagne. I watched them. I shook Pat Riley's hand, and I congratulated K.C. Jones, and it stained my brain. I never forgot how much I wanted that feeling.

As a result, the way the Pistons went about winning this season has probably never been done before in the NBA. And our statistics prove that. The fact that not a single player averaged 20 or more points per game over the regular season proves that. The fact that none of us, including Joe Dumars, was named to the first, second, or third All-Pro teams proves that. Yet we won 63 games, and that's making a pretty strong statement.

Preparing mentally for L.A. naturally made me think about last year's Finals. The thing I recall most vividly is walking into

By the Eastern Conference Finals, Isiah's hand had healed enough to allow him to go to his left, as he does here against Michael Jordan.

the shower after the seventh game and seeing Bill Laimbeer sitting in the middle of the shower room floor, water running over his body, slumped over, head down, crying. Six-foot-eleven, Mr. Tough-Guy, one of the baddest of the Bad Boys, crying real tears in the middle of the shower room. I walked in, touched him, and he looked up. "Next year is our year," he said. We promised each other right there that we wouldn't be sitting on a shower room floor crying in June, 1989.

The plane ride home from the coast last year was one of the

worst trips I've ever taken. Guys were trying to console each other, but it just didn't work. We finally landed and there were hundreds of people waiting at the airport to greet us. It made us feel better for a while, and so did the rally the next day at Hart Plaza, where thousands of people came out to cheer us. But there was still an emptiness deep inside. Isiah was home, and he was never so glad to see Lynn and Joshua in his whole life. But he had a long time to think about the loss.

22

JOHN
SALLEY

POSITION: Forward-Center
HEIGHT: 6'11"
WEIGHT: 231 Pounds
COLLEGE: Georgia Tech '86 (Industrial
Management Degree)
HIGH SCHOOL: Canarsie HS, Brooklyn, NY
BIRTHDATE: 05-16-64
BIRTHPLACE: Brooklyn, NY
WHEN DRAFTED: First Round (11th Overall)
Detroit, 1986
HOW ACQUIRED: College Draft
PRO EXPERIENCE: Three Years
NICKNAME: Spider
MARITAL STATUS: Single
RESIDENCE: Brooklyn, NY

SALLEY				FIELD GOALS			3-POINT FG			FREE THROWS			REBOUNDS							
	G	GS	MIN	FG	FGA	PCT	FG	FGA	PCT	FT	FTA	PCT	OFF	DEF	TOT	AST	PF	BLK	PTS	AVG
Through 4/23	67	21	1458	166	333	.498	0	2	.000	135	195	.692	134	201	335	75	197	72	467	7.0
Playoffs	17	0	392	58	99	.586	0	0	----	36	54	.667	34	45	79	9	58	25	152	8.9

	SINGLE GAME HIGHS						AVERAGE PER GAME						AVERAGE PER 48 MINUTES						
	MIN	REB	AST	ST	TO	BL	PTS	MIN	REB	AST	STL	TO	BLK	PTS	REB	AST	PF	STL	TO	BLK	PTS
Through 4/23	40	11	5	3	5	4	19	21.8	5.0	1.1	0.60	1.5	1.07	7.0	11.0	2.5	6.5	1.32	3.3	2.37	15.4
Playoffs	33	8	3	3	2	6	23	23.1	4.6	0.5	0.53	0.7	1.47	8.9	9.7	1.1	7.1	1.10	1.5	3.06	18.6

THIS SEASON: Played in a total of 67 games, starting 21 during the season...He missed a total of 15 straight games due to a broken bone in his left ankle...Those 15 misses were the first of his career, snapping his consecutive games played streak at 213...But, during his absence the Pistons were 13-2...Average 7.0 points and shot a career low .498 from the field...After blocking 362 shots in his first two seasons with the Pistons, he recorded just 72 rejections in his third campaign and did not lead the team in that category...Had 18 games of double figures in points...Scored his season high of 19 points at New Jersey on December 4...Grabbed double figures in rebounding in five games for the season, with his top rebounding performance being a career-high tying 11 boards at Boston on January 22...

Bill Laimbeer goes after a loose ball.

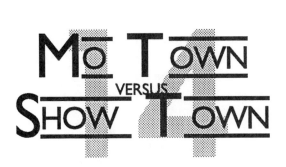

BAD BOYS

MO TOWN
VERSUS
SHOW TOWN

HE NIGHT
BEFORE THE NBA FINALS:
Detroit Pistons versus the L.A. Lakers.
This is the moment everyone on our team
has been waiting for. Before the season
even started, this was the dream we had
all envisioned. Let's face it: we didn't want
to play any opponent other than the
Lakers in the Finals. I remember back in
1987, when we were playing the Celtics in
the Eastern Conference Finals, the Lakers
let it be known that they wanted Boston
in the Finals rather than Detroit. At the
time, I really couldn't understand their
thinking. The Lakers should have wanted
us because we had never made it to the

Finals, and theoretically they would have an easier time. But in 1987 the Lakers were confident, and the Celtics were their archrival. So, what better way to win a championship than by beating the Celtics?

I injured my hamstring in the Chicago series, and although we didn't know it yet, hamstrings were going to be a hot topic of conversation throughout the Finals. I was just hoping my injury wouldn't hobble me too much or affect the way I played. I received treatment on the injury from our trainer, Mike Abdenour, just as a precautionary measure. I didn't think my injury was going to limit my play.

Last year I was real nervous before the Finals, and this year I was too, but it was a little different because we were playing at home where you're much more comfortable with the surroundings. In 1988, all the hoopla and attention our team was getting not only nationally but internationally was overwhelming. In 1989, the team was better able to deal with the situation simply because we knew what to expect.

Trying to think about anything but basketball on the eve of the NBA Finals is like a 10-year-old the night before his first trip to Disney World trying to think about something else. Throughout the regular season and even more so in the playoffs, basketball totally dominates your life. No matter what I do, I can't get the next day's game off my mind. I freely admit that the single goal of winning that ring has totally consumed my entire life. Mark Aguirre came over to the house and so did a good friend of mine, Emmett Denha. And just to show you how hard I tried to get Game One off my mind, I took them into my gym to shoot some baskets.

Again that night, I watched tapes of the Lakers. Our coaching staff of Chuck and the two Brendans (Suhr and Malone) does a tremendous job preparing us for playoff opponents. Each player on our team receives offensive tapes, defensive tapes, and individual tapes of our opponents. Plus, we have scouting reports to study, which are as extensive as college final exams. By the time we're ready to play a team, we know them about as well as they know themselves. On the other hand, I'm willing to bet the Lakers probably know the Pistons as well as we know ourselves. There weren't going to be many surprises either way concerning our offensive and defensive play calls.

On the day of the game, we had a noon shoot-around. This was an hour later than usual because the first two games in Detroit were starting at 9:00 p.m., an hour later than normal, to accommodate national television. Chuck realized coming in an hour later for practice on the day of the game would give us one less hour to kill before having to come back to the arena. For most players and coaches, the day seems to drag on from the end of practice until the start of the game.

At practice I could tell that the whole organization had been waiting for this moment. We went through the regular season, then played the Celtics, Bucks, and Bulls in the playoffs, but the Lakers were in the back of our minds the whole way.

We knew how important it was to have the home-court advantage throughout the playoffs, so during the regular season it was not hard to focus on each individual game. In the playoffs, although at this point our record was 11-2, many honestly believed we were not playing very good basketball. Granted, we were not playing great basketball, but our team was doing what was necessary to win. Our word for the whole season was "focused," and we applied that word in different ways. We were focused on the next opponent and always focused on one common goal, but with one eye on the championship, the other kept wandering over to see what the Lakers were doing.

At practice I was also aware of a sense of anger and a sense of unfulfilled accomplishment. The Lakers had gone through the 1988-89 season being called the defending World Champions. Deep down in our hearts, every time we heard that introduction, it bothered us.

The Lakers had steamrolled into the Finals, sweeping each of their first three series and were 11-0. All the basketball writers throughout the country, and even many of those from Detroit who covered our team, were picking the Lakers to win. I can understand those who saw the Lakers in the playoffs picking them because they were so impressive. But what about the ones who watched us all year long? Talk about a lack of respect! We hadn't won 74 games by using mirrors. Many writers were even calling for a Lakers' sweep in the Finals. Others even had the temerity to suggest that if the Bad Boys won the World Championship, it would give the NBA a black eye. Those who make statements like that don't know the Detroit Pistons as people. We didn't need any added incentive, but as it turned out, the media certainly helped us. All year long, the negative articles written about us had been posted on the walls in the training room as reminders of what public perceptions might be. We grew in our determination to represent the NBA and the city of Detroit in a most professional manner, win or lose.

Right after practice, we received word that Byron Scott's hamstring injury was going to keep him out of the first two games. The injury had occurred during the previous day's practice, but no one was sure how serious it was. In cases like that, we usually assume that the guy is going to play if at all possible, especially in a series like the Finals. But what the Lakers' team doctors had to take into consideration was Scott's future and the possibility of jeopardizing his whole career. They decided the risk of long-term injury was not worth the short-term benefit.

We didn't care much one way or the other; we just wanted to go out and beat the Lakers with or without Scott. They still had plenty of players to use and Michael Cooper would have to play more minutes. With the 9:00 p.m. start, my schedule, which is usually regimented, was now all out of sync. To break up the monotony of just having to wait, I drove to the Dairy Queen near my house and ordered an orange-vanilla swirl.

I am a very superstitious person. Whether it's the clothes I'm wearing or the places I go on game days, I'll follow the same routine again and again as long as we win. Well, the last time I had an orange-vanilla swirl, we won in Chicago, and I figured if it worked once, it ought to work again. We needed this first game bad, and for the good of the team I was willing to do my part by having another orange-vanilla swirl.

The rest of the afternoon, I tried to get some rest but couldn't fall asleep. My hands and feet were sweaty and even my heart was beating faster than normal in anticipation. Finally it was time for my pre-game meal. I do not like to eat anything heavy before a big game, and during the playoffs I stuck mostly to fish and pasta. A million thoughts were running through my mind on the way to The Palace, and when I finally got there, I opened my mail just to pass the time.

Game time. As soon as the game started, the ball felt like a magnet in my hand. The first time I touched the ball, I ran down the court and shot and knew it was two points. For a change, I

Magic setting the offense in Game One of the Finals.

knew I was going to have a good shooting game in a series opener. In each of the previous three series, my jump shot was erratic, but not this time. Once that first shot went in, I knew it was just a matter of us playing our game and that there was no way the Lakers would beat us. Emotionally we were really into it, and the Lakers sensed immediately that they were in for a tough, uphill climb the rest of the way.

We led after the first quarter 28-22 and started to seize control of the game in the second. With 3:30 left in the first half, we led 46-35 and another couple of baskets would really have put the Lakers in a big hole entering the second half. But Magic started to take the game over at that point, and the Lakers cut our lead to three points late in the second quarter. Dennis Rodman scored the last five points of the first half for us and we went into the locker room leading 55-48.

At halftime, the Lakers had to feel reasonably confident simply because although we had controlled the tempo for the entire first half, they only trailed by seven points.

Starting the second half, Joe Dumars, Vinnie Johnson, and I knew how important it was to take advantage of our quickness against the bigger Laker guards. With the outcome still in doubt, we quickly took control of the game. At one point we led by 20 points, 79-59, in the third quarter but the Lakers made another quarter-ending rush to close the deficit, and we led by the score of 79-66 after three quarters.

In the final quarter, the Lakers could close only to within 12 points, which they did on the last shot of the game, and we won 109-97. The key to the victory did turn out to be the play of our three-guard rotation. Between Joe, Vinnie, and me, we scored 65 points, including 39 second-half points. In that final quarter,

Vinnie scored 14 points to kill any hope of a Lakers' comeback.

The next day after practice, we had to deal with all the media questions. There were hundreds of reporters asking the same questions over and over. In last year's Finals, we totally dominated the Lakers, but we still didn't get any respect. Now we had done the same thing again, but everyone wanted to pretend it hadn't happen. What's more, we had a better chance of winning Game Two because we were at home, and last year's experience was really starting to pay dividends. Yet the media viewed it as a temporary setback for the Lakers, and still assumed it was their series.

The fierce determination shown by Rick Mahorn all season long is evident in this move to the basket in Game One.

After we beat the Lakers in the first game of the Finals last year, the Lakers looked at Game Two as a matter of life or death. Ironically, it was the Pistons this year who treated Game Two as a must-win situation. If we won it, it would put the Lakers in the difficult position of having to win four of the next five games. Plus, no matter how we played in Los Angeles, even if we lost all three, we knew the series would have to come back to Auburn Hills. That possibility seemed remote, however. But if the Lakers won Game Two, their confidence level would be high, and we didn't want to give them any advantages.

Because the game was so late, I didn't get home until 2:00 a.m., and I had to turn around and be at the arena for practice at 10:00 a.m. Over this three-day period when we played the two home games, it seemed like every waking hour was spent at The Palace. The three days went quickly.

The Lakers came out fired up for the second game, as we knew they would, and, to add to our problems, I picked up two quick fouls in the first two minutes of the game. There was no way Chuck was going to allow me any more minutes in the first quarter. It would have been a devastating blow for me to be on the bench for the rest of the first half if I had picked up my third foul.

Watching from the bench for the remainder of the first quarter, I knew we were in trouble because the Lakers were playing with all the fire and intensity and passion they were capable of. During the timeouts in the first quarter, I kept telling the guys, "Just weather the storm, just weather the storm."

With six minutes left in the first quarter, Laimbeer also picked up his second foul, and he had to sit on the bench for the rest of the period. With two starters in early foul trouble, our bench really had to respond, and both Vinnie Johnson and James Edwards played key roles. That was unusual because they rarely play many minutes in the first quarter of games.

The Lakers led by 10 points several times in the first quarter and then, finally, Joe Dumars caught fire. If there was ever a time when we needed someone to carry our offense, it was right then. Joe scored 11 points in the first quarter and the Lakers' lead was cut to six, 32-26, after 12 minutes.

In the second quarter, he continued his offensive onslaught. With Joe leading the attack, we cut the Lakers' lead to one point early in the second, but, true to form, they responded with a run of their own. Even though Joe D. had 26 points in the first half, we still trailed 62-56 at halftime. The 62 points were the most we had given up in any half during the playoffs.

In the locker room at halftime, Chuck was very upset over our defensive effort. As he likes to say, our team hangs its hat on defense. The way the Detroit Pistons have developed into a championship contender has been through defense. We rarely are going to blow out an opponent because of our offensive capabilities, but we defend so well, we simply limit the number of possessions. Allowing the Lakers 62 points in the first half was unacceptable to our coaching staff, and we were now playing right into the Lakers' style of a fast-breaking game.

Los Angeles was definitely in control of the game, but slowly in the third quarter, we cut into the lead. The score was 75-73 Lakers with 4:48 left in the third when Mychal Thompson had his shot blocked by John Salley and we had a fast break opportunity. I had the ball on the break, with a 3-2 advantage, and I faked to my right as if to pass, then passed back to my left. Mark Aguirre converted the basket to tie the score. When I released the ball, I saw Magic pull up and grab his hamstring.

Sure enough, Magic had pulled his hamstring and was in extreme pain. All I could think of was my ankle injury in Game Six against the Lakers the year before. I knew what he had to be going through emotionally. As an athlete, you don't like to see anyone get hurt, especially in a championship series. You know how hard the players on both teams have worked to get there, so the last thing you want to see is an injury. To get all the way to the Finals and then to be injured is a devastating blow.

The Lakers called timeout and we knew they were going to make another surge. Emotions so often take over in this type of situation, and when a team is shorthanded it often makes the other players step up and take charge. And that's exactly what happened. The Lakers finished the third quarter by outscoring us 13-5 over the final three minutes. We had allowed another 30-point quarter and the Lakers had already scored 92 points through the first three quarters.

None of our opponents in the playoffs had scored 100 points in a game. In fact, our playoff average was just 90 points allowed

PLAYER PROFILE

11

ISIAH THOMAS

POSITION: Guard
HEIGHT: 6'1"
WEIGHT: 185 Pounds
COLLEGE: Indiana University '83 (Criminal Justice Degree)
HIGH SCHOOL: Westchester, IL, St. Joseph
BIRTHDATE: 04-30-61
BIRTHPLACE: Chicago, IL
WHEN DRAFTED: First Round (2nd Overall) Detroit, 1981
PRO EXPERIENCE: Eight Years
MARITAL STATUS: Married (Lynn)
CHILDREN: Joshua
RESIDENCE: Bloomfield Hills, MI

THOMAS	G	GS	MIN	FIELD GOALS FG	FGA	PCT	3-POINT FG FG	FGA	PCT	FREE THROWS FT	FTA	PCT	REBOUNDS OFF	DEF	TOT	AST	PF	BLK	PTS	AVG
Through 4/23	80	76	2924	569	1227	.464	33	121	.273	287	351	.818	49	224	273	663	209	20	1458	18.2
Playoffs	17	17	633	115	279	.412	8	30	.267	71	96	.740	24	49	73	141	39	4	309	18.2

	SINGLE GAME HIGHS MIN	REB	AST	ST	TO	BL	PTS	AVERAGE PER GAME MIN	REB	AST	STL	TO	BLK	PTS	AVERAGE PER 48 MINUTES REB	AST	PF	STL	TO	BLK	PTS
Through 4/23	51	7	15	6	8	2	37	36.5	3.4	8.3	1.66	3.7	0.25	18.2	4.5	10.9	3.4	2.18	4.9	0.33	23.9
Playoffs	43	10	13	3	6	2	33	37.2	4.3	8.3	1.59	2.5	0.24	18.2	5.5	10.7	3.0	2.05	3.3	0.30	23.4

THIS SEASON: While his statistics were his lowest since his rookie years, the Pistons enjoyed the most successful season in the history of the franchise...The Pistons' captain averaged 18.2 points and 8.3 assists in 80 games played...Finished the season playing with a broken left hand suffered in a fight with Chicago's Bill Cartwright on April 7...Was suspended for two games and fined $5,000 for his fight with Cartwright in the Chicago Stadium...Those were his only missed games of the season...But, after serving the two-game suspension he returned to the lineup versus Cleveland on April 12 and played in all the games the remainder of the season...Upon his return, he came off the bench in the first two games and was shutout in each of those games for two of the few times in his career...The injury was expected to sideline him 3-4 weeks...Played with a protective glove to guard against a more serious injury...Had some outstanding individual quarters throughout the season, capped off by a 24-point fourth quarter explosion at Philadelphia on March 11...That tied the all-time Pistons' regular season record for points in a quarter also achieved by himself previously and Joe Dumars this season...Had 29 games of double figures in assists and steals ranks third on the all-time Pistons' scoring list...Connected on a career best .818 from the free-throw line...When he recorded 7 or more assists, the Pistons were 44-10...For the first time in three seasons, he was named NBA Player of the Week March 6-12...One of the league's most durable guards has missed just 11 games over the last seven seasons...In his eight-year career with the Pistons, when he does not play, Detroit is 6-15...

per game, and here the Lakers had already surpassed that total with 12 minutes still to be played.

Before the fourth quarter started, Chuck reiterated his halftime speech about defensive intensity. To this point, our defensive trademark had not yet shown through.

Trailing 92-84 entering the fourth period of the most critical game of the series, it was time for us to shut down the Lakers' offense. We scored the first 10 points of the fourth quarter and our defense was limiting the Lakers to just one shot, and with 8:31 left in the game, we led 94-92. During the following minutes, we led by as many as seven points, and with just 1:23 left we seemed to have taken control, leading 104-98.

The Lakers had one final surge left in them, and they cut the lead to 106-104 with 32 seconds remaining. We tried to run the shot clock down, but the 24 seconds ran out and we were called for the violation. Now, with eight seconds left, the Lakers had a chance to tie it up. Under normal circumstances, the Lakers would put the ball in Magic Johnson's hands and have him create something. But with Magic in the locker room, they went instead with another great option in James Worthy. He drove to the basket and Dennis Rodman was called for a blocking foul.

With Worthy at the free-throw line and two seconds left, the Lakers needed him to make both to tie. Standing there watching him getting ready to shoot, all I could say to myself was, "Please miss it, please miss it." And unbelievably, Worthy's first shot hit the rim and rolled off to the left. He made the second free throw, and on the next play I was fouled with one second left. I made both free throws and we won Game Two, beating the Lakers 108-105.

Even though we allowed the Lakers to become our first playoff opponent to score 100 points, the fourth quarter may have been our best effort defensively. We held the Lakers without a field goal for 9:27, which included 10 straight missed attempts. Their 13 points in the fourth quarter tied the all-time NBA Finals record for fewest points in a quarter.

For the second time, our guards carried the offensive load. Joe scored 33 points, his second highest playoff scoring output ever. Between Joe, Vinnie, and me, we scored 72 points and the Lakers were trying to find a way to contain us. In the Chicago series, none of us had shot the ball well, mainly because we were so preoccupied with trying to contain Michael Jordan. All our efforts were concentrated on defense, and offense almost became an afterthought. In the Lakers' series, we turned this around and adopted an offensive attitude. We were more relaxed both driving to the basket and shooting jump shots.

Going to Los Angeles, we realized that only two teams have come back from 2-0 deficits to win the NBA Finals. Although we realized that history was on our side, there was no way we wanted the Lakers to become the third.

We had a 10:00 a.m. flight to Los Angeles on Friday morning. Again, I didn't get home until 2:00 a.m. and although I was very tired, I couldn't sleep. I needed to pack enough clothes for a week, but instead I decided to go downstairs and watch the tape of the game. Any improvements I needed to make in my own game, while preparing for the next game, were going to be made after I viewed the film. As I sat in the living room watching the game, subconsciously I kept saying to myself, "You should be packing for the trip right now." But the other part of my brain replied, "Nah, you'll just get up in the morning and pack." Finally, I dozed off with the remote control still in my hand. At six o'clock I finally went to bed and was able to sleep for about an hour.

Then I woke up, and I was delirious while I was packing and had no idea what I was doing. The outfits I picked out to wear on the road trip didn't even match. Luckily, my wife Lynn woke up,

Rodman treated for back spasms before returning to Laker game.

took one look at what I was throwing in the suitcase, and told me to leave and she would finish.

At about nine o'clock, I left to go to the airport. Like I said earlier, I am very superstitious, especially about game routines. Lynn has a magic wand that a friend of hers made, and since the playoffs started, we go through this little routine in which she waves the magic wand over my head a couple of times and wishes me good luck. Then, I always kiss Joshua the same way. So, as I was walking out the door with my luggage to put the bags in the car, I realized that Lynn hadn't given me the treatment. I rushed back into the house and said, "We forgot."

She asked, "What?"

I said, "The magic wand."

Lynn ran upstairs and found the magic wand, I kissed Joshua, and I knew we would win the next game.

On the way to the airport, my mind was at ease. I really enjoy driving, so this was a release. As I approached Metro Airport, I stopped at the Union 76 gas station on Middlebelt. Again, because I'm superstitious, before every road trip I have to stop at this particular gas station. The reason is very simple. For the last three months, every time I have stopped there, we've gone on the road and won the first game. Before, I would stop just to get a Snickers candy bar. But now it's gotten to the point where I usually don't even stop. I just drive through and honk my horn. The people at the gas station probably think I'm crazy, but I can't stop my ritual.

It was a long flight to Los Angeles. Because we were up two games, everyone was talking and laughing on the plane, and even though we were all tired, we weren't going to sleep. I was talking to John Salley and he was telling me all the things he planned to do in Los Angeles. I was laughing because I knew there was no way I could keep up with him. Somehow, Salley manages to handle all the crowds.

Before I knew it, we had landed in Denver. Last year when we landed in Denver, one of the baggage handlers came up to me and told me pointedly that the Lakers were going to win the series. Well, the same guy saw me again and made the same prediction, claiming the Lakers would win the series 4-2. I was sitting on the stairs of the plane in the middle of the runway, and I had to laugh to myself. Some people never learn.

I walked inside the airport and a middle-aged woman asked if she could take a picture of me with her son. She said, "I want to get a picture of the two best smiles in the world." Then she added politely, "Yours is the second nicest."

I got back on the plane and felt like at last I could fall asleep. I probably would have if I hadn't started looking out the window at the mountains and reminiscing about how far this Detroit Pistons basketball team had come.

I can remember Terry Tyler, Earl Cureton, Kent Benson, Kelly Tripucka, and scores of others. They all had a part in this season.

Then a scary thought from 1987 popped into my head. I remembered driving to the airport with our public relations director, Matt Dobek, for a trip to Boston. I said, "This team we have together right now has three cracks at winning the championship. This year (1987), next year, and then the following year. If we don't do it by then, we'll never do it. On the other hand, we could possibly be the first team to win back-to-back championships since the Celtics, if we are lucky enough."

That year, we had a chance to get into the Finals, but in Game Seven, Vinnie Johnson and Adrian Dantley collided and couldn't play the rest of the game. Then, last year luck just wasn't on our side. A key call went against us, we had an unfortunate injury, and we didn't win the championship.

This year, according to my prediction, was our last chance with the current cast of characters. Let's face it: we were expected to win this year, and if we didn't deliver the title, I'd have to believe Jack McCloskey would have no choice but to break the team up. I didn't want to put that much pressure on myself, believing this was our last shot, so I tried to think about something more pleasant.

When we finally arrived in Los Angeles, it was rainy and cloudy. Everybody else wanted sunshine, but not I. A gloomy day does something to your emotions, and I was hoping that the weather, together with being down 2-0, would affect the Lakers. The newspapers were saying they couldn't win, and that completed the emotional climate. This was the type of setting we wanted. We wanted them feeling lousy.

We checked into an exclusive hotel in Marina del Rey. When we're on the road, especially during the playoffs, we usually don't use our real names when we register. Since acquiring the Bad

Boys reputation, fans throughout the country often threaten us. If they call the hotel and can't get our room, then they assume we're staying somewhere else. The guys on the team use names of famous and not-so-famous people, and although I won't tell you their choices, I'll tell you the name I was using, because I won't be needing it anymore.

My alias in this year's playoffs was Walter Ruether. Why him? Well, he's Mr. 696 Freeway in Michigan. Although everyone else knew him as the president of the United Auto Workers, I always saw his name when I was driving on the I-696 Walter Ruether Freeway. I figured the "I" preceding the 696 stood for Isiah, so I used it. Hey, it worked!

Last year, my name was Tony Montona from *Scarface* because I love Al Pacino. Since that name was printed in *Sports Illustrated*, I decided it was time for a change because some people started asking for Tony Montona when the Pistons were on the road.

Sitting in my room after checking into the hotel, I was waiting for an important phone call. We were in the process of doing a picture about my mother, and there were a couple of other people, including Mike Ornstein, a good friend of mine, whom I expected to call as soon as we arrived. I waited for over an hour with no phone calls, so I called down to the front desk and asked if there were any messages for Isiah Thomas. "Sorry," I was told, "there's no guest here by that name."

I eventually called a dozen or so people to tell them my alias because the hotel operators were telling everyone that the Pistons weren't staying at their hotel. About 15 minutes later, the hotel manager knocked on my door to tell me that a very irate woman claiming to be my wife was on the phone, demanding to speak to Walter Ruether.

I picked up the phone and it was indeed Lynn, and she was almost hysterical. She kept calling me Walter rather than Isiah. After we got my name straightened out, she laughed, but only a little.

When I'm in Los Angeles, I love to eat Fatburgers. But I didn't want to give in to eating that type of food during the playoffs. Fatburgers are comparable to Hunter House Hamburgers here in Detroit. I love hamburgers, but I wanted to stick with my

24

MICHAEL
WILLIAMS

POSITION: Guard
HEIGHT: 6'2"
WEIGHT: 175 Pounds
COLLEGE: Baylor '88
HIGH SCHOOL: Carver High School, Dallas, TX
BIRTHDATE: 07-23-66
BIRTHPLACE: Dallas, TX
WHEN DRAFTED: Second Round (48th Overall)
HOW ACQUIRED: College Draft
PRO EXPERIENCE: One Year
MARITAL STATUS: Single
RESIDENCE: Dallas, TX

| WILLIAMS | G | GS | MIN | FIELD GOALS | | | 3-POINT FG | | | FREE THROWS | | | REBOUNDS | | | AST | PF | BLK | PTS | AVG |
				FG	FGA	PCT	FG	FGA	PCT	FT	FTA	PCT	OFF	DEF	TOT					
Through 4/23	49	0	358	47	129	.364	2	9	.222	31	47	.660	9	18	27	70	44	3	127	2.6
Playoffs	4	0	6	0	0	----	0	0	----	2	2	1.000	1	1	2	2	1	0	2	0.5

| | SINGLE GAME HIGHS | | | | | | | AVERAGE PER GAME | | | | | | AVERAGE PER 48 MINUTES | | | | | | |
	MIN	REB	AST	ST	TO	BL	PTS	MIN	REB	AST	STL	TO	BLK	PTS	REB	AST	PF	STL	TO	BLK	PTS
Through 4/23	23	4	9	3	4	1	11	7.3	0.6	1.4	0.27	0.9	0.06	2.6	3.6	9.4	5.9	1.74	5.6	0.40	17.0
Playoffs	2	2	1	1	0	0	2	1.5	0.5	0.5	0.25	0.0	0.00	0.5	16.0	16.0	8.0	8.00	0.0	0.00	16.0

THIS SEASON: Joined Fennis Dembo as the two Pistons' rookies on the roster...Was a second-round draft choice (48th overall) from Baylor...Played in 49 games for the season with the remaining contests being DMPs due to Coach's Decision...After starting the season shooting better than 50 percent from the field, he finished with just a .364 accuracy rate for the campaign...Had his best game as a pro versus Washington on January 13 when he scored a career-high 11 points in a career-high 23 minutes of action...That was his only double-figure scoring effort of the season...During the mid-season injury to Joe Dumars, he played in 14 straight games, his longest appearance streak of the season...During those 14 games, he averaged 3.9 points per game...in the final 37 games he played, he connected on just 30-97 (31 percent)...

regimen of fish, chicken, and pasta. And at this point in the season, I was fished, chickened, and pasta'd out.

Chuck scheduled a practice for our first day in L.A. After playing the night before, and then traveling, there was no way we were going to be very effective in a practice situation.

Joe Dumars and I have a saying on days when our bodies just can't take it. Joe said, "Zeke, today it would be like trying to get blood out of a rock. If I made a hard move, every bone in my body would just break."

This was one of those days. We had played Tuesday and Thursday with 9:00 p.m. starts, and none of us had slept. In the previous 48 hours, I slept maybe five hours. Chuck is pretty smart because he knows when to push and when to pull back. We practiced for maybe a total of 10 minutes, if that. We didn't do much of anything but go over the Lakers' scouting report. Chuck wanted us to get back to the hotel and get some rest. I said, "Right on, Daddy Rich."

There were a couple hours during the afternoon before I had to make my appearance on "The Arsenio Hall Show." I stayed in my hotel room untilMatt Dobek came to the door and yelled, "Zeke, it's time to go."

The lobby was packed with all the Detroit Pistons' fans in Los Angeles for the games. During the playoffs, I usually just stay in my room, because if I go down to the lobby, all I do is sign autographs.

The limousine arrived to pick us up, but neither Matt nor I had any idea where the studio was, or whether it was five minutes or 45 minutes away. We were sitting in the back of the limo talking, when the driver suddenly slammed on the brakes, veering sharply to the right. Neither one of us had our seat belt on at the time, and we were both thrown off the seats.

We asked the driver what the problem was and he said, "These L.A. drivers are crazy, and we're in a hurry because we're late."

Both Matt and I just figured the guy got cut off. Then, about five minutes later, the same thing happened again. That was it, the seat belts definitely were going on for both of us. When we put them on, the driver looked offended, as if we were insulting his driving ability. Sorry pal, I value my life too much to spare your feelings.

Finally, after a couple more scares, we arrived at Paramount Pictures. There were three girls knocking on our window, screaming for us to open it. We could see them, but they couldn't see us. Now, I don't think of myself as a star. When I think of stars, I think of the people in Los Angeles, the people you see on television and in the movies, and the entertainers. When we finally exited the car, fans were screaming, "That's Isiah Thomas, that's Isiah Thomas."

We went inside the studio, and they took me to the makeup room. They put so much powder on my face that I felt like I was made of plastic.

On "The Arsenio Hall Show" that night, in addition to myself, Geraldo Rivera and Sherman Helmsley were also scheduled to appear. I wanted to hear what Geraldo had to say, but I wasn't able to because the show had already started by the time I arrived.

I asked the producer what Sherman Helmsley was going to talk about on the show, and they told me he was going to sing. They also told me the members of his band wanted to meet me. Sherman Helmsley is the guy who plays George Jefferson on the television show. His character is nice, but he sometimes has a chip on his shoulder. When I saw the members of his backup band, I was shocked. They were all nice-looking girls, but they were dressed like they were part of a heavy metal band. They had spikes and chains and were all dressed in black. I kept saying to myself, "They don't look like they belong with George Jefferson."

That just goes to show you the power of television. You have an image in your mind, and you sometimes forget it's just a character, not a real-life person. I assume the real Sherman Helmsley is more like the singer I saw than he is like George Jefferson. I watched them perform a song from his newest record, "Ain't That a Kick in the Head."

While I was sitting watching the monitor, they told me I was up in two minutes. And sure enough, I started to get butterflies because I had no idea what I was going to say. I was standing behind the curtain, and I was afraid I was going to trip and fall down on national television. But once we started talking, Arsenio made me feel comfortable. I looked out the corner of my eye and I saw a familiar face, but I couldn't tell for sure who it was because

I was still talking. When we went to a commercial break, I looked over and there was John Salley. He gave me the thumbs up and said everything was going great, which made me relax even more. I was Arsenio's last guest and then the show ended.

The producer from the show let us keep the limo driver, which Matt and I agreed to reluctantly, since we hadn't had a chance to buy crash helmets for the ride home. We decided to have dinner at Spago's, a restaurant where all the stars go for dinner. I had heard a lot about it, and since the stars hang out there, and I'm an admitted groupie, that's where I wanted to be. I kept turning my head looking for celebrities. Then it dawned on me. The waitress was very nice, the chef continually asked how our dinner was, and the maitre d' kept coming by our table. All the people were looking at me. They all wanted my autograph. And I figured I was going to be the one asking for autographs from other people. During the Chicago series, the Cincinnati Reds, in town to play the Cubs, stayed at the same hotel as we did, and I saw Pete Rose in the lobby and asked him for his autograph. For as long as I can remember, I have collected autographs.

Finally, the chef topped off a great meal by giving us his special dessert. We were ready to grit our teeth and face the dreaded limo driver for the return to the hotel, but this time his driving was fine. When we got back to the hotel, we fell into bed exhausted at the end of a long, long day.

We practiced at Loyola Marymount the day before Game Three. The reporters were out in force, and for about 45 minutes we kept answering the same questions. Chuck again kept the practice pretty simple, and we returned to the hotel to get plenty of rest before the 12:30 p.m. start on Sunday.

Game Three began with Magic Johnson in the lineup for the Lakers, but we could all tell by how gingerly he was moving that he was not going to be effective. Earvin played just the first five minutes before being replaced, and he did not return. After one quarter we led 27-22, but then the Lakers put together another scoring quarter with 33 points in the second. At halftime we led 57-55, but again there was concern in our locker room because we were playing right into the Lakers' hands with a fast-breaking game.

Although Chuck warned us during the intermission about our defensive intensity, there was nothing we could do to contain the

Kareem, in one of the last games of his career, launches his world-famous sky hook.

Lakers in the third quarter, and they again scored 33 points for the second straight period.

But once again, it was Joe Dumars to the rescue. The Lakers made 9 of 10 shots during one stretch of the third quarter, and under normal circumstances our deficit would have been so large that we would not have had enough time to mount a comeback. Joe D. matched the Lakers basket for basket all by himself. In one of the most memorable playoff performances ever, he scored 21 points in the third quarter, including a stretch of 17 straight

MOTOWN VERSUS SHOWTOWN

points for our team. The Lakers had given us their best shot, making 14-19 field goal attempts in the third, yet they still led by only two points. That was all because of Joe.

During the whole series, we had been trying to exploit the quickness of our guard rotation, and it was never more evident than in the third quarter against the Lakers with Joe taking full advantage. The biggest mismatch we had was James Worthy guarding Joe Dumars. This is not to say that Worthy is a bad defensive player, but Joe has a quickness advantage which allows him to get to the basket for easy shots. Our philosophy was to try to work that matchup continually. As a point guard, you look for the hot hand and then try to get that player the ball. After Joe hit his first jump shot in the third quarter, I knew he needed the ball.

I made eye contact with Joe, and both of us knew it was going to be his day the rest of the afternoon. A couple of plays later, we had a three-on-two fast break with Laimbeer, Aguirre, and me. I looked at both Bill and Mark, but I saw Joe as the trailer, behind the break. There was no way I was giving the ball to anyone but Joe. I ruined the fast break, because I waited for Joe to catch up to the play, and he sunk a 20-footer.

After that play, I turned to him and said, "Joe, what plays do you want us to run for you now?"

He looked at me and said, "Zeke, I don't care what plays we run, just give me the ball."

And that's exactly what we did for the entire third quarter. Every time down court during one stretch, Joe would either make a jump shot or a layup. I honestly believe that by his third-quarter performance, Joe Dumars made the basketball world stand up and take notice of his talents.

I am extremely, extremely happy that Joe Dumars is being recognized as a great basketball player. Night in and night out, Joe is there and ready for the challenge. He always guards the best offensive guard on the opposing team, he always does a great defensive job, and he always comes through when we need him. There's a sign in The Palace which reads: "Dumars Delivers." That's all that needs to be said.

Now that we survived the Lakers' best challenge, it was time for us to strangle them with our defense in the fourth quarter. We are the type of defensive team that locks in for five- or seven-minute stretches. In those five or seven minutes, we can virtually put the game out of reach simply by playing great defense. We were able to combat Los Angeles' rush in the third quarter with some offense of our own, and now it was up to the defense to put them away in the fourth.

Just to illustrate the depth of our team, after Joe's third-quarter explosion, he was dead tired and Vinnie Johnson came in to replace him. Vinnie was well rested because he hadn't played in the third quarter. V.J. scored 13 points in the fourth and again our defense was tremendous. We held on to defeat the Lakers 114-110 in Game Three to lead the series 3-0. It was hard to comprehend, but we were just one win away from the World Championship.

Finally realizing what the Detroit Pistons were on the verge of accomplishing, it was difficult for me to control my emotions. Last year we had also won three games, only to lose the final two and the series against the Lakers. In a series such as this, you can't really say it's over until you have checkmated the king. And to this point, the Lakers were still the kings.

Although we were up three games, we didn't want to give the Lakers any hope. After practice on Monday, the day before Game Four, I finally broke down and ate Fatburgers. It probably wasn't the most intelligent thing to do, but I figured if we won the next game, I wasn't going to have another chance. Man, did I ever break down. I had two King Cheese Fatburgers with the works. I thought I had gone to heaven. Mark wanted a Fatburger too, but I told him he was too fat already so he couldn't have one.

Monday night, all I could think about was the game. We were 24 hours from a dream. Just 24 hours from peace of mind. In 24 hours, we could say we were the best. Those 24 hours seemed like 24 years. I thought about my Chicago background. I remember how insignificant we felt and how our four- or five-block area was our entire world. By contrast, if we could win just one more game, the Detroit Pistons' would take their place in history.

That Monday night before Game Four, the War between Thomas Hearns and Sugar Ray Leonard was being fought. It was on closed circuit television, but it was being shown at the Forum and some of the Pistons' players and staff went to watch the fight. Of course, everyone on our team was rooting for the hometown hero, Thomas Hearns. Everyone, that is, except for

Rick Mahorn. Rick said he was rooting for Leonard because he's from Washington D.C. But if you know Rick, that's how he is. If everyone else is going left, he's going right, just to be different, although eventually he will go left too.

There were a number of preliminary fights before the main event. While everyone was in our locker room watching the undercard, I walked into the Forum. There was no one in the arena but me, the two baskets and 17,000 empty seats. I could feel the energy that had been created in that arena so many, many times before from guys like Kareem Abdul-Jabbar, Magic Johnson, Jerry West, Elgin Baylor, and Wilt Chamberlain. Then I remembered watching Gail Goodrich and Jerry West playing in the backcourt and dreaming someday of being like them.

Finally, I drifted back to 1988 and remembered the pain I suffered on this floor. I went to the spot where I hurt my ankle and felt an uneasiness in my body. I walked to where I lay in pain on the floor, crying because I knew I was so seriously injured. I walked over and sat on the bench and remembered seeing Chuck Daly's face, wondering as always whether his time would ever come. I walked down to the Lakers' bench, sat in Pat Riley's seat, and understood the tension he must feel every night as their head coach. I went back to center court and stood in the middle of the floor and dreamed about the game and exactly how it would be played.

I felt we were going to be in trouble. I imagined we would be down 24 points, but I also imagined us winning. Finally, after returning to our locker room, I wrote a few lines on the chalkboard:

Dreams do come true, only when you are asleep.
Dreams are shattered only in your reality.
But in your imagination, all things are possible.

The Hearns-Leonard fight was one of the best I've ever seen. After it was declared a draw, we returned to our hotel on the bus. Driving back, I said to Brendan Suhr, "Coach, I just played the game in my imagination."

He asked, "Did we win?"

I said, "Yeah, but we were down by 24 points."

Brendan said, "If we're down 24 points, there's no way we'll come back and win."

I said, "Tomorrow we are going to be down by a lot of points, but you and Chuck need to stay positive. And if we're down by 10 points or less with three minutes left in the game, I guarantee we will win."

Brendan looked at me and I know he thought I was crazy, and not for the first time. Before the series started, I watched the Philadelphia series against the Lakers in 1983. This series in 1989 has followed that one to the letter. What's the old saying? "Those who fail to remember history are doomed to repeat it."

As Game Four finally approached, the Lakers' new theme became "Let's just win one." They figured if they could just win one game, anything could happen and a miracle was still possible.

The Lakers were going to play every game from here on out like it was their last, because in all probability it would be. Right after the opening tip in Game Four, both Mark Aguirre and Rick Mahorn were called for two personal fouls each.

The Lakers were in the bonus early and the referees were not going to allow much physical play. James Worthy was unstoppable and scored 17 points in the first quarter alone. The Lakers led 42-26 early in the second quarter, when collectively our team knew it was time to play some defense or there was not going to be a Detroit Championship celebration, at least not that night.

Finally, in the middle of the second quarter, our defense stopped allowing the Lakers easy baskets. If the Lakers were going to score, they were going to pay a price. By halftime, we only trailed 55-49.

Early in the third quarter, we outscored the Lakers 12-2 and led 61-58. But as all great champions do, the Lakers mounted another furious run and reclaimed the lead, 78-76, after three quarters. In each of the previous two games, the Lakers also led after three quarters only to lose after our team depth plus our relentless defense took the game under control in the fourth quarter.

James Edwards was the offensive weapon we looked to in the fourth quarter of Game Four. "Buddha," as we all call him, scored 13 points in the last quarter, and despite all their last-ditch efforts we were finally in a position to claim the first-ever NBA Championship for the Detroit Pistons.

MOTOWN VERSUS SHOWTOWN

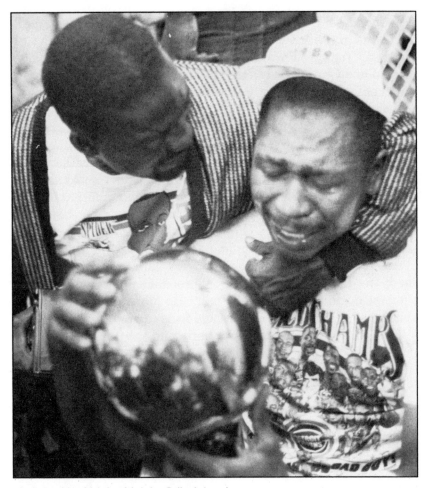
Mark Aguirre (right) with John Salley's brother

With 20 seconds left in the game, I was fouled. Up until this time, I had contained my emotions. Pat Riley took Kareem out of the game, and I knew then that they had more or less surrendered. We saluted Kareem for his incredible career and gave him a standing ovation. But with him leaving, what I finally realized was that we had won. Tears started to swell in my eyes. I'm the leader of the team and I'm supposed to be tough, but I couldn't hold back any more. Fennis Dembo came up to me and said, "Let it go."

Everything I had been holding inside me for eight years, fighting to get to that point, all rushed out of me in those few moments on the bench. I felt so incredibly high. I felt as if I were touched by God. We are Champions of the World!

At the end of the game, with five seconds to go, I had the basketball in my hand. I had a flashback to 1981 in Philadelphia when our Indiana University team won the NCAA Championship. As time was running out in that game, I remember throwing the ball to the top of the ceiling in the Spectrum. For some strange reason, that's exactly what I did again this time in the Forum. We beat the Lakers 105-97 in Game Four, completing only the fifth sweep in NBA Finals history. Joe Dumars was the unanimous choice as the Most Valuable Player in the NBA Finals. It sounds strange saying, "Detroit Pistons—World Champions." But the game had ended and it was time for the celebration to begin.

One of the Pistons' floats at the downtown pa

BAD BOYS

15 CELEBRATION

FINALLY, THE DREAM WAS REALIZED. I couldn't believe it was happening, but we were celebrating a World Championship. I was hugging all my teammates on the floor of the Forum, and the first one I remember grabbing was John Salley. "You can take your Georgia Tech ring off, baby, because you'll be getting a new one," I told him.

As I hugged Joe Dumars, I reminded him of what happened the year before after the seventh game when the Lakers had won. The Lakers' fans trampled the Pistons' players and treated us as if we were cattle. This time, we walked off with pride, and with our heads held high.

The one unfortunate thing about winning it on the road is that our fans couldn't be there to enjoy the victory. In fact, throughout the season we had often clinched on the road. When we won the division title and guaranteed the best record in the NBA, we did it in Cleveland. Then in the first round of the playoffs, we beat the Celtics in Boston, beat the Bucks in Milwaukee in the second round, and the Bulls in Chicago in the third. And now, the newly crowned NBA Champion Detroit Pistons did it on the Lakers' home court.

But to show the level of fan support we enjoyed all year long in Detroit, 21,454 fans were in attendance to watch the deciding game on the big screens at The Palace. Although they were half way across the country, those fans were with us every exciting moment of that unforgettable night.

The Bad Boys were being presented the Larry O'Brien trophy by NBA Commissioner David Stern, and the person who was more gratified than anyone else in the room was Pistons' owner Bill Davidson. For 15 long years he had labored and struggled with this basketball team, but every loss and every setback only made him that much more determined. Now, to see him finally achieve his ultimate goal was really something special to me.

Last year in the final minute of Game Six, David Stern and Bill Davidson were preparing the trophy presentation in our locker room. Then the Lakers made their comeback and won the game on a couple of free throws. One of the saddest moments in my life in sports was seeing Mr. Davidson walking out of our locker room without the trophy. I can't even describe how dejected he was in 1988 when we were on the brink of being crowned champions, only to have the championship snatched away. For a whole year, I remembered what happened that night and vowed to myself not to allow that to happen again in 1989. The sight of him in the locker room this year was one of the many things that made it all worthwhile.

Champagne was being sprayed everywhere as the Lakers' coaches and players came into our locker room to offer their congratulations. Lakers' coach Pat Riley's congratulations meant more to me than anyone else's. We looked each other right in the eye and he said, "Congratulations. You guys deserve this championship." He meant every word of it.

As you know if you saw the scene on TV, the room was a mad-

Rick Mahorn, the baddest of the Bad Boys, after the sweep

house, filled not only with media, but with a host of other well-wishers. I don't know how many suits got ruined before it was over, but it would have been nice to own a dry cleaning business in Inglewood. It went on for over an hour before we returned to our hotel for the celebration party.

I mentioned earlier about Bill Laimbeer sitting in the shower room after Game Seven last year. This year, before we left he and I took a bottle of champagne into the shower room and made a toast to each other again. But this time it was a congratulatory toast.

We never even had time to shower in the Forum, so we just grabbed our clothes and headed back to the hotel. I had been telling reporters from L.A. all week about how close our team was, that we were just like a bunch of high school kids joking around and having plenty of fun together. Now here we were sitting on the bus in our sweaty uniforms, and I started to laugh. I couldn't help remembering that it had been the same way with my old high school team at Westchester St. Joseph's—we went to away games wearing our uniforms and came home on the bus still in our uniforms.

The lobby of the hotel was jam packed with people hugging and kissing each other. I got to my room, and at that moment for the first time all night, I was alone. Even then, I don't think it had really sunk in that we were the World Champions. I showered and rejoined Lynn in the lobby, and we headed for the ballroom just like we were going to any old party.

Except that this wasn't just any old party. When Bill Davidson throws a party, he does everything first class, and it was one hell of a celebration. There was a magnificent spread with everything imaginable: shrimp, crab, lobster, caviar, and more food and drink than I've ever seen in my life. Thanks, Bill Davidson!

The bartender asked me if I wanted a drink, and I automatically asked for a Coke. Because we had decided as a team to abstain from alcohol until we won, I said it without thinking, and, like I said, the fact that it was all over hadn't really sunk in yet. Fortunately, I caught myself in time and quickly switched my order to a bottle of champagne. That was the only way to enjoy this party.

The music was playing, but nobody was dancing, so I decided that the team captain had better get things rolling and lead by example. I grabbed Lynn and soon everybody joined us on the dance floor and started letting loose. I started dancing with Mark Aguirre, and the next thing I knew I was dancing with our general manager, Jack McCloskey! Everybody's image of Jack is of the tough guy, the strong negotiator with a temper, and here he is out on the dance floor, having the time of his life dancing with a basketball player who's got a sheepish grin on his face. I couldn't believe it, but it was beautiful. Jack's dream was also realized.

After all that dancing, it was time for me to take a step back and watch everybody else. I had one arm around Lynn and the other around Matt Dobek, our PR director. All Matt kept saying was, "It hasn't sunk in yet." I think he, like a lot of other people, was still in shock.

The party went on until 2 o'clock in the morning. I had to be up at 4 o'clock to be interviewed by "Good Morning America" at 7 o'clock Eastern Time, so after going back to my room I decided to wait up instead of going to bed.

It's strange, but as much as I wanted the season to be over, and for us to win the title, when it finally happened I wanted the games to keep coming. Our team was so good, that our attitude was: We beat the Lakers, now who's next? Any teams in Europe that are any good? Let's go over there. Russia? Anywhere, we don't care. We just want to keep playing. But it was over.

The return flight from California, needless to say, was a lot more pleasant than last year's. It was the shortest flight ever for me back from Los Angeles, and when we landed at Willow Run Airport, several thousand fans were there to greet us. This was just the first of a couple of incredible turnouts by Pistons' fans.

Driving home from the airport with Lynn, I looked in her eyes and realized how big a burden my obsession with winning the championship had been on her, and I knew how lucky I was to have a wife as strong as she has been over the years. So many times when I was down, when I was hurt, Lynn was there. What's that old song by Gladys Knight and the Pips? "If anyone should ever write my life story, for whatever reason they might, you'll be there through all the pain and glory, because you're the best thing that ever happened to me."

We pulled into the driveway and I couldn't wait to see Joshua. I missed him so much. I never thought I could love anyone as much as I love this kid. And yes, Joshua will be spoiled. He looks into my eyes, and I'm like putty in his hands. I got out of the car, and he started laughing and screaming, "Da da, Da da!"

I stayed awake the rest of the day because I was too wound up to sleep. At least I didn't have to go to practice for the first time in nine months!

The parade and rally were scheduled for Thursday, and after a 10 o'clock brunch we were to leave for the parade in downtown Detroit. Before we left, I called a team meeting with the coaches and players to discuss the expansion draft. Next year, there will be two new NBA teams in Minnesota and Orlando, and each of them can choose one player from each existing NBA franchise to stock its roster. Each existing team can protect eight players, who cannot be chosen. This creates a problem for most teams, but it was an especially acute problem for us because we have virtually nine starters, who rotate and play all the time. As players, we have no idea who is on the expansion list and who is being

Isiah thanks the Detroit fans at the downtown parade.

protected by the team. I wanted to have a final meeting to talk with the guys.

I said, "After the celebration this afternoon, we'll know which one of the guys in this room will not be with the team next year. We gave a lot to each other, and made a lot of sacrifices for each other, and we just came through one hell of an accomplishment together. No matter what happens from this point on in our careers, no one can take that away from us. Whatever happens, let's be classy, let's be professional, and above all, let's remain a family."

With that, we left for downtown and the parade. There's no way you could have prepared any one of us for the type of reception the city of Detroit gave the Pistons. There were hundreds of thousands of people downtown cheering for all of us. And the theme throughout the day remained: "Bad Boys, Bad Boys, Bad Boys!"

I turned to Joe Dumars and said, "I can see why after going through something like this, you'll never settle for anything less than the Finals and winning the Championship."

To Boston and Los Angeles: I can see how you have been motivated year after year. Once you've been there, you want to come back. Being honored by your fans in this way is one of the greatest feelings in the world, and it makes all the hard work and effort worthwhile. To Detroit: You fans are the greatest in the world. We will never forget.

Before going back to The Palace for the 4:00 p.m. rally, we were to have lunch at Ginopolis' in Farmington Hills, but because the parade lasted so long and there were so many people, we were running late and decided to go straight to The Palace for the rally.

The players were the last to be introduced, after the owners, front office personnel, and coaching staff. Detroit fans are the greatest in the world, and their support is matched by no other city in America. Each player was given the chance to say a few words to the crowd, and when Dennis Rodman's turn came, he was so overcome with emotion he couldn't speak. I was sitting next to Joe, and when Worm started crying, we both knew just what he was going through. Three years ago, when he was in Oklahoma, there was nobody who really cared about Dennis Rodman, and now to know he was loved and cared for by so many people was just an overwhelming experience for him. He remained on the stage crying and I was hoping he would pull himself together. When he finally gave his speech, the applause nearly brought the roof down.

After all the players gave their brief speeches and the

Dennis Rodman, overcome with emotion

final video presentation was shown, we went back to the locker room for the last time to find out who had been selected in the expansion draft. Everyone assumed it would be either James Edwards or Vinnie Johnson, and when we heard that Rick Mahorn had been selected by the Minnesota Timberwolves, we were shocked beyond belief. We felt like someone had died. The harsh reality of losing Horn to another team was bad enough, but for him to have been on top of the world celebrating the championship with us one minute, and then to find out he's no longer a member of the family the next, was simply devastating to all of us. It was a grim reminder to us that basketball is a business, nothing more or less. We may play it because we love the game, or for other reasons, but the bottom line is performance on the court and what's best for the business. Emotions and feelings sometimes don't seem to count for much.

Losing Rick Mahorn was devastating, but we'd have been devastated no matter whom we lost, because we're a family. We are a team in the truest sense of the word, and maybe, thinking of the essence of the word "team," the best ever in the NBA. Rick's leadership will be missed, his personality will be missed, his toughness, his sensitivity, will all be missed. But most important, his friendship will be missed. We love Rick Mahorn.

All of us were obviously excited about the prospect of meeting the President of the United States. Other years we had seen the Lakers, Celtics, or Sixers meeting him, but now it was our turn. This was the final stop, the final event together as the 1988-89 Detroit Pistons. The last stop as the Bad Boys of the NBA.

The first highlight of the trip was Rick Mahorn flying with us on Roundball One. Originally, Rick was planning to fly commercially and meet the team in Washington, but instead, at 8:45 in the morning, there he was on our private plane with the other players. Knowing Rick as we do, there was no question in any of our minds that he would be with the team for this final event. He is a major part of this Detroit Piston basketball team that won the World Championship in 1989.

Every 10 steps we took, there was another security check. It is incredible how secure our nation's capitals, but I know that's the way it needs to be.

Isiah and Pistons meet President Bush.

President Bush was very impressive. I'm sure he has many more important matters to deal with other than congratulating a basketball team for winning the World Championship. Who knows how much of the Lakers' series he was able to watch, but he still knew all of us by name. I had to laugh to myself during his short speech when he called Vinnie "The Microwave," Dennis Rodman "Worm," and, of course, John Salley "Spider." He definitely is in tune with the times, and he is a nice, warm person as well.

If we learned anything about ourselves during the last two

According to Isiah: "Chuck Daly was the best coach for us."

years, it was how far we came not only as a basketball team, but as individuals. Through determination and hard work, we were successful. Joe Dumars, who was our Most Valuable Player in the NBA Finals, may have said it best. After winning the trophy, Joe said that winning the World Championship restored his faith in hard work. Over the three prior seasons, we worked hard and were determined, but each time we came up short. Coming back this year with even more determination made this championship all the more satisfying.

Hard work does pay off. Discipline and sacrifice are not just cliches. Through them we learned how to win, how to be champions. You have to pay the price to be successful. Not only in basketball, but in life.

None of us are great basketball players. We all have talent, but as individuals we don't have much more ability than many of the other players in the league. I'm 6-foot-1, and therefore I am limited in what I can and cannot do. We don't have the most dominant center in the league in Bill Laimbeer, who also has limitations. Joe Dumars may no longer be considered underrated and is a solid player. Vinnie Johnson, James Edwards, Rick Mahorn, and Mark Aguirre all came from other teams. Dennis

Chuck Daly, Isiah Thomas, Michigan Governor James Blanchard, and Pistons' owner Bill Davidson at the victory rally.

Rodman was the 27th pick in the draft a few years ago, and John Salley happened to be overlooked by several teams during that same draft. And it goes on and on. But this particular collection of individuals was the reason we won the World Championship. No individual was greater than the team.

Chuck Daly was the perfect coach for us. He realized that this team was something special, and it seemed as if he pressed the right buttons the entire season. No one's ego was insulted during the year, because the single purpose of being the best team in basketball always took precedence.

It's been said often, and at times I have had a hard time believing it, but it's true: "Anything the mind can conceive, the body can achieve." The Bad Boy Detroit Pistons of 1989 became the World Champions with some ability, but mostly through their determination.

After we won the championship, we decided among ourselves that it was time to eliminate the Bad Boys image, and because meeting the president was our last event together, this was the time to do it. For one season, the Bad Boys reigned in the NBA, but in the long run, the image was going to hurt us. Let's face facts, most of us were fined more extensively, or even suspended, because of this image. Plus, with Mahorn no longer a member of the team, the baddest of the Bad Boys was gone.

When Jermaine Jackson left the Jackson Five, they were no longer the Jackson Five, but rather the Jacksons. There will only be one Bad Boys basketball team, and that was the 1989 World Championship Detroit Pistons. From this day forward, we will be known only as the Detroit Pistons. We accomplished what we set out to do by winning the World Championship; now it is only fitting to tell the world that it is time to say farewell to the Bad Boys.

PLAYOFF
STATISTICS

FIRST ROUND PLAYOFFS:
BOSTON SERIES

NATIONAL BASKETBALL ASSOCIATION OFFICIAL SCORER'S REPORT

04-28-89 AUBURN HILLS MI   ATTENDANCE: 21,454

OFFICIALS: D BAVETTA E MIDDLETON E STROM

NO	BOSTON	MIN	FG	FGA	3P	3PA	FT	FTA	OR	DR	TOT	A	PF	ST	TO	PTS
32	MCHALE	34	10	16	0	0	7	10	2	5	7	3	5	0	0	27
35	LEWIS	45	8	20	0	1	4	7	1	2	3	5	2	3	2	20
00	PARISH	42	7	13	0	0	4	5	3	9	12	1	0	0	1	18
34	GAMBLE	29	4	11	0	1	0	2	1	0	1	2	1	1	0	8
20	SHAW	42	8	13	0	0	0	1	1	7	8	8	4	1	3	16
54	PINCKNEY	13	0	5	0	0	0	0	1	0	1	0	2	0	1	0
53	KLEINE	6	0	1	0	0	0	0	0	0	0	0	1	0	0	0
7	UPSHAW	6	0	3	0	0	0	0	0	1	1	1	0	0	1	0
3	JOHNSON	12	0	1	0	0	0	0	0	0	0	1	1	0	2	0
12	BIRDSONG	10	1	2	0	0	0	0	0	1	1	1	2	1	1	2
42	ACRES	1	0	0	0	0	0	0	0	0	0	0	0	0	0	0
33	BIRD	DNP-														
	TEAM TOTALS	240	38	85	0	2	15	25	9	25	34	22	18	6	11	91

PERCENTAGES: .447 0   .600 TEAM REB: 14 TOTAL TO: 11

(13 POINTS)

NO	DETROIT	MIN	FG	FGA	3P	3PA	FT	FTA	OR	DR	TOT	A	PF	ST	TO	PTS
23	AGUIRRE	20	7	12	2	4	3	4	2	1	3	1	4	2	1	19
44	MAHORN	21	3	4	0	0	0	0	2	4	6	1	3	0	1	6
40	LAIMBEER	38	8	13	1	2	0	0	1	11	12	2	4	1	0	17
4	DUMARS	39	11	23	0	3	3	3	0	1	1	9	2	1	3	25
11	THOMAS	37	2	7	0	0	3	3	0	0	0	10	2	2	3	7
15	JOHNSON	20	1	9	0	0	0	0	0	2	2	2	0	0	1	2
22	SALLEY	27	7	9	0	0	1	2	3	4	7	2	5	0	0	15
10	RODMAN	28	4	4	0	0	2	2	3	9	12	1	2	0	2	10
53	EDWARDS	10	0	3	0	1	0	0	0	1	1	0	4	0	1	0
25	LONG	DNP-														
24	WILLIAMS	DNP-														
34	DEMBO	DNP-														
	TEAM TOTALS	240	43	84	3	10	12	14	11	33	44	28	26	6	12	101

PERCENTAGES: .512 .300 .857 TEAM REB: 8 TOTAL TO: 12

(8 POINTS)

BLOCKED SHOTS				SCORE BY PERIODS	1	2	3	4	FINAL
BOSTON	2	DETROIT	10	BOSTON	25	10	28	28	91
PARISH	1	RODMAN	3	DETROIT	27	21	27	26	101
BIRDSONG	1	SALLEY	6						
		EDWARDS	1						

FIRST ROUND PLAYOFFS:
BOSTON SERIES

NATIONAL BASKETBALL ASSOCIATION OFFICIAL SCORER'S REPORT

4-30-89   AUBURN HILLS MI   ATTENDANCE: 21,454

OFFICIALS: J CRAWFORD   J R GARRETSON   B OAKES

NO	BOSTON	MIN	FG	FGA	3P	3PA	FT	FTA	OR	DR	TOT	A	PF	ST	TO	PTS
32	MCHALE	40	4	13	0	0	5	8	4	7	11	3	5	1	1	13
35	LEWIS	45	10	21	0	1	1	2	2	7	9	5	4	1	1	21
00	PARISH	41	11	19	0	0	3	4	2	6	8	2	4	3	3	25
12	BIRDSONG	9	0	2	0	1	0	0	0	1	1	0	1	0	2	0
20	SHAW	42	8	14	0	1	4	4	1	5	6	4	4	0	2	20
54	PINCKNEY	9	0	1	0	0	0	0	0	2	2	1	2	0	2	0
53	KLEINE	26	3	4	0	0	6	7	1	5	6	1	5	0	4	12
3	D JOHNSON	22	1	5	0	0	0	0	1	1	2	5	5	1	0	2
7	UPSHAW	6	1	2	0	0	0	0	0	0	0	2	1	0	0	2
42	ACRES	DNP-														
34	GAMBLE	DNP-														
33	BIRD	DNP-														
	TEAM TOTALS	240	38	81	0	3	19	25	11	34	45	23	31	6	15	95

PERCENTAGES: .469 0   .760   TEAM REB: 8 TOTAL TO: 15

(6 POINTS)

NO	DETROIT	MIN	FG	FGA	3P	3PA	FT	FTA	OR	DR	TOT	A	PF	ST	TO	PTS
23	AGUIRRE	29	10	19	1	2	0	3	4	1	5	1	2	0	1	21
44	MAHORN	29	1	4	0	0	0	0	3	5	8	0	4	1	1	2
40	LAIMBEER	36	4	10	1	1	1	2	2	13	15	0	6	0	3	10
4	DUMARS	33	5	14	0	0	3	3	0	2	2	5	0	1	1	13
11	THOMAS	39	9	20	0	2	8	9	2	2	4	8	2	2	3	26
53	EDWARDS	9	2	3	0	0	2	2	2	0	2	0	2	1	0	6
15	V JOHNSON	24	5	10	0	0	8	10	0	1	1	2	1	0	1	18
22	SALLEY	19	1	4	0	0	0	0	1	3	4	0	4	0	0	2
10	RODMAN	22	1	1	0	0	2	2	1	3	4	1	3	1	0	4
25	LONG	DNP-														
24	WILLIAMS	DNP-														
34	DEMBO	DNP-														
	TEAM TOTALS	240	38	85	2	5	24	31	15	30	45	17	24	6	10	102

PERCENTAGES: .447 .400 .774   TEAM REB: 5 TOTAL TO: 10

(10 POINTS)

BLOCKED SHOTS					SCORE BY PERIODS	1	2	3	4	FINAL
BOSTON 2	DETROIT	5			BOSTON	27	30	25	13	95
PARISH 1	THOMAS	2			DETROIT	31	23	27	21	102
KLEINE 1	V JOHNSON	1								
	SALLEY	2								

FIRST ROUND PLAYOFFS:
BOSTON SERIES

NATIONAL BASKETBALL ASSOCIATION OFFICIAL SCORER'S REPORT

05-02-89 BOSTON MA   ATTENDANCE: 14,890

OFFICIALS: ED T RUSH   EDDIE F RUSH   JOE FORTE

NO	DETROIT	MIN	FG	FGA	3P	3PA	FT	FTA	OR	DR	TOT	A	PF	ST	TO	PTS
23	AGUIRRE	18	6	11	1	2	0	0	1	1	2	0	1	1	1	13
44	MAHORN	18	0	1	0	0	0	0	1	4	5	0	2	2	0	0
40	LAIMBEER	18	4	9	1	2	0	0	0	1	1	0	3	0	0	9
4	DUMARS	34	9	17	0	0	6	9	0	3	3	4	1	0	1	24
11	THOMAS	34	1	9	0	2	1	3	1	4	5	10	2	2	1	3
53	EDWARDS	30	2	4	0	0	2	2	0	4	4	2	3	0	2	6
10	RODMAN	30	3	6	0	0	0	0	2	7	9	2	3	0	2	6
15	JOHNSON	28	10	18	1	1	4	4	1	3	4	5	2	2	3	25
22	SALLEY	30	5	7	0	0	4	4	2	4	6	0	4	1	1	14
24	WILLIAMS	DNP-														
25	LONG	DNP-														
34	DEMBO	DNP-														
	TEAM TOTALS	240	40	82	3	7	17	22	8	31	39	23	21	8	11	100

PERCENTAGES: .488 .429 .773   TEAM REB: 7 TOTAL TO: 11

(10 POINTS)

NO	BOSTON	MIN	FG	FGA	3P	3PA	FT	FTA	OR	DR	TOT	A	PF	ST	TO	PTS
32	MCHALE	41	6	12	0	0	5	5	1	5	6	3	3	0	3	17
35	LEWIS	35	8	14	0	0	4	4	2	7	9	1	5	1	5	20
00	PARISH	29	2	12	0	0	0	0	1	5	6	3	1	1	2	4
3	JOHNSON	25	3	9	0	0	0	0	1	1	2	3	2	2	1	6
20	SHAW	40	6	16	0	0	3	4	0	3	3	7	3	2	1	15
7	UPSHAW	12	4	7	0	0	0	0	0	1	1	2	3	1	0	8
54	PICKNEY	23	3	6	0	0	2	2	1	1	2	0	3	1	1	8
53	KLEINE	33	3	6	0	1	1	2	3	8	11	1	3	0	2	7
42	ACRES	1	0	1	0	1	0	0	0	1	1	0	0	0	0	0
12	BIRDSONG	1	0	1	0	1	0	0	0	0	0	0	0	0	0	0
33	BIRD	DNP-														
34	GAMBLE	DNP-														
	TEAM TOTALS	240	35	84	0	3	15	17	9	32	41	20	23	8	15	85

PERCENTAGES: .417 0 .882   TEAM REB: 11 TOTAL TO: 16

(15 POINTS)

BLOCKED SHOTS			
DETROIT	6	BOSTON	3
EDWARDS	2	MCHALE	2
RODMAN	3	PICKNEY	1
SALLEY	1		

SCORE BY PERIODS	1	2	3	4	FINAL
DETROIT	31	20	20	29	100
BOSTON	29	26	18	12	85

EASTERN CONFERENCE SEMIFINALS:
MILWAUKEE SERIES

NATIONAL BASKETBALL ASSOCIATION OFFICIAL SCORER'S REPORT

05-10-89 AUBURN HILLS MI   ATTENDANCE: 21,454

OFFICIALS: DICK BAVETTA   TOMMY NUNEZ   HUGH EVANS

NO	MILWAUKEE	MIN	FG	FGA	3P	3PA	FT	FTA	OR	DR	TOT	A	PF	ST	TO	PTS
31	ROBERTS	48	5	12	0	1	3	4	0	4	4	4	4	0	1	13
42	KRYSTKOWIK	32	3	7	0	0	2	2	2	2	4	0	4	0	1	8
43	SIKMA	35	5	14	2	5	3	4	0	5	5	3	5	0	2	15
4	MONCRIEF	22	3	6	0	0	0	0	3	3	6	1	1	0	1	6
24	HUMPHRIES	32	4	8	1	2	1	2	1	3	4	6	4	0	1	10
22	PIERCE	29	11	19	0	0	3	6	0	2	2	1	2	1	1	25
44	MOKESKI	11	0	0	0	0	1	2	1	2	3	0	4	0	0	1
45	BREUER	15	1	2	0	0	0	0	0	3	3	0	0	0	1	2
11	GREEN	16	0	2	0	0	0	0	0	0	0	3	1	2	0	0
35	BROWN	DNP-														
25	PRESSEY	DNP-														
34	CUMMINGS	DNP-														
	TEAM TOTALS	240	32	70	3	8	13	20	7	24	31	18	25	3	8	80

PERCENTAGES: .457 .375 .650   TEAM REB: 6 TOTAL TO: 8

(12 POINTS)

NO	DETROIT	MIN	FG	FGA	3P	3PA	FT	FTA	OR	DR	TOT	A	PF	ST	TO	PTS
23	AGUIRRE	24	6	14	1	2	0	0	2	1	3	2	1	0	0	13
44	MAHORN	16	0	2	0	0	0	0	1	4	5	0	3	0	0	0
40	LAIMBEER	43	5	10	0	3	9	10	4	13	17	2	3	0	0	19
4	DUMARS	35	2	10	0	2	5	6	1	3	4	6	3	0	2	9
11	THOMAS	37	4	17	0	2	2	4	2	5	7	5	1	0	1	10
10	RODMAN	24	1	6	0	1	0	0	4	2	6	0	4	0	1	2
15	JOHNSON	25	5	11	1	2	1	2	1	1	2	5	2	1	1	12
22	SALLEY	28	5	7	0	0	4	6	5	3	8	0	2	0	2	14
53	EDWARDS	8	2	2	0	0	2	2	0	1	1	0	2	0	1	6
25	LONG	DNP-														
24	WILLIAMS	DNP-														
34	DEMBO	DNP-														
	TEAM TOTALS	240	30	79	2	12	23	30	20	33	53	20	21	1	8	85

PERCENTAGES: .380 .167 .767   TEAM REB: 11 TOTAL TO: 8

(10 POINTS)

BLOCKED SHOTS			
MILWAUKEE	2	DETROIT	5
ROBERTS	1	AGUIRRE	1
BREUER	1	MAHORN	2
		LAIMBEER	1
		SALLEY	1

SCORE BY PERIODS	1	2	3	4	FINAL
MILWAUKEE	25	23	21	11	80
DETROIT	21	18	25	21	85

EASTERN CONFERENCE SEMIFINALS:
MILWAUKEE SERIES

NATIONAL BASKETBALL ASSOCIATION OFFICIAL SCORER'S REPORT

05-12-89 AUBURN HILLS MI   ATTENDANCE: 21,454

OFFICIALS: B SALVATORE   J MADDEN   H HOLLINS

NO	MILWAUKEE	MIN	FG	FGA	3P	3PA	FT	FTA	OR	DR	TOT	A	PF	ST	TO	PTS
31	ROBERTS	35	3	10	0	1	6	6	1	3	4	2	2	0	1	12
42	KRYSTKOWIK	43	4	13	0	2	14	16	6	7	13	1	2	0	2	22
43	SIKMA	18	1	3	0	1	2	2	0	2	2	2	6	0	2	4
4	MONCRIEF	11	2	4	1	1	0	0	0	1	1	0	3	0	2	5
24	HUMPHRIES	34	5	13	0	4	1	2	0	4	4	5	3	1	1	11
22	PIERCE	36	9	17	2	4	2	2	0	1	1	2	3	1	1	22
11	GREEN	15	1	4	0	1	2	2	0	1	1	6	1	0	0	4
45	BREUER	31	1	3	0	0	3	5	2	10	12	0	1	0	0	5
35	BROWN	17	3	4	0	0	1	2	1	1	2	1	6	1	1	7
44	MOKESKI	DNP-														
34	CUMMINGS	DNP-														
25	PRESSEY	DNP-														
	TEAM TOTALS	240	29	71	3	14	31	37	10	30	40	19	27	3	10	92

PERCENTAGES: .408 .214 .838   TEAM REB: 7 TOTAL TO: 10

(13 POINTS)

NO	DETROIT	MIN	FG	FGA	3P	3PA	FT	FTA	OR	DR	TOT	A	PF	ST	TO	PTS
23	AGUIRRE	25	3	9	0	1	0	0	2	2	4	1	3	0	0	6
44	MAHORN	20	5	8	0	0	1	1	4	3	7	0	2	1	0	11
40	LAIMBEER	34	3	9	0	2	4	4	0	12	12	1	3	0	0	10
4	DUMARS	38	6	14	1	2	0	0	0	1	1	6	1	1	1	13
11	THOMAS	33	3	9	0	0	5	6	0	3	3	10	2	1	1	11
15	JOHNSON	24	7	14	1	4	6	8	1	1	2	3	2	0	3	21
22	SALLEY	29	10	14	0	0	3	4	3	1	4	0	3	0	0	23
53	EDWARDS	14	2	3	0	0	2	2	0	1	1	2	3	0	0	6
10	RODMAN	22	5	7	0	0	1	4	4	9	13	3	5	0	0	11
25	LONG	DNP-														
24	WILLIAMS	1	0	0	0	0	0	0	0	0	0	0	0	0	0	0
34	DEMBO	DNP-														
	TEAM TOTALS	240	44	87	2	9	22	29	14	33	47	26	24	3	5	112

PERCENTAGES: .506 .222 .759   TEAM REB: 4 TOTAL TO: 5

(2 POINTS)

BLOCKED SHOTS				
MILWAUKEE	4	DETROIT	5
SIKMA	2	LAIMBEER	2
BREUER	2	RODMAN	1
		SALLEY	1
		EDWARDS	1

SCORE BY PERIODS	1	2	3	4	FINAL
MILWAUKEE	23	26	19	24	92
DETROIT	26	23	26	37	112

EASTERN CONFERENCE SEMIFINALS:
MILWAUKEE SERIES

NATIONAL BASKETBALL ASSOCIATION OFFICIAL SCORER'S REPORT

05-14-89 MILWAUKEE   ATTENDANCE: 18,633

OFFICIALS: JESS KERSEY   MIKE MATHIS   STEVE JAVIE

NO	DETROIT	MIN	FG	FGA	3P	3PA	FT	FTA	OR	DR	TOT	A	PF	ST	TO	PTS
23	AGUIRRE	33	6	12	1	2	2	2	0	4	4	4	2	0	1	15
44	MAHORN	22	4	5	0	0	5	7	4	5	9	1	4	1	3	13
40	LAIMBEER	20	4	8	2	3	2	4	0	11	11	0	4	0	2	12
4	DUMARS	41	1	5	0	0	5	5	0	4	4	10	2	1	0	7
11	THOMAS	38	11	19	2	4	2	3	2	2	4	9	1	0	2	26
53	EDWARDS	26	2	4	0	0	2	2	1	1	2	0	2	0	3	6
15	JOHNSON	15	5	12	1	1	0	0	2	0	2	2	1	0	2	11
10	RODMAN	13	1	2	0	0	0	0	1	2	3	1	5	0	0	2
22	SALLEY	28	4	7	0	0	6	7	1	5	6	0	1	0	0	14
34	DEMBO	2	1	1	0	0	0	0	0	0	0	0	0	0	1	2
24	WILLIAMS	2	0	0	0	0	2	2	1	1	2	1	0	1	0	2
25	LONG	DNP-														
	TEAM TOTALS	240	39	75	6	10	26	32	12	35	47	28	22	3	14	110

PERCENTAGES: .520 .600 .813   TEAM REB: 0 TOTAL TO: 14

(15 POINTS)

NO	MILWAUKEE	MIN	FG	FGA	3P	3PA	FT	FTA	OR	DR	TOT	A	PF	ST	TO	PTS
42	KRYSTKOWIK	1	0	0	0	0	0	0	0	0	0	0	0	0	0	0
31	ROBERTS	38	7	14	0	0	4	4	1	4	5	3	1	1	2	18
43	SIKMA	36	2	13	0	2	2	2	3	4	7	2	4	0	1	6
24	HUMPHRIES	31	7	14	0	0	2	2	4	2	6	5	4	2	1	16
4	MONCRIEF	16	1	3	0	1	3	3	1	1	2	0	2	0	0	5
45	BREUER	25	2	4	0	0	2	4	2	6	8	0	2	0	0	6
34	CUMMINGS	17	2	8	0	1	0	0	1	1	2	0	4	1	1	4
22	PIERCE	36	11	20	0	0	0	0	1	3	4	4	4	2	2	22
35	BROWN	21	0	3	0	1	2	2	0	1	1	2	0	0	0	2
11	GREEN	19	5	7	1	1	0	0	0	3	3	3	3	1	3	11
	TEAM TOTALS	240	37	86	1	6	15	17	13	25	38	19	24	7	10	90

PERCENTAGES: .430 .167 .882   TEAM REB: 0 TOTAL TO: 10

(17 POINTS)

BLOCKED SHOTS			
DETROIT 5	MILWAUKEE	1	
MAHORN 4	BREUER	1	
SALLEY 1			

SCORE BY PERIODS	1	2	3	4	FINAL
DETROIT	24	23	38	25	110
MILWAUKEE	16	22	25	27	90

EASTERN CONFERENCE SEMIFINALS:
MILWAUKEE SERIES

NATIONAL BASKETBALL ASSOCIATION OFFICIAL SCORER'S REPORT

05-15-89 MILWAUKEE   ATTENDANCE: 18,633

OFFICIALS: D GARRETSON   B FRYER   JOE FORTE

NO	DETROIT	MIN	FG	FGA	3P	3PA	FT	FTA	OR	DR	TOT	A	PF	ST	TO	PTS
23	AGUIRRE	28	7	12	0	1	1	1	0	1	1	2	1	1	1	15
44	MAHORN	29	4	6	0	0	2	3	1	3	4	0	4	0	0	10
40	LAIMBEER	34	7	11	3	7	0	0	0	7	7	0	2	0	1	17
4	DUMARS	40	7	11	0	0	8	9	2	3	5	7	3	1	3	22
11	THOMAS	40	7	14	2	2	1	2	4	6	10	13	3	0	3	17
15	JOHNSON	16	1	5	0	0	0	2	0	3	3	1	2	0	5	2
22	SALLEY	20	1	3	0	0	1	2	2	4	6	1	3	0	2	3
10	RODMAN	20	1	2	0	1	0	0	1	2	3	0	3	1	2	2
53	EDWARDS	13	3	4	0	0	2	2	0	0	0	1	2	0	0	8
34	DEMBO	DNP-														
24	WILLIAMS	DNP-														
25	LONG	DNP-														
	TEAM TOTALS	240	38	68	5	11	15	21	10	29	39	25	23	3	17	96

PERCENTAGES: .559 .455 .714   TEAM REB: 0 TOTAL TO: 18

(12 POINTS)

NO	MILWAUKEE	MIN	FG	FGA	3P	3PA	FT	FTA	OR	DR	TOT	A	PF	ST	TO	PTS
45	BREUER	25	4	8	0	0	0	2	3	6	9	3	4	2	0	8
31	ROBERTS	46	12	19	0	0	9	11	3	1	4	2	5	0	4	33
43	SIKMA	44	4	11	1	2	3	4	0	4	4	2	2	2	1	12
24	HUMPHRIES	38	4	10	0	0	4	4	1	1	2	14	0	0	1	12
4	MONCRIEF	26	2	7	0	0	2	3	1	2	3	2	0	2	1	6
22	PIERCE	33	9	17	0	0	3	4	0	4	4	1	2	1	0	21
35	BROWN	28	1	4	0	0	0	0	1	3	4	2	2	1	0	2
	TEAM TOTALS	240	36	76	1	2	21	28	9	21	30	26	15	8	7	94

PERCENTAGES: .474 .500 .750   TEAM REB: 0 TOTAL TO: 7

(10 POINTS)

BLOCKED SHOTS					SCORE BY PERIODS	1	2	3	4	FINAL
DETROIT	5	MILWAUKEE	1		DETROIT	20	24	32	20	96
AGUIRRE	1	SIKMA	1		MILWAUKEE	33	21	17	23	94
MAHORN	1									
LAIMBEER	1									
THOMAS	1									
SALLEY	1									

EASTERN CONFERENCE FINALS:

CHICAGO SERIES

NATIONAL BASKETBALL ASSOCIATION OFFICIAL SCORER'S REPORT

5-21-89   AUBURN HILLS MI   ATTENDANCE: 21,454

OFFICIALS: J CRAWFORD   J H EVANS   T NUNEZ

NO	CHICAGO	MIN	FG	FGA	3P	3PA	FT	FTA	OR	DR	TOT	A	PF	ST	TO	PTS
33	PIPPEN	45	5	13	0	3	4	6	1	10	11	6	4	0	0	14
54	GRANT	24	2	5	0	0	0	0	5	2	7	1	6	1	2	4
24	CARTWRIGHT	31	4	9	0	0	2	4	2	2	4	1	4	0	1	10
23	JORDAN	45	10	29	2	6	10	13	2	9	11	4	5	0	3	32
14	HODGES	29	5	9	4	7	0	0	2	1	3	4	4	1	1	14
40	CORZINE	21	6	12	0	0	0	0	4	1	5	0	0	2	1	12
5	PAXSON	19	0	2	0	0	0	0	0	1	1	3	2	2	0	0
22	DAVIS	20	3	5	0	1	2	2	2	1	3	0	5	0	3	8
11	VINCENT	3	0	0	0	0	0	0	0	0	0	0	0	0	0	0
2	SELLERS	3	0	1	0	0	0	0	0	0	0	0	0	0	0	0
15	HALEY	DNP-														
32	PERDUE	DNP-														
	TEAM TOTALS	240	35	85	6	17	18	25	18	27	45	19	30	6	11	94

PERCENTAGES: .412 .353 .720   TEAM REB: 14 TOTAL TO: 13

(8 POINTS)

NO	DETROIT	MIN	FG	FGA	3P	3PA	FT	FTA	OR	DR	TOT	A	PF	ST	TO	PTS
23	AGUIRRE	30	6	12	0	2	2	2	1	3	4	1	2	1	2	14
44	MAHORN	26	7	11	0	0	3	5	4	3	7	0	4	0	1	17
40	LAIMBEER	37	6	11	2	3	1	2	4	11	15	3	3	0	4	15
4	DUMARS	34	5	16	0	1	0	0	1	3	4	6	1	0	3	10
11	THOMAS	42	3	18	0	5	3	6	2	2	4	10	3	2	1	9
15	JOHNSON	20	3	11	0	0	2	2	2	2	4	1	2	0	0	8
10	RODMAN	23	3	5	0	0	3	6	5	3	8	0	1	0	1	9
22	SALLEY	17	0	4	0	0	1	2	4	1	5	0	5	0	1	1
53	EDWARDS	11	2	3	0	0	1	1	0	2	2	0	0	0	1	5
25	LONG	DNP-														
24	WILLIAMS	DNP-														
34	DEMBO	DNP-														
	TEAM TOTALS	240	35	91	2	11	16	26	23	30	53	21	21	3	14	88

PERCENTAGES: .385 .182 .615   TEAM REB: 11 TOTAL TO: 14

(12 POINTS)

BLOCKED SHOTS				
CHICAGO 3		DETROIT	6
PIPPEN	2	MAHORN	1
GRANT	1	LAIMBEER	1
		RODMAN	2
		JOHNSON	1
		SALLEY	1

SCORE BY PERIODS	1	2	3	4	FINAL
CHICAGO	33	17	21	23	94
DETROIT	17	17	29	25	88

EASTERN CONFERENCE FINALS:
CHICAGO SERIES

NATIONAL BASKETBALL ASSOCIATION OFFICIAL SCORER'S REPORT

05-23-89 AUBURN HILLS MI   ATTENDANCE: 21,454

OFFICIALS: EARL STROM   MIKE MATHIS BILL SAAR

NO	CHICAGO	MIN	FG	FGA	3P	3PA	FT	FTA	OR	DR	TOT	A	PF	ST	TO	PTS
33	PIPPEN	30	5	9	0	2	2	4	1	4	5	3	2	3	3	12
54	GRANT	43	7	13	0	0	2	3	7	13	20	2	1	0	4	16
24	CARTWRIGHT	33	3	12	0	0	3	4	1	6	7	0	4	0	2	9
23	JORDAN	38	9	20	0	2	9	11	1	3	4	4	5	2	4	27
14	HODGES	19	2	7	0	3	2	2	0	0	0	1	5	0	1	6
5	PAXSON	26	1	3	0	0	4	4	0	0	0	6	3	3	0	6
22	DAVIS	20	2	4	0	0	0	0	2	3	5	0	3	0	2	4
40	CORZINE	16	2	4	0	0	1	2	1	1	2	0	2	0	1	5
11	VINCENT	15	1	3	0	1	4	6	0	0	0	5	1	0	0	6
2	SELLERS	DNP-														
15	HALEY	DNP-														
32	PERDUE	DNP-														
	TEAM TOTALS	240	32	75	0	8	27	36	13	30	43	21	26	8	17	91

PERCENTAGES: .427 0   .750   TEAM REB: 9 TOTAL TO: 17

(5 POINTS)

NO	DETROIT	MIN	FG	FGA	3P	3PA	FT	FTA	OR	DR	TOT	A	PF	ST	TO	PTS
23	AGUIRRE	36	4	8	0	1	0	0	0	8	8	1	1	1	0	8
44	MAHORN	23	0	0	0	0	1	2	1	2	3	1	3	1	2	1
40	LAIMBEER	26	3	7	1	3	0	0	1	4	5	2	3	1	1	7
4	DUMARS	36	5	13	0	1	10	11	1	2	3	3	2	2	2	20
11	THOMAS	38	12	27	1	2	8	12	2	1	3	4	3	2	6	33
53	EDWARDS	21	0	2	0	0	1	2	1	2	3	0	4	0	1	1
10	RODMAN	17	2	4	0	1	4	4	2	10	12	1	5	1	0	8
15	JOHNSON	20	4	11	2	4	6	7	2	1	3	0	2	0	0	16
22	SALLEY	20	1	2	0	0	4	6	3	1	4	0	3	1	1	6
25	LONG	2	0	0	0	0	0	0	0	0	0	0	0	0	0	0
24	WILLIAMS	1	0	0	0	0	0	0	0	0	0	0	0	0	0	0
34	DEMBO	DNP-														
	TEAM TOTALS	240	31	74	4	12	34	44	13	31	44	12	26	9	13	100

PERCENTAGES: .419 .333 .773   TEAM REB: 9 TOTAL TO: 13

(13 POINTS)

BLOCKED SHOTS					SCORE BY PERIODS	1	2	3	4	FINAL
CHICAGO	6	DETROIT	2		CHICAGO	23	26	21	21	91
PIPPEN	1	LAIMBEER	1		DETROIT	19	30	26	25	100
GRANT	2	EDWARDS	1							
CARTWRIGHT	1									
JORDAN	1									
DAVIS	1									

EASTERN CONFERENCE FINALS:

CHICAGO SERIES

NATIONAL BASKETBALL ASSOCIATION OFFICIAL SCORER'S REPORT

05-27-89 CHICAGO ATTENDANCE: 18,676

OFFICIALS: JACK MADDEN BILL OAKES ED T RUSH

NO	DETROIT	MIN	FG	FGA	3P	3PA	FT	FTA	OR	DR	TOT	A	PF	ST	TO	PTS
23	AGUIRRE	36	9	16	1	5	6	8	1	2	3	4	3	0	1	25
44	MAHORN	12	4	6	0	0	1	2	1	3	4	0	3	0	1	9
40	LAIMBEER	32	2	9	0	3	0	0	3	3	6	5	4	1	1	4
4	DUMARS	29	3	8	0	1	6	7	1	1	2	4	4	0	3	12
11	THOMAS	39	2	8	0	1	1	2	2	3	5	11	3	2	4	5
22	SALLEY	19	4	4	0	0	0	0	0	3	3	0	3	1	1	8
10	RODMAN	26	4	6	0	0	0	0	4	9	13	0	5	0	3	8
15	JOHNSON	25	6	14	2	4	5	5	1	2	3	1	2	0	1	19
53	EDWARDS	19	2	3	0	0	0	0	0	1	1	2	4	0	0	4
25	LONG	3	0	0	0	0	3	3	0	0	0	0	0	0	0	3
24	WILLIAMS	DNP-														
34	DEMBO	DNP-														
	TEAM TOTALS	240	36	74	3	14	22	27	13	27	40	27	31	4	15	97

PERCENTAGES: .486 .214 .815 TEAM REB: 0 TOTAL TO: 16

(14 POINTS)

NO	CHICAGO	MIN	FG	FGA	3P	3PA	FT	FTA	OR	DR	TOT	A	PF	ST	TO	PTS
33	PIPPEN	43	2	10	1	2	2	4	1	7	8	4	5	4	3	7
54	GRANT	33	2	5	0	0	3	4	1	2	3	1	4	0	1	7
24	CARTWRIGHT	34	5	6	0	0	5	6	0	4	4	1	4	0	2	15
14	HODGES	25	1	7	0	4	0	2	0	0	0	5	3	0	0	2
23	JORDAN	45	16	26	0	3	14	15	3	4	7	5	2	5	2	46
22	DAVIS	13	3	4	0	0	0	0	2	1	3	0	2	0	0	6
5	PAXON	26	6	9	0	0	0	0	0	1	1	4	5	0	0	12
40	CORZINE	16	2	4	0	0	0	0	1	2	3	0	2	0	1	4
11	VINCENT	5	0	2	0	0	0	0	0	0	0	1	0	0	1	0
2	SELLERS	DNP-														
32	PERDUE	DNP-														
15	HALEY	DNP-														
	TEAM TOTALS	240	37	73	1	9	24	31	8	21	29	21	27	9	10	99

PERCENTAGES: .507 .111 .774 TEAM REB: 0 TOTAL TO: 10

(5 POINTS)

BLOCKED SHOTS			
DETROIT	1	CHICAGO	5
LAIMBEER	1	PIPPEN	1
		CARTWRIGHT	1
		CORZINE	3

SCORE BY PERIODS	1	2	3	4	FINAL
DETROIT	28	28	21	20	97
CHICAGO	27	18	21	33	99

EASTERN CONFERENCE FINALS:
CHICAGO SERIES

NATIONAL BASKETBALL ASSOCIATION OFFICIAL SCORER'S REPORT

05-29-89 CHICAGO   ATTENDANCE: 18,676

OFFICIALS: J O'DONNELL   JESS KERSEY   WALLY ROONEY

NO	DETROIT	MIN	FG	FGA	3P	3PA	FT	FTA	OR	DR	TOT	A	PF	ST	TO	PTS
23	AGUIRRE	15	2	2	0	0	2	2	1	3	4	0	1	0	1	6
44	MAHORN	14	0	2	0	0	0	0	1	2	3	0	2	1	0	0
40	LAIMBEER	28	1	5	0	2	0	0	2	3	5	1	1	0	2	2
4	DUMARS	33	5	13	0	0	5	6	2	1	3	1	3	0	1	15
11	THOMAS	43	9	20	1	1	8	10	4	6	10	6	2	3	2	27
22	SALLEY	33	2	10	0	0	5	10	4	4	8	0	2	1	2	9
53	EDWARDS	21	3	9	0	0	7	10	0	2	2	1	4	0	1	13
15	JOHNSON	21	3	8	0	0	1	2	1	2	3	4	3	1	0	7
10	RODMAN	32	2	6	0	0	3	6	8	10	18	2	3	0	2	7
25	LONG	DNP-														
24	WILLIAMS	DNP-														
34	DEMBO	DNP-														
	TEAM TOTALS	240	27	75	1	3	31	46	23	33	56	15	21	6	11	86

PERCENTAGES: .360 .333 .674   TEAM REB: 9 TOTAL TO: 12

(12 POINTS)

NO	CHICAGO	MIN	FG	FGA	3P	3PA	FT	FTA	OR	DR	TOT	A	PF	ST	TO	PTS
33	PIPPEN	42	8	18	1	6	1	2	4	7	11	3	6	2	0	18
54	GRANT	46	5	8	0	0	2	2	3	9	12	4	3	1	1	12
24	CARTWRIGHT	34	3	7	0	0	3	4	1	2	3	1	4	0	3	9
14	HODGES	30	6	13	4	6	0	0	1	3	4	5	5	0	1	16
23	JORDAN	43	5	15	1	3	12	17	0	2	2	4	5	1	1	23
5	PAXON	22	0	5	0	4	0	0	0	2	2	2	2	1	1	0
22	DAVIS	6	0	0	0	0	0	0	0	1	1	0	2	0	3	0
40	CORZINE	13	0	2	0	0	0	0	0	5	5	1	3	0	0	0
15	HALEY	1	0	0	0	0	0	0	0	0	0	0	2	0	1	0
11	VINCENT	3	0	1	0	1	2	2	0	0	0	0	0	0	0	2
2	SELLERS	DNP-														
32	PERDUE	DNP-														
	TEAM TOTALS	240	27	69	6	20	20	27	9	31	40	20	32	5	11	80

PERCENTAGES: .391 .300 .741   TEAM REB: 7 TOTAL TO: 13

(10 POINTS)

BLOCKED SHOTS			
DETROIT	3	CHICAGO	8
AGUIRRE	1	PIPPEN	3
LAIMBEER	1	GRANT	1
RODMAN	1	CARTWRIGHT	2
		HODGES	1
		CORZINE	1

SCORE BY PERIODS	1	2	3	4	FINAL
DETROIT	22	20	22	22	86
CHICAGO	26	13	21	20	80

EASTERN CONFERENCE FINALS:
CHICAGO SERIES

NATIONAL BASKETBALL ASSOCIATION OFFICIAL SCORER'S REPORT

05-31-89 AUBURN HILLS MI   ATTENDANCE: 21,454

OFFICIALS: D GARRETSON   DICK BAVETTA   HUE HOLLINS

NO	CHICAGO	MIN	FG	FGA	3P	3PA	FT	FTA	OR	DR	TOT	A	PF	ST	TO	PTS
33	PIPPEN	39	3	7	1	2	0	0	0	9	9	2	2	0	2	7
54	GRANT	26	1	5	0	0	2	2	0	1	1	1	5	0	4	4
24	CARTWRIGHT	35	5	9	0	0	6	8	1	11	12	0	1	0	5	16
23	JORDAN	46	4	8	0	1	10	11	0	5	5	9	3	1	4	18
14	HODGES	32	7	12	5	9	0	0	1	1	2	1	2	0	6	19
2	SELLERS	22	3	7	0	0	0	0	2	4	6	2	2	0	1	6
5	PAXSON	14	2	4	0	1	2	2	0	0	0	0	3	0	1	6
40	CORZINE	13	3	5	0	0	1	2	2	2	4	0	1	0	0	7
11	VINCENT	6	1	2	0	0	0	0	0	0	0	1	1	0	1	2
22	DAVIS	7	0	0	0	0	0	0	0	0	0	0	2	0	0	0
15	HALEY	DNP-														
32	PERDUE	DNP-														
	TEAM TOTALS	240	29	59	6	13	21	25	6	33	39	16	22	1	24	85

PERCENTAGES: .492 .462 .840   TEAM REB: 5 TOTAL TO: 24

(24 POINTS)

NO	DETROIT	MIN	FG	FGA	3P	3PA	FT	FTA	OR	DR	TOT	A	PF	ST	TO	PTS
23	AGUIRRE	29	8	14	1	2	2	4	2	1	3	1	2	0	1	19
44	MAHORN	10	0	0	0	0	0	0	0	2	2	0	4	1	1	0
40	LAIMBEER	24	3	8	1	4	0	0	2	1	3	1	0	1	1	7
4	DUMARS	41	4	11	0	0	1	2	0	1	1	2	3	1	1	9
11	THOMAS	32	8	17	0	1	1	1	0	3	3	12	1	2	2	17
22	SALLEY	31	3	6	0	0	2	2	2	3	5	1	4	3	0	8
10	RODMAN	26	0	1	0	0	0	0	2	12	14	0	4	1	2	0
15	JOHNSON	23	8	14	1	2	5	5	1	1	2	4	3	0	1	22
53	EDWARDS	24	5	9	0	0	2	3	1	0	1	1	4	0	1	12
25	LONG	DNP-														
24	WILLIAMS	DNP-														
34	DEMBO	DNP-														
	TEAM TOTALS	240	39	80	3	9	13	17	10	24	34	22	25	9	10	94

PERCENTAGES: .488 .333 .765   TEAM REB: 1 TOTAL TO: 11

(9 POINTS)

BLOCKED SHOTS		SCORE BY PERIODS	1	2	3	4	FINAL
CHICAGO 2	DETROIT 2	CHICAGO	25	20	19	21	85
PIPPEN 1	MAHORN 1	DETROIT	17	24	24	29	94
GRANT 1	RODMAN 1						

EASTERN CONFERENCE FINALS:
CHICAGO SERIES

NATIONAL BASKETBALL ASSOCIATION OFFICIAL SCORER'S REPORT

06-02-89 CHICAGO   ATTENDANCE: 18,676

OFFICIALS: HUGH EVANS   EARL STROM   JOE CRAWFORD

NO	DETROIT	MIN	FG	FGA	3P	3PA	FT	FTA	OR	DR	TOT	A	PF	ST	TO	PTS
23	AGUIRRE	32	3	8	0	2	4	4	1	6	7	4	2	0	2	10
44	MAHORN	22	2	2	0	0	0	0	1	2	3	0	4	0	0	4
40	LAIMBEER	33	4	10	1	4	2	2	4	6	10	5	4	0	1	11
4	DUMARS	40	5	12	0	0	2	2	2	2	4	9	2	2	3	12
11	THOMAS	40	12	28	0	2	9	10	1	4	5	4	1	3	4	33
10	RODMAN	32	3	5	0	0	3	4	6	9	15	0	3	0	0	9
15	JOHNSON	16	3	13	0	1	2	4	1	0	1	2	1	0	1	8
22	SALLEY	10	2	3	0	0	1	2	2	1	3	0	5	1	0	5
53	EDWARDS	14	3	9	0	0	5	7	0	2	2	0	3	0	1	11
25	LONG	1	0	0	0	0	0	0	0	0	0	0	0	0	0	0
24	WILLIAMS	DNP-														
34	DEMBO	DNP-														
	TEAM TOTALS	240	37	90	1	9	28	35	18	32	50	24	25	6	12	103

PERCENTAGES: .411 .111 .800   TEAM REB: 0 TOTAL TO: 13

(10 POINTS)

NO	CHICAGO	MIN	FG	FGA	3P	3PA	FT	FTA	OR	DR	TOT	A	PF	ST	TO	PTS
33	PIPPEN	1	0	0	0	0	0	0	0	0	0	0	0	0	0	0
54	GRANT	33	4	6	0	0	5	6	4	9	13	2	4	0	1	13
24	CARTWRIGHT	41	1	8	0	0	2	4	1	5	6	0	3	0	0	4
14	HODGES	39	6	12	3	8	0	0	0	2	2	2	2	1	2	15
23	JORDAN	42	13	26	1	2	5	12	0	4	4	13	5	3	8	32
2	SELLERS	38	4	10	0	0	8	8	3	4	7	3	3	1	0	16
5	PAXON	16	4	6	1	2	1	2	0	1	1	1	6	0	1	10
40	CORZINE	10	0	2	0	0	0	2	0	1	1	0	1	0	1	0
22	DAVIS	16	1	4	0	0	0	0	5	0	5	0	2	0	0	2
11	VINCENT	4	1	2	0	0	0	0	1	0	1	0	1	0	0	2
32	PERDUE	DNP-														
15	HALEY	DNP-														
	TEAM TOTALS	240	34	76	5	12	21	34	9	31	40	21	27	5	13	94

PERCENTAGES: .447 .417 .618   TEAM REB: 0 TOTAL TO: 13

(13 POINTS)

BLOCKED SHOTS				SCORE BY PERIODS	1	2	3	4	FINAL
DETROIT 1	CHICAGO	5		DETROIT	24	25	28	26	103
MAHORN 1	GRANT	1		CHICAGO	26	21	22	25	94
	CARTWRIGHT	1							
	JORDAN	2							
	SELLERS	1							

NBA FINALS:
LOS ANGELES SERIES

NATIONAL BASKETBALL ASSOCIATION OFFICIAL SCORER'S REPORT

06-06-89 AUBURN HILLS MI   ATTENDANCE: 21,454

OFFICIALS: JAKE ODONNELL   JESS KERSEY   JACK MADDEN

NO	LOS ANGELES	MIN	FG	FGA	3P	3PA	FT	FTA	OR	DR	TOT	A	PF	ST	TO	PTS
42	WORTHY	39	6	18	0	0	5	8	0	2	2	3	1	1	1	17
45	GREEN	25	3	8	0	0	2	2	2	6	8	1	3	0	1	8
33	JABBAR	14	4	7	0	0	0	0	0	2	2	0	4	1	1	8
21	COOPER	25	1	5	1	4	0	0	0	2	2	1	5	1	0	3
32	JOHNSON	41	6	12	0	2	5	6	1	4	5	14	2	3	5	17
0	WOOLRIDGE	24	3	5	0	0	3	3	1	4	5	1	4	0	1	9
43	THOMPSON	37	5	8	0	0	5	11	4	1	5	0	4	1	1	15
19	CAMPBELL	25	4	9	0	0	4	6	0	2	2	0	5	2	2	12
3	LAMP	4	2	2	0	0	0	0	0	0	0	0	0	0	0	4
31	MCNAMARA	3	0	0	0	0	0	0	0	0	0	0	0	0	0	0
14	RIVERS	3	1	1	0	0	2	2	0	1	1	1	0	0	0	4
4	SCOTT	DNP-														
	TEAM TOTALS	240	35	75	1	6	26	38	8	24	32	21	28	9	12	97

PERCENTAGES: .467 .167 .684   TEAM REB: 11 TOTAL TO: 12

(16 POINTS)

NO	DETROIT	MIN	FG	FGA	3P	3PA	FT	FTA	OR	DR	TOT	A	PF	ST	TO	PTS
23	AGUIRRE	27	4	11	0	1	4	6	4	6	10	1	3	0	1	12
44	MAHORN	21	1	4	0	0	0	0	2	6	8	1	3	0	0	2
40	LAIMBEER	21	2	4	0	0	0	0	0	8	8	1	4	1	2	4
4	DUMARS	39	11	16	0	0	0	0	0	2	2	7	1	0	2	22
11	THOMAS	32	9	16	1	1	5	6	0	0	0	9	2	0	2	24
22	SALLEY	21	2	5	0	0	1	2	0	2	2	1	3	0	2	5
53	EDWARDS	25	5	9	0	0	5	5	2	2	4	0	4	0	1	15
15	JOHNSON	21	9	14	0	0	1	1	0	1	1	2	3	0	0	19
10	RODMAN	27	2	3	0	0	0	1	1	9	10	3	3	1	3	4
24	WILLIAMS	2	0	0	0	0	0	0	0	0	0	1	1	0	0	0
25	LONG	2	1	1	0	0	0	0	0	0	0	0	0	0	0	2
34	DEMBO	2	0	0	0	0	0	0	0	0	0	0	1	0	0	0
	TEAM TOTALS	240	46	83	1	2	16	21	9	36	45	26	28	2	13	109

PERCENTAGES: .554 .500 .762   TEAM REB: 6 TOTAL TO: 13

(20 POINTS)

BLOCKED SHOTS
LOS ANGELES 2   DETROIT 5
WORTHY   1   SALLEY 5
WOOLRIDGE   1

SCORE BY PERIODS	1	2	3	4	FINAL
LOS ANGELES	22	26	18	31	97
DETROIT	28	27	24	30	109

NBA FINALS:
LOS ANGELES SERIES

NATIONAL BASKETBALL ASSOCIATION OFFICIAL SCORER'S REPORT

06-08-89 AUBURN HILLS MI   ATTENDANCE: 21,454

OFFICIALS: D GARRETSON   HUE HOLLINS   JOE CRAWFORD

NO	LOS ANGELES	MIN	FG	FGA	3P	3PA	FT	FTA	OR	DR	TOT	A	PF	ST	TO	PTS
42	WORTHY	43	7	19	0	0	5	8	2	3	5	4	3	0	3	19
45	GREEN	34	3	6	0	2	4	4	2	7	9	0	3	0	2	10
33	JABBAR	28	4	12	0	0	3	4	1	1	2	2	3	0	3	11
32	JOHNSON	29	6	12	1	3	5	5	2	4	6	9	2	0	0	18
21	COOPER	44	6	12	4	8	3	3	1	0	1	4	3	3	0	19
43	THOMPSON	20	2	6	0	0	2	2	3	1	4	0	3	0	1	6
0	WOOLRIDGE	20	1	2	0	0	5	6	3	2	5	1	2	0	3	7
19	CAMPBELL	21	6	8	1	2	2	2	1	3	4	1	3	0	1	15
3	LAMP	1	0	0	0	0	0	0	0	0	0	0	0	0	1	0
4	SCOTT	DNP-														
14	RIVERS	DNP-														
31	MCNAMARA	DNP-														
	TEAM TOTALS	240	35	77	6	15	29	34	15	21	36	21	22	3	14	105

PERCENTAGES: .455 .400 .853   TEAM REB: 12 TOTAL TO: 14

(12 POINTS)

NO	DETROIT	MIN	FG	FGA	3P	3PA	FT	FTA	OR	DR	TOT	A	PF	ST	TO	PTS
23	AGUIRRE	33	7	11	0	2	0	0	2	4	6	2	5	0	4	14
44	MAHORN	21	1	3	0	0	0	0	0	2	2	2	4	0	0	2
40	LAIMBEER	14	1	3	0	0	0	0	2	3	5	0	4	0	1	2
4	DUMARS	36	10	16	0	1	13	14	1	1	2	6	2	0	0	33
11	THOMAS	34	9	21	0	2	3	4	1	3	4	7	4	2	3	21
15	JOHNSON	27	8	14	1	3	1	1	1	2	3	2	1	0	0	18
53	EDWARDS	32	3	8	0	0	2	2	3	1	4	2	4	0	1	8
10	RODMAN	26	1	1	0	0	0	0	2	5	7	0	3	0	1	2
22	SALLEY	17	4	4	0	0	0	0	1	1	2	0	4	1	0	8
24	WILLIAMS	DNP-														
25	LONG	DNP-														
34	DEMBO	DNP-														
	TEAM TOTALS	240	44	81	1	8	19	21	13	22	35	21	31	3	10	108

PERCENTAGES: .543 .125 .905   TEAM REB: 3 TOTAL TO: 11

(21 POINTS)

BLOCKED SHOTS

LOS ANGELES	3	DETROIT	9
WORTHY	1	MAHORN	3
JABBAR	1	THOMAS	1
COOPER	1	JOHNSO	1
		SALLEY	3
		EDWARDS	1

SCORE BY PERIODS	1	2	3	4	FINAL
LOS ANGELES	32	30	30	13	105
DETROIT	26	30	28	24	108

NBA FINALS:
LOS ANGELES SERIES

NATIONAL BASKETBALL ASSOCIATION OFFICIAL SCORER'S REPORT

06-11-89 INGLEWOOD   ATTENDANCE: 17,505

OFFICIALS: HUGH EVANS   MIKE MATHIS   ED T RUSH

NO	DETROIT	MIN	FG	FGA	3P	3PA	FT	FTA	OR	DR	TOT	A	PF	ST	TO	PTS
23	AGUIRRE	24	0	6	0	0	2	2	3	6	9	3	3	2	1	2
44	MAHORN	21	3	4	0	0	1	2	1	3	4	0	4	0	0	7
40	LAIMBEER	29	4	7	0	1	2	3	0	2	2	6	3	1	0	10
4	DUMARS	35	12	21	0	1	7	7	0	2	2	5	1	2	3	31
11	THOMAS	43	9	20	1	2	7	9	1	2	3	8	3	2	2	26
10	RODMAN	28	3	6	0	1	6	6	7	12	19	1	4	1	4	12
53	EDWARDS	19	0	2	0	0	0	0	0	2	2	1	4	0	1	0
22	SALLEY	23	4	6	0	0	1	1	0	3	3	3	5	0	0	9
15	JOHNSON	18	8	11	0	2	1	2	2	1	3	2	3	0	2	17
25	LONG	DNP-														
24	WILLIAMS	DNP-														
34	DEMBO	DNP-														
	TEAM TOTALS	240	43	83	1	7	27	32	14	33	47	29	30	8	13	114

PERCENTAGES: .518 .143 .844   TEAM REB: 7 TOTAL TO: 13

(13 POINTS)

NO	LOS ANGELES	MIN	FG	FGA	3P	3PA	FT	FTA	OR	DR	TOT	A	PF	ST	TO	PTS
45	GREEN	37	3	6	0	0	5	9	4	4	8	1	6	3	3	11
42	WORTHY	42	9	18	0	0	8	9	5	2	7	4	3	1	2	26
33	JABBAR	33	10	19	0	0	4	4	3	10	13	2	1	1	2	24
21	COOPER	48	6	14	3	8	0	0	0	0	0	13	2	1	2	15
32	JOHNSON	5	0	2	0	0	0	0	0	0	0	1	0	0	0	0
19	CAMPBELL	23	3	4	0	1	5	7	0	1	1	1	5	1	2	11
43	THOMPSON	22	3	6	0	0	2	3	2	1	3	2	2	0	0	8
0	WOOLRIDGE	18	3	4	0	0	3	4	0	4	4	1	2	0	1	9
14	RIVERS	11	2	6	0	2	2	3	0	1	1	2	3	0	2	6
3	LAMP	1	0	0	0	0	0	0	0	0	0	0	0	0	0	0
32	JOHNSON	DNP-														
4	SCOTT	DNP-														
	TEAM TOTALS	240	39	79	3	11	29	39	14	23	37	27	24	7	14	110

PERCENTAGES: .494 .273 .744   TEAM REB: 7 TOTAL TO: 14

(19 POINTS)

BLOCKED SHOTS

DETROIT	3	LOS ANGELES	5
DUMARS	1	GREEN	1
RODMAN	1	WORTHY	1
EDWARDS	1	COOPER	1
		THOMPSON	2

SCORE BY PERIODS	1	2	3	4	FINAL
DETROIT	27	30	29	28	114
LOS ANGELES	22	33	33	22	110

NBA FINALS:

LOS ANGELES SERIES

NATIONAL BASKETBALL ASSOCIATION OFFICIAL SCORER'S REPORT

06-13-89 INGLEWOOD   ATTENDANCE: 17,505

OFFICIALS: EARL STROM   JACK MADDEN   JESS KERSEY

NO	DETROIT	MIN	FG	FGA	3P	3PA	FT	FTA	OR	DR	TOT	A	PF	ST	TO	PTS
23	AGUIRRE	23	1	5	0	0	0	0	0	2	2	0	2	0	2	2
44	MAHORN	35	5	7	0	0	3	4	3	4	7	1	6	1	1	13
40	LAIMBEER	30	5	8	2	2	4	4	1	5	6	2	4	0	0	16
4	DUMARS	37	5	13	0	0	13	17	0	1	1	6	0	0	2	23
11	THOMAS	32	5	9	0	1	4	6	0	3	3	5	4	2	3	14
10	RODMAN	13	1	5	0	0	0	0	3	1	4	1	2	0	1	2
22	SALLEY	20	3	4	0	0	2	4	1	2	3	1	2	0	0	8
15	JOHNSON	29	5	11	0	0	4	7	0	6	6	5	2	0	0	14
53	EDWARDS	21	4	8	0	0	5	9	1	3	4	0	4	0	0	13
25	LONG	DNP-														
24	WILLIAMS	DNP-														
34	DEMBO	DNP-														
	TEAM TOTALS	240	34	70	2	3	35	51	9	27	36	21	26	3	9	105

PERCENTAGES: .486 .667 .686   TEAM REB: 15 TOTAL TO: 9

(11 POINTS)

NO	LOS ANGELES	MIN	FG	FGA	3P	3PA	FT	FTA	OR	DR	TOT	A	PF	ST	TO	PTS
45	GREEN	38	2	5	0	1	2	4	3	9	12	0	3	1	0	6
42	WORTHY	46	17	26	2	3	4	6	0	3	3	3	3	0	1	40
33	JABBAR	29	2	8	0	0	3	4	1	2	3	3	3	0	2	7
19	CAMPBELL	14	2	3	0	0	2	2	2	1	3	2	6	0	1	6
21	COOPER	46	4	14	1	7	2	3	0	3	3	9	4	2	0	11
14	RIVERS	12	1	5	0	0	0	0	0	1	1	2	3	0	2	2
43	THOMPSON	24	3	10	0	0	5	6	3	4	7	1	3	0	0	11
0	WOOLRIDGE	25	4	7	0	0	5	6	1	6	7	3	3	0	1	13
3	LAMP	5	0	1	0	0	1	2	0	1	1	0	2	0	0	1
31	MCNAMMRA	1	0	0	0	0	0	0	0	0	0	0	0	0	0	0
32	JOHNSON	DNP-														
4	SCOTT	DNP-														
	TEAM TOTALS	240	35	79	3	11	24	33	10	30	40	23	30	3	7	97

PERCENTAGES: .443 .273 .727   TEAM REB: 14 TOTAL TO: 7

(7 POINTS)

BLOCKED SHOTS			
DETROIT	4	LOS ANGELES	6
SALLEY	3	WORTHY	3
EDWARDS	1	JABBAR	2
		WOOLRIDGE	1

SCORE BY PERIODS	1	2	3	4	FINAL
DETROIT	23	26	27	29	105
LOS ANGELES	35	20	23	19	97